The Boy Who Invented Skiing

ALSO BY SWAIN WOLFE

The Woman Who Lives in the Earth

Lake Dreams

The Parrot Trainer

The Boy Who Invented Skiing

A MEMOIR

Swain Wolfe

ST. MARTIN'S PRESS
NEW YORK

www.stmartins.com

Library of Congress Cataloging-in-Publication Data

Wolfe, Swain.
    The boy who invented skiing : a memoir / by Swain Wolfe.—1st ed.
      p. cm.
    ISBN-13: 978-0-312-31093-6
    ISBN-10: 0-312-31093-5
    1. Wolfe, Swain—Childhood and youth.   2. Novelists, American—20th century—
Biography.   3. Novelists, American—Homes and haunts—West (U.S.)   I. Title.

PS3573.O5257Z46   2006
813'.54—dc22
[B]   2006042225

First Edition: June 2006

10 9 8 7 6 5 4 3 2 1

ACKNOWLEDGMENTS

Thanks to Diane Reverand, editor extraordinaire.

This is a book of memories and the insights evoked by those memories. The events described are not metaphorical. There was drama enough without the need for fiction. Obviously, our memories warp, and I've had to write what I remembered. The names and backgrounds of some individuals were changed, and some timelines were altered.

CONTENTS

Introduction

Tootsie Honyocker and the Devil   *1*

PART ONE
Woodman

Grandfather's Bricks and the Secret Room   *7*
The Radio People   *12*
Pack Rats   *15*
The First Bad Thing   *18*
Uncle Bud's Painting   *25*
Tunnels   *30*
The Board of Directors   *35*
How I Almost Lost My Pecker   *37*
Vicki and the Egg   *39*
The Bulls   *41*
School   *44*
Jodhpurs, Silo Sex, and the Fall   *47*

PART TWO
Mountains and Rivers

Snakes and Sulfur 51

Spring Creek 52

The Tin-Can Man 60

Poker Chips and the Tent Fire 62

The Cabin 65

The New Allen Hotel 68

Colorado Springs 73

Montana 77

The Taylor River Ranch 80

I Invent Skiing 95

Spring Thaw 104

Rarick Creek and the Secret of the Universe 106

Fishing 109

Bovine Bigotry 113

The Outsiders 116

The End of an Era 120

Bucktoothed 130

Slide Rock 134

Killings 137

Our Bank Robbers 140

The Elk 143

The Hole in the Wall 146

The Big Snow 148

Bighorn Sheep 151

Final Spring 153

PART THREE
Monkey Town

Leaving Colorado — *167*

My Uncle's Crowd — *169*

Town — *174*

Almost Sex and High School — *183*

Some Jobs — *190*

Running Away to California — *197*

Vicki — *202*

An Education, Sort Of — *206*

Commies and Moralists — *210*

PART FOUR
Work

The Fours — *215*

The Fire — *221*

The Woods — *228*

The Bitterroot Ranch — *232*

The Slaughterhouse — *236*

The Most Powerful Man in Butte — *240*

The Thirty-Two and the Cold-Hole — *248*

The Bar: Steve and Gracie — *256*

The Grizzlies — *260*

Station of the Cross — *268*

Billy Tolley and His Girl — *271*

The Junior League — *275*

Blown to Bits — *277*

Reincarnated from Dirt — *279*

Buddhists with Headlamps — *284*

The Boy Who Invented Skiing

Tootsie Honyocker
and the Devil

When she was a child, they called her Tootsie Honyocker—Tootsie for endearment and Honyocker for bullheadedness. The European roots of *honyocker* referred to a maker of hay. To city people, it meant a rustic or hick, but the Icelandic homesteaders who migrated to Eastern Montana in the early nineteenth century accepted the term with a wry sense of humor. Farming at the edge of the Badlands was an unfortunate misconception. Tootsie's father suggested that some Norwegian's thick tongue got twisted around a fancy word for farming-where-you-ought-not-to-be-farming, and the result was *hon-yock*.

The Badlands were beautiful and desolate. It was said that while God was dealing with the rest of creation, the devil was busy clawing out that maze of ravines and gullies across the prairies. Even the Indians, who had a significantly better relationship with nature than those Icelandic farmers did, believed the Badlands were evil.

In 1918, Tootsie spent the summer she turned four investigating the hills and arroyos above the family cabin. Her grandmother claimed the arroyos led up to a prairie crawling with diamondback rattlers and beyond that to the Badlands and the Norse demons who had tracked the family all the way from Iceland. While Tootsie's parents worked the field, Grandmother watched the child, cleaned, washed clothes, and prepared meals. Grandmother was a formidable woman.

Tootsie was rebellious. She wanted to explore the world beyond the cabin, to find one of those terrible snakes slithering through the prairie, or with luck, the demons lurking in the Badlands. Every time escape seemed possible, Grandmother came thundering over the hill and snatched her back. That stern, old woman became the one to defeat.

There was a showdown on a hot August afternoon in the sheep shed—a test of wills between the ill-tempered grandmother and the determined four-year-old. For the second time that day, Tootsie had escaped into the prairie to look for diamondbacks. Grandmother was angry, gasping, and sticky by the time she caught up with her granddaughter. She gave her a severe scolding, marched her back through the sagebrush and down the hill to the sheep shed. Tootsie was going to the devil.

Grandmother had warned her. Anyone who sought out snakes and demons must be the devil's daughter. Now she was about to meet her true father. The devil had been invoked many times before and described in detail. Intrigued that a creature with horns, a long tail, and goat's hooves could be her real father, the child's interest grew with each invocation.

Her grandmother believed the mere threat of seeing the devil would terrify the defiant girl into obedience, once and for all. She gave Tootsie a stern look and began to open the sheep shed door. Tootsie did not resist. She slipped into the shed ahead of her grandmother, who had no choice but to follow.

The shed was dark and hot and stank of manure. At the far end, thin rays of light shone through the weathered boards. Light and dust fused into a soft haze. Tootsie stared into the expanding glow.

As grandmother had promised, the devil revealed himself—standing at the far end of the sheep shed, so tall he had to bend forward, and even then his back scraped the roof. His long tail arced around his body. Sharp horns sprouted from his bloodred forehead, and his hooves were cloven and black as patent leather slippers.

Tootsie was enraptured. The devil was everything she could wish for in a father. She leaned forward, pulling her grandmother toward the far end of the shed. The old woman's ploy had unintended consequences. She knew Tootsie was seeing something she shouldn't, and the child's response was more than improper. Grandmother was spooked and frightened. Still holding her straining granddaughter by the hand, she backed out and shut the sheep shed door.

The grandmother never mentioned the devil again, but his image stayed with her granddaughter to the end. Tootsie said she'd come to embrace the devil, that in some respect he was her father. To her grandmother's credit, Tootsie learned early to distrust proper authority.

Tootsie liked to tell the story of the sheep shed devil to respectable people. It shocked some, no doubt her intent, and put God's fear in others. Probably no one had met a progeny of the devil—at least not one so willing to claim birthrights to the beast.

Tootsie died with her eyes wide open. She looked straight up as if she were staring at an incredibly bright, universal revelation.

But that wasn't the case at all. Her pupils were huge. They were not focused on the blinding secret of the universe. She was staring into a night sky, gathering every speck of light in the galaxy's haze, searching the stars for the tail and horns of her cloven-hooved father.

Tootsie Honyocker was the woman who raised me, and the mother I loved.

PART ONE

Woodman

Grandfather's Bricks and
the Secret Room

A doe stood on the hillside, still as a stone. I couldn't tell if she was real or a statue. The ambivalence made me dizzy. Then she turned and looked at me. Others came into view—four doe and several fawns, grazing on the sparse, pale grass, working their way up the slope through the pines and evening shadows toward the sandstone house of my childhood. They were stately, fragile animals— pets to the Catholic nuns who nurtured them, fed them treats, and talked to them in quiet, nun voices.

I moved a step at a time toward the grazing deer until I reached the end of the path, where steps descended the hill to the old hospital grounds. The deer were only a few feet away. They stopped and lifted their heads. When I said hello, their bodies tensed. The soft, whispering murmur of nuns had been replaced by an unexpected male voice. They turned and walked away, down the hill and into the trees. The last time I was here, there was neither deer nor trees, only grass.

I turned to go back to the car and noticed I'd been standing on a patch of white firebricks. There were no other bricks anywhere around, only these. They'd been carefully laid faceup to display the words "Denver Fire Clay Company." Firebricks were not meant for a footpath or even a building. They were heavy, oversize bricks used to line industrial boilers and ceramic kilns, made to withstand temperatures over 2,000 degrees Fahrenheit.

It took a moment to grasp how the bricks came to be at the end of the path and what they meant. These bricks had been made by my father's father. Grandfather must have carried them home one or two at a time in his lunch pail and given them to my father, whom he'd put through medical school by working ten- and twelve-hour shifts loading and unloading the hot kilns. Whether the bricks were Grandfather's idea or my father's, they were dense, guilt-laden bricks.

I tried to recall if the bricks were there when I was a child, to imagine my father on his knees, nearly sixty years before, bending over his work, carefully adjusting each brick to fit flat against the next. I had no memory of the event, but I knew these were serious bricks.

Grandfather had fled the czarists across the Caucasus, found a Russian wife in Austria, and made steerage to the land of peace and plenty. He'd survived to work under slave labor conditions in Denver's factory gulag. At that time, Denver was 300,000 souls a mile high, infusing the air with the scent of desire and desperation that still clings to the men and women of the West.

I stood on the guilty bricks, watching the deer drift down through the long-needled pines, thinking of my father in his suit and white shirt, on his knees, struggling with his tribute to the man who had worked half his life in a Colorado brick factory to raise his six children and put his brightest son through medical school. It was no accident that Grandfather's bricks were the first thing your feet touched after you climbed the 105 steps to the top of the hill— where you could turn and look down on the magnificent little valley and see my father's hospital.

I once saw a photograph of my grandfather wearing a porkpie hat and a rumpled suit not made for the muscular, hunched-over torso of a working man. You couldn't tell from the snapshot that his hands were thick and strong—more mechanical grippers than hands. What it did show was a man who knew life was work and work was his duty.

I met him only once. My father drove our beautiful red Buick down the clay driveway and stopped behind Grandfather's Model A Ford. Grandfather was standing in front of his small house as though he'd been waiting.

Grandmother did not come out. She might have been ill, but knowing what I know now, she was probably angry and humiliated, because her son was ashamed of his family. He never introduced them to my mother, never took them to see the hospital where he saved people, and never invited them to the big stone house on the hill for Christmas dinner.

The day I met him, Grandfather had just come home from the brick factory. It was the middle of summer, 1943. He was wearing three pairs of pants, a heavy wool shirt, and several sweaters. The third day after the burners were shut down on the huge beehive kilns, and the bricks had cooled to around 300 degrees Fahrenheit, the company required the men to remove the bricks. All those layers of clothes were insulation from the searing heat. To keep his face from blistering, Grandfather wore a wet gunnysack over his head.

My father owed his grand position, his beautiful wife, and his fine life to his parents, but he was embarrassed by their ignorance and their backward, Old Country habits. No amount of education and status could wash that off. My father regretted anything associated with his parents, including hard labor, poverty, and, obviously, himself. Much of his life was devoted to the inventions and rationalizations necessary to conceal his shame.

I looked up at the house of my first memories. It was two stories high and stood on a hill overlooking the small valley. When I was little, the valley seemed vast, stretching off toward the rim of the

known world, marked by monumental sandstone pillars eroded by
wind and water into alluring shapes with bands of soft yellows, or-
anges, and reds. Their tops were mushroom caps of harder sedi-
ment. On the valley floor were several buildings made of stone,
including father's hospital. To the east of the hospital were a hundred tiny, white, six-sided cottages where individual patients lived.
The place was called Woodman. It was a tuberculosis sanatorium.

From the window of my room on the second floor, I could see the
grass stretch down across the valley and up the other side through
the sandstone pillars with their mushroom caps. Our house was
made of the same sandstone. The other houses were white with
porches.

My room had windows on three sides. When the sun came in,
the room would glow. I would sit in the bright room and think
about how the world worked. I understood nearly nothing and was
often unsure of what little I'd learned. Every day there were new
things, so many things. Sometimes, on warm days, I'd fall asleep on
the blue rug and dream and wake up and wonder if what I'd
dreamed was real. Everything was a mystery. It was my job to explore, to understand the mysteries.

Late in the afternoon on a summer day when the sun slanted in, I
woke from a nap and noticed something new near the chest of drawers on the wall without windows. It was a door I'd never seen. The
door was white like the walls and about four feet high. A small glass
knob left a faint blur of rainbow daggers scattered through its long
shadow. I lay on the blue rug, wondering what was on the other side
of the door.

I got up and walked over to the wall and felt along the edge of
the door. I pulled the knob, which was just right for my small hand,
and the door opened. The room was nearly black except for a bright
doorway on the far side. I thought I saw a boy standing in the door-

way. How could someone be living in there without my knowing? I waited. Nothing happened. Then Mother called from downstairs. It was dinnertime. I walked down the steps wondering about the boy in the secret room.

By the next morning the door had disappeared. I made several passes along the wall, running my hand over the plaster between the bureau and the windows. I stood for a long time with both hands and an ear pressed to the wall, listening. Mother and the maid were making noise downstairs, so it was hard to tell where the sounds came from, but it seemed like something was on the other side. It occurred to me that the door appeared only when the sun struck the wall, and I'd have to wait until later in the afternoon. For several days, when I woke in the morning, and later, when the sun stretched across the wall, I searched for the door, but I never found it again.

The Radio People

Mother and Father talked a lot. She said he had a great mind. He'd had rheumatic fever when he was a boy, and his heart was weak. My father was running out of time. I wanted to ask about the boy who lived in the secret room, but they were talking away and Father was running out of time. I wasn't even sure what that meant.

We ate dinner in the evening. In the summer it was still light out, and the sun streamed in across the white tablecloth and reflected off the big plates. Sometimes I had to squint. I could have said something, but maybe I liked squinting.

One evening when dinner was finished, my parents said they were going for a walk and I could come or stay with Pando, the Great Dane. I wanted to stay. They walked slow, and they talked only to each other. Besides, I wanted to think about the radio.

When they left, I went to the room with the bench under the leaded windows made of many squares of beveled glass. The radio sat on a low table between the seats. I'd already spent a significant part of my life peering through the radio back, trying to make sense of the glowing tubes.

I turned the radio's dark brown knob. It made a soft click. Sometimes I turned it back and forth just to feel that particular click. The click made the radio people talk. It turned them on. But where were the people?

I often thought about the radio tubes. I couldn't imagine what they did. Perhaps there were no people at all, and it was the tubes that talked. Did the tubes have thoughts? They were smoky and dark and they glowed from deep inside—they sure looked like they were thinking. If I was thinking about them, I wondered if they could be thinking about me.

There was another radio puzzle. Did the radio people wait for me to turn the knob or were they always talking? Did they ever stop? It was perfectly reasonable to think they waited, since the entire world existed for my benefit. It took a lot of clicking before I accepted the fact that they went on without me. Radios were tiny cottages with people in them, and people were like radios without knobs.

My parents came back from their walk and found me asleep, curled up on the floor next to Pando, who slept with one paw over his nose and one paw in his mouth. Father carried me upstairs and put me to bed.

Besides Pando, who was so huge I could ride him around the house, we had a Dalmatian that had puppies. I watched Mother weigh the puppies on the balance scales. She did it every day. We had a box of squirmy puppies with black spots. She drew little pictures of each puppy and its spots and wrote numbers next to the pictures. They were special, purebred puppies, and when they got big enough, she sold them.

We had a red, slope-backed Buick with a long, eight-cylinder engine. My father parked it in the driveway and forgot to set the brake. The car rolled headfirst down the sloping lawn, tipped over the retaining wall, and landed on its nose in the road below. The rear end was propped up against the wall. A commotion followed. Men came with a truck and a winch. They laughed themselves silly.

The doctor forgot to set the brakes. The men hooted. It was funny—the car nosed into the road with its tail in the air. Father was flustered. Mother thought he was a little cuckoo. She smiled at me and did the thing with her eyes—she'd flutter her eyelids and move her eyes from one side to the other, then blink, and glance up as though she were watching something fly away. Maybe she was pretending to fly away.

They pulled the car up and over the wall, examined the inside and outside, and declared that only the bumper was damaged, but with the war on, parts were hard to find. They might be able to get a bumper from a wreck, since Father was a doctor. One day we had a new bumper. I didn't notice when this happened. It was just there, and nobody said a thing.

Pack Rats

Woodman was near Colorado Springs, just north of the Garden of the Gods, a famous monument to erosion. Dying people who coughed up blood came to the sanatorium to get well. Getting a good rest and breathing clean air may have been their best medicine. At least they weren't at home, coughing TB germs on their families. I never knew how many survived, or how many died, never saw an ambulance or a hearse. I don't remember a single patient. It was as though the sanatorium had been sanitized of its patients. How could I have lived in the midst of all those dying people and not have seen even one of them? No doubt, patients were kept well isolated. It was important not to draw attention to the ones who died. Perhaps the place was a myth—people going to work, stone buildings, white cottages, and sandstone mushrooms—tricks of the mind, as tangible as the radio people.

My father's title, chief of staff, sounded important. I was told that when the patients first came they stayed in the hospital. After a while they were moved to one of the six-sided cottages set in neat rows.

Inside there were six things—a bed, chair, lamp, table, washbasin, and towel rack. I looked in one once when no one was around and counted the six things. The cottages made me anxious—where did people go after they left the cottages? Maybe that was where time ran out.

On the sanatorium grounds, there were miles of walks and stone walls and tall lampposts with round globes on top. There were vine-covered gazebos with stone benches. Sometimes I took naps under the vines, and I remember sitting on a cool bench on a hot day, making little people out of the hollyhocks that grew against the stone walls.

I found a gully that led up into the hills through bands of pale yellow sandstone and whitish clay to the mesas above the sanatorium. Deep crevices and gnarly, stunted oaks and junipers—trees with limbs warped like flames, dust green leaves, and tight gray bark—inhabited the expanse of reddish stone. The mesa's twisted trees were like dancers on a stage.

There were crevices deep enough that you could fall in and never be seen again, and fissures wide enough for small hands to explore. The thousand fissures contained decades of collected treasure. I had no idea why earrings, finger rings, small toys, keys, and shiny things like a tiny spoon were hidden in the mesa's cracks and crevices, but they were there for the taking. If it hadn't been for the things people valued, mixed among the gum wrappers, buttons, paper clips, and bits of this and that, you would think I'd found hundreds of little garbage dumps.

One day Mother opened a cigar box full of my best things. She asked where I got them, and I told her about the cracks in the mesa. She said I'd found where pack rats nest. They were traders. They came down from the mesa and stole things from houses and the little cottages, then packed their loot back to hide in the cracks in the rocks, but they always replaced one thing with another, which explained why sometimes small objects magically appeared or disappeared.

When pack rats took something, they gave something back, which meant they had a conscience. That made them very interesting animals, worthy of a small boy's consideration.

Of course, the pack rats were only leaving objects of lesser interest behind when they found something more to their liking, but I didn't know that. To me, pack rats were noble. I felt guilty. I should've left something for them when I raided their treasures, but there was a dilemma. I had to find things they would consider valuable enough to trade for what I wanted—the basic riddle in the endless quandary in the game of tit for tat. I wanted to do business with pack rats.

Mother warned me not to go up to the mesa again. Long, fat snakes with diamonds on their backs lived in those crevices. They slithered through the gullies and over the mesa hunting for pack rats and small boys.

I was never surprised by a snake on the mesa even though I continued to explore the crevices and the surrounding hills. What did surprise and mystify me was a house I discovered in the late afternoon in the grass-covered hills above the dairy barns. I don't remember shadows, so it was probably a cloudy day. It was a place I'd never been. I was climbing a hill and looked up and saw the house. No one was around. There was no car, no garage, no horses. Just this house all by itself in the middle of a lot of grass.

I remember being inside and looking around. Everything was in perfect order. There was a big trunk with a rounded top, full of stuff like bedding and clothes. The table was set with a single plate, a spoon, a pointed knife, and a tin cup. I decided it was a witch's house and ran away.

I could never find that house again. It got lost in the hills.

The First Bad Thing

Long before the sanatorium became my playground, giant stone mushrooms and twisted pillars in human forms were scattered along the rim of the valley. It had taken wind and water half a million years to shape them from the sandstone. But what phenomena allowed everything else to be washed away, leaving only the pillars? Perhaps the ancient gods unleashed monumental lightning strikes into the soft stone, fusing columns deep in the ground, leaving wind and water to carve away the rest.

In ways, the Woodman monuments were more astounding than the Garden of the Gods. They stood like sentinels looking out in all directions, protecting the little valley from the world beyond the mountains. Geologists called these formations hoodoos. The Indians believed they had magic powers. It took twenty Scottish masons less than two years to bust up nature's ancient handiwork and construct the buildings and retaining wall. Hammer-and-nail men quickly replaced the stone monuments with the one hundred cottages.

The Dutch wedding rocks, whose mushroom caps joined at the top, were allowed to stand. What was the story behind that singular romantic gesture? Was there an impassioned plea, a board member's threatened resignation, or a surveyor's zealous wife, late at night, erasing the stone lovers from the master plan?

The valley opened up where the road passed a cornfield on the right. Across the road from the field were a tall redbrick silo that fermented the cornstalks and leaves into silage for the milk cows, a stone milking barn, a white, two-story wood barn, pens for bulls, and a low-stone-wall paddock for the cows.

Farther on, the road left the sanatorium property and passed the farm of a dirt-poor family whose bony cows stood in mud up to their hocks in a grassless pasture. The road led to the highway. If you turned right, you went to Colorado Springs, or the Springs for short. If you turned left, you ended up on a stretch of road known as the ribbon of death, because the curves banked the wrong way. According to Mother, after several people died in crashes, the engineer was sent to an asylum for the criminally insane. That story seemed a little fantastic, but it was a treacherous road. If you survived the ribbon of death, you got to go to Denver.

To the west at the foot of the mountains was the dormitory for single men who worked at the sanatorium. Next to the dormitory was a garage for repairing trucks and farm machinery. In front stood a tall cast-iron gas pump painted red and crowned with a clear-glass cylinder. The gasoline sloshed up into the cylinder when you worked the pump. Numbers and fine lines for exact measurement were painted on the glass. Sunlight turned the gasoline bright amber and illuminated streams of tiny bubbles that rose through the liquid light and vanished.

At the far end of the garage was a greenhouse with a scum green pond. Brightly colored goldfish with flecks of red and streaks of silver lurked among the roots in the pond. I was three years old when I first discovered a stairwell hidden by ferns in one corner of the greenhouse. At the bottom of the stairs was a door and behind the door a tunnel. I opened it and looked in. It was dark, of course.

Night after night, the tunnel was in my dreams. I went back to the greenhouse several times. I would hide in the stairwell behind the ferns and breathe the dank tunnel air. The tunnel was waiting. I could feel its pull.

I didn't have to ask. This was a forbidden place. If I said anything about it, I would be told never, ever to go there. When I went anyway, I'd have to lie. It was better to say nothing about the tunnel. It was more than a year before I found the courage to investigate, and when I did, I found places I was not sure existed anywhere but in my imagination, but that, I would discover years later, is the nature of tunnels.

Beyond the greenhouse were the horse barns in the mouth of a narrow canyon that led into the Garden of the Gods. That was where the first bad thing happened.

The beginning of a snowstorm had kicked up, whipping past the big arched windows of our house. It was before Christmas, because Mother was standing on a ladder in the living room decorating a tree. Pando, the galumphing dog, sat in the middle of the room watching. Mother reached down as far as she could, and I would stretch up to hand her a glittering strand of tinsel. They were all tangled and kept breaking, and I couldn't keep up. When Mother answered the phone, I had a chance to untangle the tinsel.

A life pattern was in the making. When I was overwhelmed, the unexpected would happen, giving me a chance to reshape the chaos of the moment and escape failure. Sublime intervention.

Mother talked while I sorted tinsel. The day man at the dormitory called to tell her a new parolee named Otis had just come in. She wanted to be sure the new man got something to eat. They could call Jack, the cook, and get him to warm up leftovers. I knew it would be meat loaf, because that morning I'd sat on a counter in the kitchen watching Jack make it. Mother listened for a while and said to tell the man she'd be down the next day.

During the war, hired help was hard to find, but Woodman was qualified to accept parolees from federal prisons. Some men got early parole if they had a job and a sponsor and minded their manners. The sanatorium had a ready-made work pool of cheap, well-behaved labor. Nobody wanted to go back to prison. More than half the nonmedical staff were ex-cons.

Grant Willis, who was on parole from a Texas prison, called the parolee system soft slavery. He said he could live with it, considering the alternative. In the late thirties, Grant had killed a man. I never knew the particulars. He was good with horses, so he worked in the stables. Mother liked him. She told Father that Grant was her favorite ex-con, then she laughed. I didn't know why that was funny. I liked Grant, because he had a soothing, deep voice and he knew thirty-two versions of "Frog Went a-Courtin'." His skin was a shade darker than most, his nose was a little flared, and his eyes were black and glinty. He had a devilish side to him. He couldn't have been more different from my father, who was a pale Russian, quiet and analytical.

Father came home late from the hospital. He was covered with snow, and his shoes were wet. Mother fixed him scrambled eggs and a gin gimlet and told him about the parolee. I sat in the dark in the radio room with Pando and listened to them.

The army had given Otis a 4-F for a missing finger. He'd been working for a contractor building a bridge near Salida and took to going into town in the evenings, where he met a waitress. He fell for her. Of course, she didn't know he existed, and he didn't get the message. He wanted to stay, but the bridge job was almost finished, and he couldn't find work in the area. He was stumped.

"So what do you think he did?" Mother asked.

Father sipped his gimlet, then looked up, gave her a little shrug, and waited for the punch line. He could do that for what seemed like hours—sit and wait with almost a smile. Mother took a sip and went on with her life of Otis.

"He got the bright idea to burn the bridge down so they'd have to rebuild it. His big mistake was confiding in his dream girl. She must not have believed him, because she didn't go to the police right away. After he'd burned the bridge, she got scared and turned him in. They charged him with sedition."

Father couldn't believe that a man would be charged with sedition for burning a bridge for love.

Mother was always telling Father he was naive. "Bridges," Mother explained, "are strategic structures."

"Strategic structures?" Father smiled and raised his glass. "Don't burn your bridges." They thought that was pretty funny. Mother said, "Don't burn your strategic structures." They giggled. They were in their gimlets.

The storm was worse the next day. In the late afternoon the wind picked up, and the temperature dropped well below freezing. The phone rang, and I heard Mother say, "Oh God, no." I was sure Otis, the bridge burner, had set the dormitory on fire, but that wasn't what happened. He'd walked out into a snowstorm stark naked— not even wearing shoes.

While Mother dressed me in sweaters and a heavy coat until I felt like a stuffed bear, she told me about Otis, repeating most of what she'd said to Father the night before, but this time she was depressed and sad. Otis wasn't normal, she said. He had to be a little off-kilter to fall so crazy in love with a girl he hardly knew. The fact she'd turned him in must have been a horrible shock.

Mother took two heavy blankets, and we shuffled through the snow to the Buick. I stared out at the swirling snow as Mother negotiated the twisted road down the hill to the stables.

Otis had a hungry heart. It was big and empty, and he'd found somebody who made it stop hurting, then he lost her, and he hurt more than ever.

Otis was scary, and Mother was going to look for him in a snowstorm. I have no idea what she thought she could do when she found him. When we got to the stable, she wrapped me in one of the blankets and told me to stay put until she got back. I've never understood why she didn't leave me at home.

She disappeared into the stable. I sat in the front seat and waited. By now the snow was a foot deep and drifting. She came out leading her jittery, jet black Arab mare, got on, blew me a kiss, and disap-

peared into the storm. The mare's black rump faded into the blowing snow.

It was a long wait, maybe an hour, but for a child, particularly a
cold child, it seemed like hours. It was dark, and gusts of wind
rocked the car and swung the stable light back and forth, making
things appear and disappear. I would see something, then the light
would swing back. I'd wait for the next swing, but whatever I'd seen
would be gone. I don't remember being afraid, but I was probably
terrified. Then I saw the black mare coming through the blowing
snow toward the car. Mother got off and opened the car door. She
was crying. She said she'd put the mare up, and we could go home.
As we drove back to the house, she told me she'd found Otis's bare
footprints and followed them as far as the Garden of the Gods. His
feet had begun to bleed, at first only spots of blood, then blotches.
He'd stopped at one point and turned around, perhaps he'd heard
the mare, then he turned back toward the Garden. She'd been very
close to him, because the snow hadn't covered the blood. The light
was fading, and it was hard to see. His bloody prints disappeared.
She crisscrossed the hill above the hidden Garden, but lost him in
the storm.

It was the first time I remember her crying. For several weeks after Otis's death, Mother was slow and distracted. She stared into
space and had to search for words when Father asked her something. She stopped talking to me altogether. Nothing was more
frightening than that. It was like we were waiting for the next bad
thing to happen.

In early February, somebody saw Otis and the waitress in Denver getting on a train for Los Angeles. The story was that the waitress had a change of heart and really loved him. He'd called her late
at night from the dormitory, and she'd driven all night through the
storm to save him. They'd met near the trading post in the Garden
of the Gods and escaped, just as they'd planned.

Mother didn't believe a word of that. She'd seen his bloody footprints. It was too cold and the trading post too far. Besides, he

would've needed permission to use the dorm phone, and there would have been a record. What happened to the bridge burner seemed to overwhelm us. It affected Mother more than anyone— she'd come so close, and she'd failed.

The snow and the cold slowed our lives all through January and February. The snow melted off in March, and things came to life. In early April, a young couple bundled up for a spring picnic in the Garden of the Gods, drove up into the hills, and stumbled on a half-frozen body in a gully.

There were people who still wanted to believe Otis and the girl had escaped. After all, someone saw them getting on that train in Denver. There was a rumor that the police were never a hundred percent about who they'd found in the gully. It was said another man had gone missing that winter. And Otis could have made his phone call before he got to the dormitory. I wanted to believe he'd gotten away, that he and the waitress escaped to a secret hideout, far, far away in California. Over the years, their escape became more than a wish, it became a necessity.

Uncle Bud's Painting

In March Mother's brother, my uncle Bud, came to visit. I never learned much about his childhood, but he must have been born about the time the family left the Badlands farm. Mother's mother found work in the oil fields in Eastern Montana, cooking for the drilling crews. Grandfather abandoned his family along with the farm. He got a job with Standard Oil and traversed Montana and Idaho promoting the company's line of petroleum products to service stations and hardware stores.

I never learned what became of the old woman who was bent on redeeming her granddaughter's soul with the threat of the sheep shed devil. Perhaps the Norse demons swooped down out of the Badlands and grabbed up my great-grandmother before the devil could get his claws in her.

If you hold stock in the taint of blood, Mother's side of the family claim they've traced our bad behavior to the murderous, ravaging, drunken Icelandic poet Egil Skallagrimsson, born in A.D. 900. As an old man, in jealousy, spite, and anger at his son, he forced two Irish slaves to bury a treasure of gold, then killed the slaves to seal the deed. The bones of the Irishmen are still out there, nestled next to Egil's gold in the marsh somewhere below the hay fields of Mosfell.

Three years before he'd come to visit us at Woodman, Bud managed to escape Montana to Denver, where he studied painting. He was younger than Mother by two or three years, but his thoughtfulness made him seem older. Bud painted landscapes, flowers in vases, and portraits. Mother was impressed. She told people that Bud's teacher was a master painter. She saw greatness in Bud.

Mother tried to be grand by making everyone around her grand, including me. She talked me up to her guests and dressed me in little suits and caps and took pictures. In several, I'm standing on a sandstone ledge with two of her Dalmatians. At first the attention was okay, but even I began to see through her. Both Father and Bud would tell her to get off her high horse, but it never did any good. She rode that horse to the end.

Bud painted portraits that were more about who people were than what they looked like. The paintings were too revealing and therefore threatening to his subjects. You can spend hours looking at one of his portraits, finding clues to his thinking and what he was able to see in people. His landscapes may have been influenced by the early work of Paul Gauguin. Mother said that while Bud painted, they would talk about light and color, and painters and styles. Bud's mountains and mesas were flat like Gauguin's haystacks. His colors were subtle and cut with raw umber.

The Bud who spent the summer with us was very unlike the Bud I would know years later when he became an insurance man and started making money. When I was little, he was quiet and gentle like Father. And very patient.

On Easter morning Mother woke me up while it was still dark, because we were supposed to go to the sunrise service in the Garden of the Gods. I was up and dressed and struggling with my shoelaces when Bud came to get me. I'd created a tangle. I was in awe of my uncle and embarrassed that he had to take time to show me how to tie shoes. I'd invented my own way, which I wish I could remember, because it made Bud laugh.

The service took place at the base of a big rock. A gust of wind blew the hats off a few ladies, but they had stiff perms that were something like hats anyway. The hats were candy-color greens, blues, and pinks. The bleachers were steel and concrete, the speakers were loud, and the wind was cold. The harsh ceremony was a contrast to the warm burnt-orange and yellows of the sandstone. The preacher talked into a microphone. His words screeched and echoed through the Garden of the Gods and bounced back to the bleachers. He talked about God, but not the gods. I wondered how the other gods felt about that. It was their garden, too.

When we got home, I went across the road and sat in the mouth of my cave in the sun. It wasn't a deep cave, more of a shallow depression in a clay bank—the ideal place to contemplate the meaning of life.

The cave was warm and out of the breeze, and I was pondering the question of God and the gods. Bud came out with his paints, sat on the trash can, and began painting. I wondered what he was painting, so I crawled out of my cave, brushed the white clay off my pants, and walked over. He was painting my cave, but I wasn't in the picture.

I asked why he wasn't painting me, since I was in the cave. Besides, it was my cave, but I didn't say that.

"You move around too much. You couldn't sit still if your life depended on it." I went back and sat in the cave like an eye under a brow. I tried to sit still, but evidently, not still enough. I never got painted. Wound-up little boys were not good subject matter.

Soon afterward he started a portrait of Mother sitting on the love seat in the parlor. She was wearing her favorite dress, a pink satin gown circled from the waist down by four evenly spaced chocolate brown bands of plush velvet. The narrow collar band was made of the same velvet, and just below it she wore a ruby brooch. One arm was draped behind the rise of the love seat, the other lay in her lap.

She was holding her head up, her chin tucked in very slightly. She was posed—stiff and aloof like a show horse.

Bud worked on her expression for a long time. At one point he put his board and brush down and looked at Mother. She didn't look normal. He asked what she thought she was doing.

"I'm posing for your painting."

"You're not natural."

She told him to paint what he saw. She had things to do. So Bud painted, not necessarily what was on the surface, but what was underneath.

Looking at that painting today, I can see that what Bud saw would haunt Mother all her life. She had a forced regal look that only emphasized her self-doubt and anger.

She had been abandoned by her mother's early death to breast cancer and by her phony, pillar-of-the-community father. She felt betrayed, as did many intelligent women who were ignored as people while they were exploited for their skills and abilities. The rage Bud had seen would cut a path through her life. Mother had learned to mistrust the world—knew she would always be betrayed and abandoned. That was what she expected, and the world would match her expectations.

I believe our failures as human beings stem from fear of not being all right. We need lovers, mommies, and children to hold us in the night. My mother had been abandoned, by nearly everyone, and the scent of those betrayals always lingered in the room.

Mother found the finished portrait disturbing. She flared at Bud. "You bastard. You made me look fat."

In his defense he said, "You're pregnant. That's how you look."

Later she became fascinated by the painting. I don't know if she saw Bud's vision of insecurity and rage, or if she saw only what she'd meant him to see—the regal woman of status. Throughout the rest of her life she would spend hours staring at that painting. As her waning eyesight dimmed the details, looking at the painting became an exercise of memory and imagination.

The morning after Bud had finished Mother's portrait, I came down the long, wide staircase and found the painting leaning against the love seat in the living room. I was hypnotized by the beautiful brooch. It seemed to float slightly off the canvas, inviting my grasp. I reached for the glittering rubies my uncle had created with his brush, but my fingers came away sticky and red.

Though he never said anything to me about it, Mother told me Bud was upset. He'd been proud of that brooch. Though he tried several times, he could not get the brooch exactly right. He took the brooch-grab personally. I was never the same in his eyes.

Bud had painted Mother's dilemma. You can see she felt lost. Before she died, she said that during the period Bud did her portrait she thought she was crazy. She would lose track of time, of where she was, and would walk aimlessly through the sanatorium, asking questions of everyone. She wanted to know what people did and how they did it. I think she wanted to know what other people were like and what it meant to be normal. She blamed her loneliness on my father, who was always busy and rarely had sex with her for fear his damaged heart would burst.

She wanted me to be her little man, but I ran away often and far. When I was three, she saw me climbing down the drainpipe to make my escape. She said I made it to the foot of the hill before she caught me, but I never really stopped running.

Tunnels

I was almost four. My father and I were standing near the faucet on the lawn. It hadn't occurred to me that he might have anything life-changing to say. We were just having a chat when a glint in the grass caught my eye. I picked it up for Father to see. He bent down and looked at the thing in my hand and said it was a fifty-caliber machine-gun shell. It was wet and shiny. The war had come to our lawn. The week before, a bomber flew into the mountain above the sanatorium and exploded. Father assumed the shell had come from the explosion. That didn't seem possible. The wreck was so far away.

Then he told me he was going to get Mother from the hospital in Colorado Springs, and when she came home, she would be bringing a new baby with her. I would have a sister. I stood there, holding the shell, wondering if it could still explode, and watched him walk to the red car and drive away. I went to my little cave in the white clay cut bank in back of our house and stared at the shell and wondered how it really came to be by the faucet. It seemed as if I were there for a week.

I remember Mother weighing my new sister, Vicki, on the puppy scales. I stood on my toes and peered at the small, wiggly pink body, and asked, ever hopeful, "Are we going to sell Vicki when she's old enough?"

There was a brief period when the shallow cave behind the house was sanctuary against all misfortune and intrusions into my perfect life, such as my baby sister's existence or a fight with Juanita, the mean babysitter whose brief stay was traumatic and memorable—for both of us. The end of Juanita came when she was chasing me, intent on inflicting pain, and I locked her out of the house. We could see each other through the glass. She was screaming at me to open the door, when her eye caught sight of an open window behind me in the dining room. We raced for it. She had longer legs, but I had the shorter route. Her hands were on the sill when the window came down.

An hour later Mother returned—no doubt from showing off her new baby daughter. Juanita was sitting outside making up lies and excuses and going over her resignation speech. Mother nodded and smiled, indifferent to what either I or the babysitter had to say. She wrote Juanita a check and went upstairs with her bundle of joy.

I progressed from the shallow cave in the hillside to the tunnel door in the greenhouse, next to the goldfish. I'd been thinking about the tunnel for more than a year, trying to guess where it went and getting up the courage to find out. I imagined it went deep underground, but had no idea what I'd find. I made my way through the greenhouse ferns to the door. The tunnel was made of concrete with an arched roof. I would explore a little farther every day, gaining courage. I discovered a lightbulb in a little wire box in the tunnel wall. A pipe led from the box to a switch. The underground was visible but dim, because the lights were spaced far apart. The steps were different sizes—long-shallow, long-shallow, short-deep, long-shallow, short-shallow, short-deep. Trip and stumble, stumble and trip. There was a lot of shin whacking.

The tunnel connected all the sanatorium buildings—the garage, the hospital, the kitchen, the dormitory, the machine shop, and the boiler plant that sent steam through the asbestos-wrapped pipes bolted to the tunnel ceiling. Today, only workers dressed like astronauts with face masks and air tanks are allowed in.

The boiler plant was the starting point for the tunnel I'd entered from the greenhouse. There was another that took off to the right as you entered from the boiler room. The lights in this mystery tunnel were spread out so far it was nearly dark in between. It went on and on, and I kept stumbling on the stupid steps. The first time I ventured into this tunnel I had to give up and go back. I knew Mother would start a search if I was gone much longer. The entire sanatorium staff would be on my trail.

I waited until Mother went to the Springs one day and left me behind. This gave me several hours. It turned out I needed them. I left the house in the morning and didn't get back until evening. After a very long time, the tunnel came to a series of uniform, easy-to-climb stairs. Near the top was a wide beam of light from under a door, which, like all the others, was unlocked. I balanced on the top step and listened. It was quiet. I turned the knob, waited for a moment, then pushed the door open. I stood there, not moving, because I was blinded by sunlight.

I was in a room with many windows along one side. As my eyes adjusted to the light, several tables appeared. They were long and white. I had no idea where I was. When I stood on a chair to look out the windows, I saw only a gully but nothing recognizable. I got down and looked around the room. The tables had stone tops and porcelain sinks with sets of curved chrome pipes and porcelain knobs.

A human skeleton hung from a hook on a stand in the far corner of the room near the windows. I had seen pictures of skeletons, but never a real one. I walked over and touched it. Wires held the bones together. It was the strangest thing I'd seen in my life. It had been a person once. It had been alive, had a name, and was a father or a mother. I couldn't even tell if it was a man's or a woman's skeleton.

I took its hand in my hand, and thought: Underneath my skin, I look like this. I studied the bones for a long time, until I'd seen each separate bone. The complete skeleton was ugly, but the separate bones were beautiful.

It was late, and I had to get back, but I noticed a set of stairs to another door. It opened to a huge slanted room filled with seats facing a large platform.

The seats were lined up in long rows. Two aisles ran up through the seats toward swinging doors that opened to an entry hall with coat racks and a set of large locked double doors to the outside. In one corner of the entryway, narrow stairs went up to another locked door.

I walked back down the aisle and climbed the stairs to the platform and looked out on all those seats. I noticed four small windows above the swinging doors at the high end of the huge room. That had to be where the narrow staircase went. It was like a little house up there. I wondered if anyone lived in it.

In the back of the platform I discovered several ropes stretching up into the dim recesses of the ceiling. I pulled a rope and a giant canvas came down. It stretched from ceiling to floor and across the width of the platform. I walked around to the front of the platform and discovered the canvas had a picture painted on it. The painting was several times the size of anything my uncle had done.

I pulled down all the paintings. There was a painting of stone columns with mountains in the background and clouds coming over the mountains, another of a lake with mountains and clouds coming over the mountains, and one of a log cabin with mountains and clouds coming over the mountains. One was just white. The thought of that huge room filled with grown-ups staring at huge pictures was troubling.

Several days later I made another trip through the tunnel to the building of many seats and big paintings. I was sitting near the swinging doors just under the room with the four windows when I heard a car on a gravel road. My palace was about to be invaded. I crouched on the floor, waiting for the intruders, and heard my mother's voice. She unlocked the double doors and came in with a man with big feet. They went up the small staircase to the little house. The man unlocked the door, and they went in.

I left my hiding place under the seats and crept up the stairs. I could see their legs and a black machine with chrome knobs. On its front was a fat spyglass, and on the sides were tin wheels on spindles. I heard little and understood nothing of what they said. They were talking about movies.

It was years before I told my mother I'd gotten into the sanatorium's theater through the tunnel and spied on her that day. She explained she'd gone there to check out the equipment, because she was thinking of reestablishing the long-forgotten practice of movie night for the staff and noncontagious patients. She didn't remember if they started showing movies again or not. That sort of entertainment wasn't high on her list—movies were a bad influence or not worth the time.

She took me to a movie once, several years later. It was about a beautiful girl who couldn't stop dancing, because her shoes were cursed. In the end she fell off a balcony and got run over by a train. I remember the movie in black-and-white, but the girl's shoes were red.

The Board of Directors

Mother said Woodman was a disaster. When my father first took the job as the medical chief of staff, the hospital, laundry, and kitchen were poorly maintained, marginal operations. The dairy had not passed state inspection for the last year, and the milk was being fed back to the cows and their calves. Within a few months my father had the hospital in decent shape, but the rest of the operation was run by an indifferent bureaucrat who had kept the board of directors at bay for years.

When the directors got wise, they fired the superintendent and started looking for a replacement. After Father had been running the hospital for several months, the directors came to inspect his progress and discuss the vacant superintendent's position. They offered to double Father's salary, but he wasn't about to take on that thankless task. The hospital was all he could handle.

It had been arranged that the directors would come to dinner at the house the last night of their stay. They came, sat around having cocktails, had dinner and more drinks, and discussed their dilemma. After they'd finished eating, everyone got comfortable in the living room and kept drinking. Mother was, by her own account, near the height of her mental instability. She'd been listening all through dinner and hadn't said much more than thank you when the house-keeper brought her another drink.

Finally she'd heard all she could take and launched into a martini-fueled diatribe, telling the directors what was wrong with their little operation. Her forays into the sanatorium with her intense, endless questions had given her an understanding of why the place was so wasteful and badly run. Father listened with his almost smile.

Two weeks later he came home and announced the sanatorium had a new director.

Mother smirked. "So who's the sorry bastard?"

Father stared at her. She waited for an answer, but he didn't say a thing. He just stared at her.

"Oh Christ, no," she moaned and held her head in her hands. He convinced her to do it. She was going crazy doing nothing in the time-free zone of the sanatorium, and together, they would have twice his $225-a-month income. There was a catch, however. She wouldn't be the official superintendent. The Woodman directors were afraid to tell the stockholders that a woman had been hired to do a man's job.

Father was named director in addition to his position as chief of staff, and his salary was doubled. Though she would not get credit, there was compensation—she controlled the money and she had the power, but more important, she had a job that required her intelligence and competence, which put her feet back on the ground.

How I Almost Lost
My Pecker

My world was filled with adventures and pranks played on the staff, with getting in their way and causing grief. I have a vague memory of running the length of a long steel table, bright lights, lots of clanging and banging and shouting men. Evidently I'd climbed up on the steel prep room table and run its length while cooks screamed at me. I have no idea why I'd done something like that.

I ran away into the hills in search of the witch's house, into the mesas looking for pack rat treasure and snakes with diamonds on their backs, or disappeared for hours at a time in the tunnels, where no one knew to look for me. Eventually Mother stopped organizing search parties.

I did learn not to mess with the Mexicans. I was in the cornfield pestering two Mexican field hands with endless questions about their big knives, their large mustaches, the color of their skin, where they came from, and what crimes they'd committed, for I assumed they were convicts like most of the workers. The Mexicans laughed. They had dark eyes that gleamed under their huge hats.

It was late in the afternoon, and Mother stopped on the road to ask if they had seen her son. I was hidden by the corn and wanted to play a trick on her, so I told them not to tell and started toward the car. They played along, pretending not to understand what she said and followed me through the tall corn. Mother was waiting, leaning against the car. When I jumped out of the corn, she laughed. She was happy to see me and pretended to be surprised. I was giddy and laughing, until I realized her eyes were large and staring at something behind me. The Mexicans had followed me up the bank to the car. Each man was holding a fat, headless rattlesnake. They convinced me I'd just stepped over death. Being brave men with machetes, they'd cut off the snakes' heads and saved my life. The Mexicans made a belt for my mother from the skins.

I was impressed by their big knives, big hats, loud laughter, and their talent for doing terrible things. One day I said something to the Mexicans I shouldn't have. What that was I don't remember, because they proceeded to terrify me as I have never been terrified. They chased me through the sanatorium, waving their machetes, screaming that they meant to cut off my little pecker.

They caught me in the street near the stair that led up to the stone house. There was a struggle and screaming and finally pleading. Instead of cutting off my membership to manhood, they cut the suspenders on my coveralls. Whatever I said, I'm sure a suspender cutting was minor punishment, but I went up the steps shaking. Mother's maternal self got the better of her good judgment. She knew the Mexicans' display of crossed machetes in their dormitory window had everyone at the sanatorium scared, so maybe my cut suspenders were an excuse to act. She marched down the hill to the dormitory, up the stairs, into their room, snatched the machetes from the window, and left. They applauded her bravery. As she climbed the steps up the hill, the Mexicans laughed and whooped. They loved my mother.

Vicki and the Egg

When my sister, Vicki, was two years old, she had an allergic reaction to a bite of an egg Mother had given her. Vicki turned blue. Mother called Father at the hospital, grabbed Vicki, and started running. They met near the stairs at the foot of the hill. Father gave Vicki an injection of Adrenalin and saved her life, but the damage to her brain was permanent. Before the Adrenalin did its work, part of her died. A single bite of egg changed Vicki from who she would have been to someone altogether different.

I don't know when I found out about the egg incident, but Vicki must have been four or five before I understood something wasn't right with my sister. She was slow to learn and seemed disconnected from her surroundings.

Decades later, cousin Ellen wrote me a tormented letter. Ellen's story was that she and her mother and father had visited us at the sanatorium in 1945, the year her father came back from the war. Ellen would have been seven or eight at the time. She wrote about the morning a happy, sparkling Vicki came dancing down the stairs, singing a song of her own, and about Vicki's intelligence and beauty.

Ellen's letter went on to describe the rest of the day—playing hide-and-seek with me and some other kids. She had run into the house and hidden behind the big sofa just when my father came back from the hospital and confronted Mother about poisoning their daughter. He was angry and shouting. He accused Mother of feeding eggs to Vicki even though she knew eggs could kill her. He wanted to know why. Mother didn't have an answer; all she could say was, "I just gave her one little bite."

Ellen was convinced Mother was insanely jealous of Vicki, whose beauty and happy optimism drew attention away from Mother. Ellen claimed that Mother, in a jealous rage, tried to kill her own daughter. Insecurity and jealous rage were standard toxins in Mother's cabinet, but I don't know if she intended to harm her daughter.

It would have been logical for Father to have his children tested for an egg allergy, as eggs were common in vaccines. So Mother probably knew Vicki was allergic to eggs, but she could have been distracted. Maybe it was a mindless act.

The Bulls

The summer I was five was very hot. Heat made the Holstein bulls crazy. Fortunately, their individual corrals were surrounded by stone walls on three sides. The fourth side was enclosed by a fence of six-inch steel pipes embedded in stone at one-foot intervals. The bulls were huge and mean—a danger to one another, to the cows they serviced, and especially to people. They really hated people. The only person who could handle them was Al, the foreman of the dairy barn. His job with the bulls consisted of teasing them into a chute, hoisting their loins up with a truck tire, and masturbating them with a yellow rubber glove. Later Al diluted the bull cream and shot it into the milk cows with a turkey baster. The overbred bulls were too vicious to be let in with the dairy cows to make calves naturally. They would have gored the docile cows.

By the time a bull had his second trip to the tire, Al could bellow, "Bull-la, Bull-la, Bull-la," hold up the tire, and that bull would trot from the holding pen into the chute. Fortunately, tires on cars were not perceived as sex objects, or, for incomprehensible bovine reasons, were considered out of bounds.

An elegant lady named Alice Longstaff came to visit the

dairy. She said her family were dairy people. She wanted to see the bulls. She was tall and pretty, but spindly. Her long white dress covered down past her ankles, revealing only the white tips of her shoes.

Once when Mother and I were having hot fudge sundaes at the Broadmore Hotel in Colorado Springs, she pointed out that women's skirts always got shorter during a war. I didn't get the connection, but there was a war on and skirts were short. Mother suggested that good men were hard to find. Then she laughed.

Usually only old women wore long dresses like Alice Longstaff's. She was only in her thirties, but she was odd. Mother didn't tell the elegant Alice about Al masturbating the Holsteins, but she did tell her the bulls were treacherous and not to put her hand inside the corral pipes.

Mrs. Longstaff did something I never understood—maybe being told what not to do irritated her. She slid a gloved hand over the steel pipe and with the other reached in to pat the broad, curly head of a huge bull. In an airy tone of confidence Mrs. Alice Longstaff said, "Oh, he's such a pretty bull, he wouldn't hurt a—" Then she screamed. The bull had slammed its monstrous head against Alice's thin wrist and began rolling his thick skull back and forth, crushing her elegant, bird-thin bones against the steel pipe. The scream became a siren wail and went on and on and on. Where there had been a silky white glove was a mushy red sack filled with pulp.

The bull kept Mrs. Longstaff pinned against the pipe until Al appeared with a bullwhip. He cracked the whip on the animal's testicles—the bull bellowed, and with a final twist of its head, sheared the mushed hand halfway free of the woman's arm. As she collapsed, the blood left her contorted face, spurting from the broken wrist, across her long white dress.

Mother slipped the loop of her riding crop over the woman's wrist and twisted it to stop the bleeding. Alice Longstaff stared at the blood splattered down her white dress to the pointy toes of her

fine calf shoes. Before she fainted, she whispered faintly, "You could
have warned me."

Al had told me about a man who was painting the barn and dropped
his brush in the pen. In spite of shouted warnings, the painter
climbed down to retrieve it. The bull charged, got a horn in him,
and pitched him over the stone fence into the next corral, where another bull picked the man up and flung him back over the fence. The
bulls played pitch until Al came with his big whip and beat them
back into their stalls. I was already terrified of the bulls. Mrs.
Longstaff was just icing on my fear.

School

My first day of school Mother dressed me up. I was a little man going off into the world. She stopped me before I went out the door and bent down for a kiss. I shook my head. I was going to school. I was different now, too old for kisses.

She was insistent. I was defiant. I stared at the design in the door-knob. There was a high shriek from Mother, a stream of swear words; then her fist caught me under the jaw and lifted me into the air. I arced up and over the dark red carpet into the bundled laundry.

Then I was sitting at a desk in the one-room schoolhouse, wondering how I got there. The back of my head had a small sticky spot, which proved to be blood. Apparently, I'd bounced off the laundry and hit the wall.

My teacher dressed a little like Mrs. Longstaff, except for the fancy shoes and the gloves. She was old. I think her name was Miss Worth, but I'm not sure. The school was half a mile past the dairy. It had an enclosed porch attached to its front. That's where we took our galoshes off and hung our coats and scarves on our own hook. There were steps and a door on either side of the porch. The schoolhouse was a white clapboard building with a high peaked

roof. There was a little basement with a furnace and coal bin. The
school was usually too hot or too cold.

Each chair was attached to a desk. Each row of desk chairs was a
different grade. Eight grades and eight rows. She taught all eight
grades, about thirty kids in all. I went to first and second grade in
the Woodman school, and Miss Worth, if that was her name, was
my teacher.

In the second grade during recess, we dug a tunnel in the hillside
behind the school. We moved a lot of dirt. One day Miss Worth discovered the tunnel went far into the hill. She made us fill in the en-
trance. The tunnel is probably still there along with a rubber bunny
key chain and a cache of milky blue marbles in a matchbox—
lessons from the pack rats.

After the tunnels were off-limits, we had to find other ways to
entertain ourselves. Sliding down the steel posts that braced the
swings was a big thrill—my first sexual experience. We also played
Annie, Annie Over, a game that involved shouting, "Annie, Annie
over," and throwing the ball over the roof of the schoolhouse to a
bunch of kids on the other side, who caught it, shouted, "Annie,
Annie over," and threw it back. Maybe you missed a point if you
didn't catch the ball. The main thing was shouting and throwing.
Miss Worth got irked when the ball went down the chimney and she
had to retrieve it from the ash box. I'm sure she was equally enter-
tained by all that shouting and the ball bouncing off the roof. We
never played Annie, Annie Over in the winter, because the ball
would have burned up when it went down the chimney.

Lucy was in third grade when I was in second. She had golden
curls woven into long braids. She also had a huge jar filled to the
brim with pennies. Never having saved anything myself, I wondered why she did that.

One weekend we went for a walk and discovered an abandoned
chicken coop. Someone had written *fuck* on the issing-glass. Neither
of us could speak for an hour. That *fuck* in black crayon made the

world extremely risky. Everything became charged. I couldn't look at the clouds for fear she might look up and we would see an *F* cloud or humping-cow clouds. I certainly couldn't look at Lucy. When we were near her house, I whispered, "I have to go now," and ran until I was out of her sight.

The next week at school we both had to take a pee break from Annie, Annie Over and went to our respective sides of the back-to-back outdoor biffie. Of course, there was a wall between the boys' side and the girls' side, but I'd never checked to see if the wall went all the way down. Inspired by my love for Lucy, I climbed up on the seat, turned around, and knelt down. I took a deep breath and stuck my head through the hole so I could see my beloved's bare bottom. What I saw were dangling long blond braids and Lucy staring back.

Jodhpurs, Silo Sex, and the Fall

In the late summer after the corn was harvested, the stalks and leaves were put through a chopper then onto a conveyer that lifted them to the tops of the silos. Gradually the silos would fill, the foliage would ferment and turn into silage, which the cows ate and turned into milk. I don't remember what we did with the corn, probably what everyone does with corn—sold it, ate it, and gave it away.

Mother came in to check on the silage operation one day. She'd been out riding in the hills with Major Williams, a neighbor who raised thoroughbreds. She was wearing jodhpurs and carrying her riding crop. After she rode away, some workers made cracks about the pants with the baggy sides. One of the Mexicans asked me what Mother had in those bags. He walked around bowlegged, whipping his butt with a leather strap, and shouting, "Giddy up, boss, giddy up, boss." I was embarrassed. The other workers smiled at the Mexican but didn't laugh.

The silo was a refuge from grown-ups. Most of the staff, who weren't ex-cons, had families. There were about a dozen kids around my age. Sometimes in the evening after dinner, we'd climb up the enclosed ladder on the outside of the silo to the iron door that opened above the top level of the silage. Another ladder let us down inside. During the year the silage level would drop to the next door, then the next, and so on. We could hear if someone was coming up the outside ladder, and we'd have time to get our clothes on. The reason we had our clothes off was because we were having sex. Of course, we'd all seen animals doing it, but I'm not sure we knew what they were doing. I have a vague memory of being in a ring, both boys and girls, and bumping into one another. I don't even know if my pecker got hard. The grown-ups would have considered us a gang of little perverts. Even though we were just curious, we knew better than to let anyone outside our ring of naked butts know about sex in the silo.

By second grade, everyone was old enough to absorb their parents' attitudes about my mother, that woman who bossed their fathers. Mother was the administrator. It was her job to see that everyone did his job. Many of the men didn't like a woman telling them what to do. Even worse, she could fire them. The wives developed an intense dislike for the boss lady. There was a lot of bellyaching. By second grade, the kids began to apply their parents' prejudices to me. It got so it wasn't good being me.

I was standing alone in the cornfield in early spring, staring up at the sky, watching the birds circle and dive, when the sky started spinning. I looked at the ground, at my feet. They seemed far away. At that moment I lost my confidence. I was not the center of the world. I felt confused and dizzy. I looked up at the blur of sandstone monuments that rimmed the valley and wondered if they were there to keep an eye on me. In a single instant, I'd lost my footing—I went from being a self-centered, overconfident little boy to being afraid.

PART TWO

Mountains and Rivers

Snakes and Sulfur

At the end of second grade, the sanatorium closed. After the war, penicillin replaced the little six-sided houses, and our lives changed. I don't remember any details of when or how we left.

Mother and Vicki and I spent two or three weeks at some kind of resort. The rocks around there were red, and the dirt was red. Our house was just plain boards, and for some reason it was up on blocks. There was a hot springs, which was probably the reason for the resort. The water was extremely hot, and the place smelled of rotten eggs.

I don't remember why we were there. It wasn't a vacation. I think mother may have been renting out horses. I only remember red rocks, red dirt, rotten egg smell, the channel of steaming water running through the rocks, and snakes with red, yellow, and black bands. Most of the snakes I saw were dead. They died in the hot water and settled in clear pools in the rock. After a couple of days the colored bands bleached out, and the snakes turned pinkish white. I spent my time climbing the rocks, looking for banded snakes. Then one day we left.

My memory of Colorado was blue mountains, blue water, and blue skies. The resort was a reddish-orange stripe in a blue memory.

Spring Creek

Father set up a private practice in Gunnison, Colorado. His office was in a storefront on the main street. He lived in the New Allen Hotel, which was expensive. It never made sense that he didn't get an apartment. Maybe he got a room for the night and just stayed.

Mother and Vicki and I were living in a huge green canvas tent at the Spring Creek Lodge, a resort in the mountains about twenty miles north of Gunnison. There were cabins for the guests— tourists in the summer, hunters in the fall. The main lodge was where the guests got drunk and played poker. There was also a tiny store where we could buy eggs, milk, bread, Spam, cigarettes, and candy.

It was curious to me that people could leave where they lived, come clear across the country to lollygag around in those cabins with nothing to do except drink and fish or drink and shoot something with horns sprouting out of its head.

Our tent was army surplus, probably twenty by twenty, but it seemed much bigger then. Its canvas top and five-foot side walls were coated with wax to keep the rain out. Mother brought eight horses to start a business that catered to tourists and hunters. She also brought along Grant Willis, the ex-con, as a guide and packer. He had his own tent off in the woods somewhere.

Grant had completed his parole, but he joked about being Mother's slave. When his parole was over, I thought he'd take off. He could've gone if he wanted. I wondered if Grant was in love with her. She wasn't holding a gun to his head.

When you're a kid and your family moves, the first thing you do is find a place that's your own, where you can hide out. It can be in a closet, a garage, an attic, a shed, an old car, even a big box. When you're older, it can be a library or a movie theater, but you need a place. It's important to know, in the back of your mind, that you have someplace to go—a sanctuary. And if you don't find it, you're always a little off-kilter. Sometimes you can see that look in a migrant worker's kid, who lives a kind of concentration-camp life. He has nowhere to hide out, and wherever he goes, there's a good chance he's going to get hassled.

The tent was the office, kitchen, tack room, horse barn, and where we slept. I didn't have rights anywhere else. It was very different from the tunnels of Woodman. I felt strange, and that didn't go away until I took a hatchet into the woods and built a small fort by a spring. It was a kid house made of branches. It didn't have a door, but it had a piece of canvas for a roof and branches on top for camouflage.

I caught my first fish, a cutthroat trout, with my bare hands in Spring Creek. It was the first fish I'd ever seen in the wild. I was so excited I splashed through the creek after the fish until it trapped itself in some shallow rocks and I grabbed it, but it kept slipping away until it flopped up on the bank and I got both hands around it. That might have been the most thrilling moment of my life.

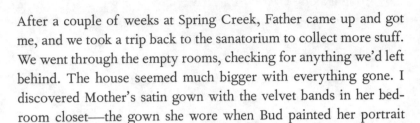

After a couple of weeks at Spring Creek, Father came up and got me, and we took a trip back to the sanatorium to collect more stuff. We went through the empty rooms, checking for anything we'd left behind. The house seemed much bigger with everything gone. I discovered Mother's satin gown with the velvet bands in her bedroom closet—the gown she wore when Bud painted her portrait with the glittery brooch.

Except for the gown and some wire hangers, the closet was empty. Why had she left her gown? How could she forget something so beautiful, something she loved so much? I asked if we should bring it. Father stared at the gown for a moment then turned away. He whispered, but I couldn't hear what he said or can't remember. He shook his head slightly and glanced around the room, looking for something he'd misplaced. The emptiness in my father made the house feel as though it had been abandoned for years.

Mother and I built a fence down the middle of our tent—one side for horses, the other for people. In one corner we made a kitchen. It had a card table for eating and another for apple crates that held dishes, silverware, spices, and canned goods. There was a zinc-lined wooden box with a hinged lid and a brass clasp, where we kept milk and eggs and meat on a block of ice.

We got the ice from Sam Wolfe, a rancher who had an icehouse. He was about six-four or -five and strong as a bull. He'd go down to the river in the winter, make long saw cuts across the ice, cut the longs into blocks, and tong the blocks onto a sled. His team would pull the sled up to the icehouse, which was dug into the ground and full of sawdust for insulation. Only the roof showed. You went down through a small door in the thick log walls, and inside, even

in the hottest of August, it was cool as a mild winter day. Sometimes, river ice had things in it, like rose hips, willow twigs, and
grass.

In early June the feeder creeks from every drainage were over their
banks, gushing toward the main canyon. The mud was so thick the
creeks smelled of earth. For two weeks Spring Creek roared night
and day, overflowing into the meadow below the lodge and edging
up toward the cabins, the store, and our tent. The nights were cold
and slowed the snow thaw in the high mountains. Anxiety reduced
most talk to speculation about weather and kept us checking the
thermometer. The only thing worse than spring rain was August
drought. Some Einstein said the problem with nature was there was
too much of it. That spring was the proof in the hypothesis.

The fast-rising creek carried uprooted trees, a dead calf, and a
little black bear clinging to a branch. If I'd saved that little bear, I
could've had a bear of my own.

Spring Creek advanced on the corral and our tent. We waited for
the rains to take it all away. Then the creek began to subside. A family of foxes came down to the meadow in the moonlight to fish for
trout trapped in shallow pools left by the receding flood. Trout,
spooked by fox shadows, wiggled over the matted grass in the shal-
lows, leaving a trail of waves in the moon's reflection. The foxes
leaped and pounced at the gleaming backs of the slithering fish. A
small fox caught a trout so large it had to drag its dinner backward
out of the water, holding tight while the powerful fish flopped the
fox's head from side to side. The other foxes rushed in, chomped
down on the prey, and held it for several minutes after the trout
stopped struggling. When they were certain it was dead, they began
yipping and tearing at their fresh feast.

Things began to dry out. The sun cooked dead fish and other

critters along the banks and in the meadow. The air was thick with decay until the hawks, magpies, cougars, and fly larvae gorged themselves on the leftovers. It was an exhilarating, stinky time.

We had to wait for a county crew to rebuild the bridge before dude season started. A dude was someone who didn't know his butt from the moon. They came from the cities and knew nothing of horses or "net-ture," as some called it. They were scared of things that weren't a threat and weren't scared of things that were. I knew about horses and the difference between an elk and a deer. That was about it, but it was enough to fool the dudes.

That summer I had to take dudes out every day or wait around to take them out. Too often it was a dudeless day, which meant no money, and I'd waited around all day for nothing.

In our big green tent, Mother fixed breakfast for Grant, Vicki, and me—usually bacon, toast, jam, and eggs. Of course, Vicki didn't get eggs. Lunch was Spam and a potato, and dinner was canned salmon and a potato, or lunch was salmon and dinner was Spam. Canned salmon was cheap. It cost about the same as Spam and tasted good, especially the string of crunchy vertebrae that ran down the middle.

After Mother fixed breakfast one morning, she sat straight and stiff with her hands flat on the oilcloth and waited for Grant to sit down. When she spoke, she was too calm and precise, and she stared at the center of the table. "I understand that the Spring Creek store was broken into last night. The money in the till was taken." She paused long enough for the dangerous-looking man with a hang-over to realize she knew he'd done the breaking-in and taking. "I want that money returned by tonight." She picked up her fork and started eating and didn't say another word to Grant all day. That night the store was broken into, the money put back, and nothing was said about it again, though things seemed to go downhill be-tween Grant and my mother after that.

I slept on a cot next to the horse pen. My favorite horse was Joe. He liked to hang his head over the gate at night and put his muzzle next to my cheek. Sometimes I would wake up to his warm breath on my face. If I lay still and pretended I was asleep, he would snort. I could never fool Joe. On hot days, if they weren't working, the horses came into their side of the tent to get out of the sun. By evening the place smelled of horses, hot wax, and Spam.

The four of us would go into town on Saturday evening. Grant would go off to drink. Mother would take Vicki and me to see our father. He was usually happy and wry. I liked him like that, because he was funny. He would make jokes and tease, but it was never mean. He'd always let us know it was teasing.

One evening, after visiting my father, Mother and I tracked Grant down in his favorite watering hole. He passed out in the backseat on the way home. It was dark by the time we turned off at Almont and started up Taylor Road. The single-lane dirt road wound its way through the canyon up into the mountains toward Spring Creek Gulch. In places you could look down at the river in the gorge below. It was remarkably steep. I preferred the ride home, because I was on the passenger side, away from the river. Anyone who slid off that road was a goner.

Mother was complaining that Father was going through their savings and we were eating Spam. She had to feed us off the dudes, which was pretty iffy. Besides that, she had to pay Grant and feed him, too. He didn't like Spam, either. I was the only one who did. I don't think Vicki was voting. Mother was still muttering about Father, the money, and Spam, when there was a flicker in the headlights. She hit the brakes. The moonstone eyes of a deer shone back at us. He stood in the middle of the road, paralyzed by the lights. Mother set the handbrake, got out, got the rifle from the trunk, braced herself against the car, and fired. The deer dropped. Grant was still out. I don't think he even heard the shot. Mother drove up to the deer. We grabbed its hind legs and dragged it around to the back of the car. It was a big buck, and we couldn't lift it into the trunk. Downriver, headlights flashed through the trees and against the sides of the canyon. She shouted at Grant until he woke up and crawled out onto the road. Mother leaned over and explained about the deer and the car coming up the canyon. I knew this wasn't going to work. He was way too drunk. We were going to get caught. Grant raised his head and looked down the road at the approaching lights. Then something sparked in his brain. He jumped up, took three long steps to the back of the car, and lifted the buck into the trunk. We got out of there. Mother managed to turn off Taylor Road and up Spring Creek Gulch before the headlights caught up with us. Mother's distaste for Spam had turned her into a poacher.

Once we were safe at our camp, we dragged the buck down to the creek. I held a flashlight while Grant gutted, skinned, and quartered. Even drunk, he managed not to nick the hide. After the lodge closed, we carried the quarters through the back door into the kitchen and cut and wrapped the meat. There was cold storage in the lodge for the legal game the hunters shot in the fall, but Mother didn't want anyone at Spring Creek knowing she'd poached a deer. She negotiated with the rancher on the Taylor River. A bunch of steaks got us the use of his icehouse.

If we'd been caught, the sheriff would have taken the deer, we would've paid a fine, and they could have put Mother and Grant in jail. But that didn't happen. Instead we had a lot of tough venison to contemplate. There were several families in the valley who would've gone hungry if they didn't hunt out of season. It was what people did to get by.

A black bear and her two cubs came down to my little fort in the gully. They sat under a tree and watched. I was nervous about bears. Maybe they were thinking about eating me. They weren't far away, just across the gully and a little up the hillside. We looked at one another for a long time, then I talked to them. It was kind of a whisper. I said they were pretty bears. They cocked their heads like dogs will and listened. I thought they were trying to understand. I asked what their names were and where they lived, but they got irritated and looked away. I decided they didn't like the tone at the end of a question, so I just told them about everything I could think of. After they'd had enough education, they left.

Except for the bears, no one found my fort. I could have hidden there for years. Grant had told me a story about an Indian whose tribe was all killed by cowboys. He lived alone in the hills for years. He hunted and raided cow camps for flour, salt, and sugar. That was my plan. I would hunt deer with a knife, catch fish in the meadow with my bare hands, and swipe bread, potatoes, and Spam from the lodge. It was a pretty good plan.

The Tin-Can Man

Gardner was a small man, four-foot-eight in boots, who lived in a little underground house near the Spring Creek Lodge. His rabbit hole of a house had a shallow-pitched roof covered with grass and moss. He kept his cars in a long shed. He had two—the Model T Ford he drove and the one in crates. Being short, he raised the seat and lengthened the pedals with blocks. Gardner had learned to drive on a tractor, where he could keep an eye on the front wheel. He never learned to look down the road when he drove. He watched the front wheel. Since it was hard for him to see the wheel on the newer cars, he ordered a second T from the dealer. Ford hadn't made a Model T in years. They found one in a warehouse. It arrived in crates. That was the story, and the proof was a stack of crates on the far side of his long shed. The crates were stamped FORD MOTOR COMPANY, so it must've been true.

Gardner's pastime was putting tin cans in the road and letting cars run over them. When he'd collected a wheelbarrow of flat cans, he nailed them to the side of his shed like shingles. He had several layers of cans on the side of that shed.

I was afraid of Gardner because he was strange, so I never asked what he was up to, but it was obvious he had a plan. The different colors made nice patterns on the shed. After several weeks the words KILL THE JAPS emerged. It was hard to make out up close. You had to study it. Then he'd nail up more cans and change everything.

Poker Chips and the Tent Fire

When hunting season came, I was in school five days a week and stayed in town with Father. I spent weekends at Spring Creek, helping guide hunters. They were usually from the East. They drank, stayed up all night playing poker, and staggered out in the morning. Sometimes they had to be boosted onto their horses. Mother had special horses for those gentlemen. She claimed it was a legal requirement in Colorado that hunting guides provide staggering-drunk-tolerant horses.

Mother didn't like trophy hunters. She thought it was obscene that some hunters would take the horns or head of an animal and leave the rest to rot. She said it should be a law that people had to eat everything they killed. Grant gave that some thought, then he said, "It'd sure as hell put an end to war."

I would sit at the poker table in the lodge at eye level, hoping to go unnoticed, and watch until somebody ran me off—usually a guy who was losing and thought I was bad luck. Once I saw a man nod that he'd meet a bet, then cup his chips, push them into the pile, and draw them right back out. No one noticed except me, and I wasn't saying a word.

The next morning Mother went up a draw near the lodge with

two hunters. Grant took two downstream, across the Taylor River, and into the mountains. I got Mr. Chips, the guy who'd skimmed his bet off the table the night before. We went about eight miles up Spring Creek to the edge of a small meadow, then cut off into another canyon and followed the trail along a little creek for a mile. Most mornings a herd of elk came down the trail to graze in the mist along the edge of the meadow. It was early in the season, so the odds of getting an elk were pretty good—they hadn't been spooked up high yet.

My guy had both hands on the saddle horn and was swearing to himself. Mother's strategy was to bring her hunters back exhausted and saddle sore. If they didn't get an elk, at least they had a little emotional and physical trauma to brag about.

On orders from Mother, I took Chips into the same place I took all my hunters. If I was out too long, Mother or Grant would know where to look. My camp was a flat spot on soft ground a hundred feet off the trail near a spring. I stayed there with the horses, built a fire, and waited. Chips disappeared into the mist to "hunt." Half an hour later, he came puffing up the trail, yelling, "I just shot the biggest goddamned moose-thing you ever saw." I followed him back to his kill. He'd shot somebody's jackass. The guy acted like a little boy with a Christmas pony, or a drunken card cheat with a dead moose. Jacks have long ears and long legs—which made it a moose-thing. Chips was so happy. Maybe that's why I managed to keep my mouth shut.

After Grant got back to Spring Creek that evening, he drove up the canyon looking for me. I met him coming up the trail, and we went back for the jack. Grant buried the head and the hooves. I don't think it had shoes. The rest we quartered and packed on the horses down to the pickup. Chips insisted on riding in the truck with Grant and left me to bring the horses, which was a blessing— there was a moon, and I liked to ride alone. Being on a horse on a warm night under a bright moon was as perfect as life could be.

That night, after the lodge closed, Grant and Mother cut and wrapped the jack and put it in the freezer. Two days later, Chips left with several boxes marked moose ribs, moose steak, and moose roast. That was as close as I came to seeing a moose in Colorado.

It was late September and snowing. I woke up after Mother had started the fire and gone to the lodge to count the hunters who were conscious enough to get on a horse. There was a strange smell in the air, but I couldn't tell where it was coming from. I put my boots on, went outside, and tried to pee perfect circles in the snow—my private art form. I turned back to the tent and watched the nickel-size snowflakes drift down and melt on the dark green canvas. Then the horses whinnied. The smell was hot wax and burning cotton. The first flames flickered above the canvas around the stovepipe. Vicki ran out in her bare feet and flannel nightgown, and yelled, "Fire." I ran around to the other side to open the gate. The horses panicked and thundered out, knocking me down. When I stood up my head was ringing, blood was running down my shirt, and the top of the tent was in full blaze. The sides sucked in just before the big *wump*. The *wump* brought everyone out of the lodge. That tent couldn't have burned faster if it were soaked in gasoline. Everything inside, including saddles and bridles, were burned. We were out of the dude business in a flash.

Grant Willis took his guitar, his pasteboard suitcase, and caught a ride to the bus station in Gunnison. No more "Frog Went a-Courtin'."

The Cabin

After the tent burned, Mother rented a small log cabin from Sam, the Taylor River rancher whose icehouse had preserved our poached deer. The chinking in the cabin was loose. The wind came in and, later, the snow.

The hills were covered with dusty-green sage. In the gully above the cabin was a forgotten assortment of rusty iron and weathered wood objects that had been drawn by horses. These included dump rakes, mowers, wagons, manure spreaders, and a buck rake. There was a pickup, a faded-red kids' wagon with the handle busted off, a washing machine with a broken wringer, and a rusty shell of an old boiler with a cast-iron eagle on its front. There were wood wheels scattered in pieces—the iron rims that held them round long ago reforged into knife blades, hinges, swivels, and pins. Slantwise on the hillside, the remnants of a chuck wagon crowned with listing hoops rested on its oak axles. I studied the mechanical mysteries of obsolete machines, while magpies contemplated what the featherless one found of consequence in their sacred grasshopper-hunting ground.

From high above, the meadow below the cabin would have looked like giant lips, defined on the near side by Taylor Road and on the far side by the Taylor River. Upstream, the road and the river separated at the Spring Creek turnoff and came back together two miles downriver at a bridge. At the midpoint, a lane cut through the meadow from the road to the river. Below the bridge, they twisted down through six miles of a steep, jagged canyon to the Almont store, where they joined the Gunnison River and the paved road between Gunnison and Crested Butte.

Sam lived in a big old house across the road from the cabin. The lane branched off Taylor Road, passed Sam's place and the icehouse, crossed the irrigation ditch bridge, passed the machine shop, went through the hay meadow for half a mile, then down a gentle slope that flattened out before the river. There were six or seven small cabins lined out along the river that Sam rented to tourists in the summer and hunters in the fall.

Next to Sam's house was an open yard wide enough to maneuver a cattle truck. On the far edge of the yard was a cabin for a hired man. Beyond that were a big barn and a smaller barn, corrals, paddocks, pens, a squeeze chute, and the loading chute.

Mother cooked and cleaned for Sam, who lived alone in his tall house. She said it was Victorian. There were three stories, although the top one was crammed in under the roof.

Sam's father was the chief justice of the Utah Supreme Court. The Honorable James H. Wolfe and his wife, Carolyn, lived in a mansion on a hill in Salt Lake City. I was impressed by the fact that they traded in their cars every year or two. The judge didn't care about staying current in cars, but his wife knew the importance of appearances. She helped make him a judge and got them into the mansion. Sam had three brothers and a sister. It was a smart and idiosyncratic family.

Sam was his mother's favorite son, and he was deeply attached to her. He claimed she'd played a major role in FDR's presidential campaign. Evidently she got out the vote—Franklin and Eleanor would visit them in their mansion on the hill. Sam said Roosevelt was confined to a wheelchair by polio and had to be carried up the steps by his sons or the Secret Service men. The newspapers had been so quiet about FDR's affliction that I was surprised to hear about his wheelchair, but it was a time when the news hardly traveled at all.

Sam had been in the war. The army air force gave him a pistol and a small airplane. Every time the generals thought about making a bomb run, they had him fly across the English Channel to check the weather. The pistol was in case the Germans caught him, and it wasn't the Germans he was supposed to shoot.

He went into the war a first lieutenant and came out a first lieutenant—never promoted, never busted—a deliberate act in wartime. Sam had a bad attitude. Sam hated the army. He'd gone to Swarthmore, and at the age of twenty, he graduated magna cum laude in engineering from the University of Utah. He believed intelligence mattered more than rank. The army must have looked incredibly stupid to Sam. He taught me the meaning of *oxymoron*, as in, "Military intelligence is an oxymoron." I thought he'd invented that.

After the war, Sam decided he wanted to be a rancher, so his parents helped him buy the Taylor River place. It was the perfect life. Then he met my mother.

The New Allen Hotel

That school year, I stayed in Gunnison during the week with my father. We lived and ate in the New Allen Hotel. Father went through the family savings within a year. He was unusually emotional in those days. I later learned he was shooting morphine and nicotine between his toes. The morphine was supposed to be for his heart. The nicotine constricted the blood vessels, which slowed the release of the morphine, resulting in a sustained high. I don't know when or how often he shot up, but he tended to fall apart in the late afternoon.

After he left his office, he'd come back to our room in the New Allen and beat me up. Father had never hit me. The first time he hit me, it was fast and short—three or four hard slaps. For a moment, I didn't even understand what he was doing.

It didn't happen every day, but often enough that I came to expect it. I would watch out the window between the blinds and wait for him to come home. It got so I could tell by the way he walked if a beating was headed my way. He used his flat hand, sometimes his fists. Once he ripped the cord from the venetian blinds and used it as a whip on my back. I don't remember black eyes, which meant he had some control. When I yelped, he'd stop—the New Allen's walls were thin, and there'd been complaints.

After he'd gotten that out of his system, he'd loosen his tie, sit on the edge of his bed, and drop his head in his hands. Sometimes the head holding went on for a long time. It could seem like an hour. When he was quiet like that, I couldn't or wouldn't move. I'd keep my eyes on him and listen to the air going in and out of our lungs. The silence was worse than the beating. For one thing, I couldn't do anything but sit there and watch him breathe.

I didn't take any of this personally. Whatever tormented Father, I knew it wasn't me. It was lack of money, lack of Mother, or his bad heart, but it wasn't me. I wasn't that bad. Not then, anyway.

He sat on the bed while remorse filled the vacuum left by his subsided rage. He would look up and say what he always said, "How about a banana split," and we'd go to the drugstore on the corner across the street and sit on swivel stools that had green and black triangles around the cast-iron seats and eat ice cream until we forgot about beatings and dinner. He'd ask about school. Was Mother all right? How was I getting along? Was Sam a good guy? Did I want to be a rancher when I grew up? How was Mother? How was I doing? What did Vicki do all day? Was Sam nice to me? What did I want to be when I grew up? Beatings, remorse, breathing, banana splits, and the damned questions—life with Father.

I never told anyone Father beat me. Mother learned from the hotel staff. Children don't want their parents to be found out. They'd rather lie than admit Mom and Dad behave badly. Besides, kids can't afford to snitch on their parents, and there's that familial knot. When they're older and discover "sharing" is a great attention getter, they shed tears in public about their terrible childhoods. Sharing also absolves them of being screwups.

Being beaten as a child taught me to distrust people with too much power. The last generation whose parents had unrestricted whipping rights was the one that challenged the Vietnam War.

Protesting authority begat the Magna Carta, the ideals of democracy, and the closest thing to freedom since hunting with spears.

Father invested in a gold mine and a single-engine airplane. There was no gold, and he never learned to fly. He'd already drained the bank account, so I don't know where the money came from. He also bought a big black Hudson. Certainly not a doctor's car. It looked like a long, giant beetle on wheels. Hudsons were acquired by outsize, eccentric men in need of room. Traveling salesmen snapped them up. Occasionally, small farmers bought secondhand Hudsons to haul small animals to market. I'm not sure what possessed Father to spend money on these things, probably the morphine he was shooting between his toes.

Something happened to him after we left the sanatorium. Maybe he never recovered from the loss of Mother and status. He knew he was going to die. It could have happened at any moment, day or night. I'm surprised he didn't die while he was beating me. Luckily, I missed that. Would I have felt guilty? Without a doubt.

What I remember most about the New Allen, besides Father's erratic behavior, was going down to the restaurant and ordering waffles for breakfast and lunch. If Father was late, I'd order them for dinner. Once I carved a rocket body for a CO_2 bottle and shot it the length of the second-floor hallway. It made a hell of a noise going down the steel exit stairs.

I could always make things. A schoolmate and I built a unicycle in his father's garage. It even worked. We rode it down alleys, but kept it in the garage. Father never found out about the unicycle. Maybe I overreacted, but he'd become extremely unpredictable, and I didn't know how he'd take it. He'd probably be afraid I'd kill myself.

I think that was third grade—the year the Russians set off their first A bomb, and I was forced to stand in front of school assembly to announce that riveting bit of history to my peers. The A bomb and cleaning up at marbles were the most noteworthy things third grade had to offer, beside the fact that I was late to discover the silent *k* in *knife*. Another day of school, another humiliation.

When school was out, I went back to the cabin. Mother and the rancher horsed around a lot. She was never like that with my father. One afternoon Mother and Sam ran me out and locked the door. I walked down along the irrigation ditch and caught a young magpie that had fallen out of its nest. I took it back to the cabin and made a place for it in the catch tray under a discarded icebox on the front porch.

Sam bought us a refrigerator and moved the old birchwood icebox with its brass hinges and latches as far as the porch. Either beauty or lethargy saved it from the dump in the gulch behind the cabin, but the trend of the porch icebox was established. I was convinced this cultural phenomenon was Sam's doing. He started that.

The little magpie had a distinct personality. I named him Inspector. He was very curious about the sounds that came out of my mouth. I tried to make sense of his squawks and cries and spent hours teaching him to talk. I would point to an object, say its name, and he would make a sound. I became convinced he was learning to talk.

I found another young magpie and brought him home, thinking he'd be good company for Inspector. I put them together under the icebox and gave them a piece of ham fat. The next morning Inspector was dead, his eyes pecked out by the new magpie. As I held Inspector's limp body, my guilt turned to rage against the other magpie. I grabbed the bad bird by the head and swung him around, trying to wring his neck. In midswing the screen door flew open, and Mother was looking down, giving me her stern face. "What the hell are you doing?"

I was in tears. "He killed Inspector. I was tryin' to wring its neck."

"Give me that bird," she demanded.

I handed her the bad bird, then watched as she lifted it above her head and brought it down with a snap. She handed it back, dead. "That is how you wring a bird's neck," she said and disappeared into the cabin. There didn't seem to be much wringing involved.

Colorado Springs

Not long after the magpie-neck wringing, Mother, Vicki, and I de-camped for Colorado Springs. The only reason Mother might have given for the move was that she needed to find a job that paid better than cleaning house for Sam.

Vicki was six. Mother held her back from first grade. My little sister was slow, quiet, and kept to herself. For the most part I lived my life without her. She just disappeared.

For a while, we lived in a tenement in a run-down part of town called Manitou Springs, sharing the toilet with at least three other families. It was after the war. Everyone was coming to America. The roaches and rats drove Mother bonkers—too bad, because the other tenants were very interesting to me. They spoke Spanish fast and made lots of gestures, not like the Mexican field hands, who talked slow and moved slow—except when they were after my pecker.

Our next find was an overpriced one-room basement apartment where the three of us shared a soft, saggy bed. When there was a decision to be made, Mother would always consult me and turn things around so I thought she was taking my advice. She was try-ing to teach me to think. Her strategy had its effect. It made me consider failure. If we made a mistake, I learned to see it as my mistake. The basement apartment was a mistake. It was damp and noisy, and the bed ruined my mother's back. We lasted a week and lost the deposit. My mistakes changed the way I looked at the world. If you know your ass is on the line, you devote considerable energy to thinking things through from every angle, a trait shared by doctors, attorneys, and peasants.

Mother found a job designing neon signs, and we moved to a motel that rented rooms by the month. Next door was a Mexican restaurant and not far away was Lincoln School, which was clean and new. I went to fourth grade there. The girls were nice and taught me jacks, but I lost interest when I learned boys didn't play jacks.

Jacks, hopscotch, and jump rope were girl things, which involved rhythm and timing and often chanting. They were instinctive tools that developed coordination and inspired social harmony. The objective of marbles—the choice of young males—was to blast the other guy out of the ring with a strong, well-aimed shot. We naturally gravitated to our destinies. Were one of us to deviate, the others would set him straight.

Mother's job was on the other end of town. She took a bus to work every morning and left Vicki at an orphanage during the day. They were strict at the orphanage. Day children were to be picked up by six or they had to stay overnight. That was the rule. And you got charged extra.

I hung out at the restaurant a lot. The Mexican waitresses and the cook tried to get me to eat hot peppers. I wanted them to think I was brave, so I tried. My mouth burned all night. They thought it was funny, and their laughter made me laugh. I told them stories about the sanatorium and Spring Creek. They fed me and gave me food to take home. I was a breadwinner.

Mother found another motel closer to the orphanage and her job. At least it was on the same side of town. I still went to Lincoln. After school, I took a city bus across town to the orphanage, picked up Vicki, caught the next bus, and got off near the motel. It was important to remember Vicki because of the six o'clock rule. We couldn't afford to pay for her to stay overnight, and she would have been terrified.

One day, Mother came home and asked, "Where's your sister?" I was paralyzed. I couldn't speak. Mother knew. She stood in the kitchen and screamed, "How could you forget your sister? How could you forget your sister? How could you forget your sister?" like she was stuck. Then she grabbed her purse and ran out the door. Not knowing what else to do, I followed. We caught a bus and got off at the orphanage. She ran down the sidewalk and rang the buzzer. A little iron door opened at Mother's eye level. She started to talk into the dark rectangle. A voice said, "Too late." The door snapped shut. Mother began to cry. It wasn't just crying. It was a grief-stricken wail, as though she'd lost Vicki forever.

The next day I picked Vicki up on the way home from school. Her eyes were red and her hair matted. She was convinced we'd forgotten her. When she saw me walk into the muggy waiting room, she ran up, wrapped her arms around me, and sobbed. We escaped the dank dungeon and ran like fugitives for the bus.

Soon after the drama at the orphanage, I got chicken pox. It was contagious and itched like crazy, and light made it worse. I was quarantined to the motel room. To escape the light, I'd built a fort with the sofa cushions. Mother had left for work, and I was snugged up in my cushion fort, trying not to scratch and reading comics from a crack of light when it dawned on me that Mother was going to divorce my father and marry Sam. I was a slow ten, ignorant of life beyond horses and cows. Worldly ways, like divorce, zinged right by. I had the facts right but the reasons wrong. I felt like a lump. Even the pox stopped itching.

Father had orchestrated the divorce and paid for it. Someone, probably Sam's mother, wanted things to look proper, so Mother, Vicki, and I went off to the Springs for a while. I doubt the Gunnison gossips even once used the word *proper* in regard to Mother. Father was going to die soon, and he wanted Vicki and me taken care of—who better than a rancher with rich, doting parents. Father didn't care about the six thousand acres and the four hundred head of cattle. It was the parents who'd captured his attention. He couldn't keep a set of books, but he knew raising cows was a losing proposition. Ranches were largely a paradise for indentured fools.

Montana

After school was out, Mother, Vicki, and I left the Springs and went to Missoula, Montana, to stay with Mother's brother. Bud had moved back to Missoula, where he'd gone to college. He'd gotten married, had two kids, and discovered painting didn't pay the bills. He started an insurance business and was in the process of making his first fortune. He knew the right guys, knew how to drink, and made a million bucks. He would lose nearly everything and start over. He made and lost three fortunes before he died.

We spent part of the summer on the Hobble Ranch near Flathead Lake, about fifty miles from Missoula, while Mother trained some of Mr. Hobble's Arabian horses. The horse ranch was near the lake at the foot of the Mission Mountains, whose tops stayed white until the end of August.

A thin cowboy named Oscar Pittman worked at the ranch. He had a long nose and a narrow, sun-weathered face. I got to watch him try to break a tough horse. The horse bit him and wing-kicked him. Pittman said the horse was a mean bastard and needed his spirit broke. One day the horse laid its ears back, planted its front feet, dropped its head, and threw Oscar Pittman into the rocks. It was Oscar's spirit that broke, along with his jaw and his pelvis. I saw

him years later. One leg still dragged a little, skimming the ground
so a broken stream of dust trailed behind him.

For a while we stayed with Mother's father in his big stone house
near the university in Missoula. Grandfather wanted to be important. He joined everything. In public he had important posture. People thought he was rich, because that's what he wanted them to
think. He liked women, but males were a threat, even little boys.

One evening Grandfather was showing slides of roses from his
garden. It was warm, and the French doors between the garden and
the living room were open. A bunch of grown-ups were sitting
around *ooh*ing and *aah*ing each time Grandfather shuttled a slide. I
liked flowers, but pictures of flowers were a bore. I was standing in
the wide doorway, looking back and forth between the garden and
the slide show. The real flowers were in the garden, lovely as flowers
can be, and a few feet away were Kodachrome pictures of the same
flowers. I was puzzled. Maybe, when I grew up, I'd like pictures of
flowers. I don't remember growing up, but I was twenty-seven before I saw a picture of a flower and thought it was beautiful.

In the fall Sam came up to Montana and married Mother in my
grandfather's garden. She would have been about thirty-five. He
was five years younger. Sam drove us back to the ranch in Colorado in his black prewar Ford sedan with treadless tires—one of
many clues that my stepfather would risk his and others' lives to
save a buck.

Sam's mother, Carolyn—Mrs. James H. Wolfe—had helped elect
one man to the presidency of the United States and establish another
as the chief justice of the Utah Supreme Court. She knew Sam's
strengths and weaknesses and was his self-appointed protector.
When my mother came into Sam's life, Carolyn, who understood human motivation and character better than most, took one look and

saw a smart, determined, manipulative woman driven by anger and self-doubt—the woman destined to destroy her helpless son.

As it turned out, Sam was, if not altogether helpless, considerably troubled. He and Mother had their first fight outside the Hotsprings Lodge before we got out of Montana. His face was red, and he was bellowing—Mother had given Vicki and me a Coke. For reasons I no longer remember, flavored sugar water was a sin in Sam's world. The phrase "fear of God" has the right ring. It was the moment I knew I'd made a big mistake. Yes, I'd been consulted. Yes, I had agreed—living on a big ranch would be great fun, and Sam had been nice. Be wary of nice.

Before Mother died, I asked her why she had come to hate my real father so much. She had to think about it for several minutes, then she said, "He forced me to marry Sam. It couldn't have been worse if he'd pushed me down a flight of stairs and broken every bone in my body." She had to think of her answer too long to be convincing. She may have hated Father because he had pushed her—not down Sam's stairs, but simply away. He abandoned her. Yes, Father had given the union his blessing for the sake of his children, but Mother and Sam were co-conspirators in their own anarchy of love.

The Taylor River Ranch

In the beginning Sam had the right look and feel for the good-man job. His stock and trade were stability, persistence, an ability to focus and to go about in dependable skin.

Ranching suited Sam. I think he actually liked cows—not something I ever understood. Saddle horses he didn't like, and they didn't like him—he was heavy and tall and had bad hands. He didn't know how to read a horse. To Sam, a saddle horse was a badly designed machine that required too much care. He liked draft horses. They did their job, complained little, and looked strong and beautiful. He had a sense of beauty, but almost never let it show. Sometimes I would catch him looking at something and smiling to himself. It might be hoarfrost on the willows along the river or a red-tailed hawk hanging in the sky. Only once did he ever comment on the beauty of something, and that indirectly. We were visiting a neighboring rancher, and Sam took me down to a shed near the creek. He pointed to a beautiful hand-forged iron latch with a serpentine handle, watched my expression as I examined the design and workmanship, then said, "Maybe you can do something like that someday."

For the most part, he was an instructor of things and would explain a rock formation or why one kind of grass had taken over in a particular draw. He was good at the mechanics of the world.

The forge was his refuge—hammering on salvaged pieces of iron, making latches, hinges, and straps, mending traces, shaping a piece for the mower—things you had to do if you wanted a ranch to work. I think he would have liked to make beautiful things, but no one encouraged that. Making things that worked was satisfaction enough.

Just before we returned to Colorado to live with Sam, he was in the machine shop hammering away, when a heavy, acrid stench wafted through the open door. What he smelled was a fire in the chimney of his ancient house. By the time he smelled the fire, it had spread from the first floor to the roof. A Roman-candle display of flames and sparks shot out the top. He'd been proud of his fancy house. It had bay windows and solid oak banisters.

That winter all of us lived in the little cabin across the road. Vicki and I had bunks on one end with a curtain on a wire to separate us from the kitchen. In the opposite corner of the cabin, Mother and Sam screamed, bellowed, landed thudding punches, blackened eyes, threw both blunt and sharp objects, then made up—the usual fighting and fucking scenario that played out in the farmhouses of the West, not the pastoral idyll of little houses on the prairie. Winters were real killers. Ranch families didn't need town culture. We made our own fun.

At first, when Mother and Sam fought, I would stand between them and plead with them to stop. That didn't work. In fact, it was dangerous. I was quick to discover I could escape by mumbling "outhouse" and disappearing with a lantern and a book. No matter how cold it was, I would go down to the barn and read.

Once Mother and Sam had shattered a few of Mr. Woolworth's best pressed-glass plates and vented their hatred, Sam would put on his plaid wool jacket and come looking for me. Sometimes I'd have fallen asleep, and he would carry me back to the cabin. One night, to make me smile, he told Mother I'd frozen solid, and he had to burn down the barn to thaw me out. During a particularly terrible fight, they'd forgotten about me for two hours when it was five below. I must have gone into hibernation. Mother told a friend that she and Sam nearly killed themselves to get me to read. She said it with a straight face, but she slid me a look and winked.

Life with Sam had side effects. That winter, Mother began to change. I'm vague on specifics—the screaming and shouting turned my mind into a prickly pulp. They fought about money, but mostly she was jealous—she saw him making "sheep's eyes" with the hired man's wife, the girls who rented summer cabins, women on the street in town, elusive, phantom girls who fell from the sky—threats came from everywhere. If we were snowed in—six miles and tons of snow between Sam and another woman—threats lingered in the rafters from the summer before. They fought about the hussy cook who worked for three weeks in August—the one who waved her "knockers" at Sam and made him "all gaga." Mother stayed on high alert through every season. Sheep's eyes, knockers, all gaga. The air inside the house had that odor of rancid electricity old fan motors give off as they die.

After Mother and Sam married, my plans and daydreams seemed less about secret treasures and more about escape. Every weekend after chores—milking cows, chopping wood, helping feed the herd—I would saddle Joe and ride up through the foothills into the mountains. Joe's markings made him a pinto. Mother called him an Indian pony. If he had only a smidgen of Indian pony in him, he'd still be called an Indian pony. Mostly, he was quarter horse. Joe was good at cutting calves from a bunch and for roping and holding. I never got interested in different breeds. To me horses were long, tall, thick, thin, short, blocky, crazy, smart, quick, or dumb. They had the same personality traits people had. Maybe all I was able to understand about horses was what I knew about people.

We had a beautiful and very smart dappled mare. I was standing in the horse barn watching her nuzzle another mare through the paddock fence. They were definitely sweet on each other. Then the dapple turned around, put her rump against the heavy pole gate, pushed it open, and set the other mare free to join her. They raced out into the meadow, tails high, flaunting their liberty and superior intelligence.

Then there was Peaches. She was a giddy horse, which was un- usual, because she was part Percheron and large. I'd just washed the sleep off and gone out to feed the horses. Peaches was standing in the middle of the corral, probably asleep herself. I must've startled her, because she kicked. I saw the hooves shoot straight out from her rump. There was a blank space, then I was standing in front of the house, staring up at the sky, holding my jaw. My hand was warm and sticky and blood was seeping through my fingers. The ground came up with a *whoosh,* and I was lying on the backseat of the car listening to the tires thump across the bridge planks. There were bright lights, and a man was bending down, peering at my neck. He said, "Grab the bars and hold on." I felt around and found cold steel bars on the sides of the table. My hands were still sticky. He pushed a long, curved needle through the skin under my jaw and started stitching me up with catgut. I guess he didn't know about novo- caine. He said, "You're a very lucky young fellow." I gave Peaches a wide berth after that.

Joe and I had certain places we had to check. There was Gardner, the little man in Spring Creek Gulch, to spy on—nothing much happened up there, just a plume of smoke, except one day he came out of his underground cabin, snow to his chest, fired his twelve-gauge into the air, listened to the boom ricochet through the canyon, and went back inside. Maybe he remembered an old fight and was settling a score, or he'd just turned 101, or at the moment Joe and I crested the hill, he felt like celebrating his quiet, peaceful life.

Once we saw mountain lion tracks, but actual lions eluded us. We followed the trail of a big cat chasing a deer in the crusty snow. The deer's small, sharp hooves broke through, but the wide paws of the cat stayed on top. We followed for an hour and gave up when Joe winded. I assumed the deer didn't have a chance. I'd started out hoping to see the kill played out in the snow. Before we turned back, I was rooting for the deer. No doubt Joe was. Maybe we gave up early for a reason.

One weekend we found an elk trail that led us over the frozen river and up the bank to a small meadow. The elk had crossed the meadow to a grove of aspen then turned left and gone up a steep, barren mountain to a line of trees. Probably a hundred years before, a fire had burned up to that line, and the trees had never grown back. We followed the elk trail into the trees, to a ridge, and doubled back above the meadow. From up there we could see the bridge at the tip of the lower hay field.

When Joe was ready for home, we dropped down out of the sun into the shadow of the blue canyon. He had to plunge through deep drifts in places; in others, a skim of snow over shale made the descent more of an event than we needed. Near the bottom, windfalls forced us up the hillside where the trees thinned and we could see the river. We came out on a hill above the road. Beyond the road and a bank of plowed snow, the frozen river snaked its way through the deep canyon toward Almont and the Gunnison River. The air was still. Joe didn't move. He was poised over the road, listening. Nothing moved except the column of steam that rose off Joe's withers and rump and went straight up into the air.

After he'd satisfied his curiosity—sometimes a horse just gets it in his head to be curious—we dropped down onto the road. His interest was the barn and grain, but he stopped on the bridge and looked down between the trusses. In this cold-to-the-bone world, there was a tiny realm of color and motion in the frozen river. A warm spring fed into the river beneath the bridge, heating the water for a hundred feet downstream. It was the one place on the river that never froze. The open water attracted a colorful exhibition of swimming, diving, darting birds—fluorescent green ducks with yellow bills, golden-eyed ducks, water ouzes, cinnamon teals, and red-billed mergansers. We watched for several minutes before Joe remembered rolled oats. I could've watched for an hour, but I let him have his rein. It was my way of getting him to cooperate when it mattered.

It's good to negotiate with a horse. Treat him well, and he'll keep you out of trouble. He'll pay attention to where he's going instead of thinking bad thoughts about the jerk on his back. A really smart horse is smarter than a dumb man. There're some things a run-of-the-mill horse understands that would fly right past a man.

Sam, even though he was smart, didn't notice a lot of things. Very little got by Mother. She believed the strong, silent type didn't say anything because he didn't have anything to say.

I climbed into the loft to fork hay into the manger. The hay dust made me sneeze—always twice. Between the ecstacy of sneezes, I saw an oddly curved board on the far side of the loft. I climbed through the hay to investigate. The curved end of the board tapered to an odd square peg. I pulled the hay away and found another. The pegs had been whittled by hand, without much thought given to their look—one tapered slightly, the other was straight.

These were the first actual skis I'd laid eyes on. I pulled the boards from the hay and laid them out on a bare spot near the loft doors where there was enough light to illuminate my find. The boards were over seven feet long and flat, except on the end. In the middle of each one, there were leather straps riveted together with copper pins hammered flat against iron washers. The copper made the washers greenish. The straps were meant for boots.

No one skied in the valley anymore. I'd been told that old Gardner

used to ski to Almont and back for groceries, but Sam had started taking groceries up to him. So, I'd never seen anyone ski. I worked my
galoshes into the straps and stood in the loft looking down at the
gracefully tapered boards with funny pegs on their ends. The skis
were too close together. I wobbled, then tipped, waving slowly then
wildly to save myself, and fell on the floor. The thump of my fall startled Joe. He reared back. I heard his halter rope snap against the
manger. He snorted, and I called down to reassure him. I got the galoshes free of the straps, crawled to the hole above the manger, and
peered over the edge. Joe's head was turned back, looking up at the
place he'd heard me fall. I put my tongue against the roof of my
mouth and made a *tsu, tsu* sound. Joe turned and raised his nose,
sniffing to see if I was all right. We stared at each other—the horse
thinking horse thoughts and me wondering what he smelled. Did he
smell the fear of falling or was he searching for the smell of blood?

Once when I cried, Joe caught the scent of salty tears. He put his
large nose near my face and inhaled. When he exhaled, I drew his
breath into my lungs and blew it back into his nostrils. He pressed
his silky muzzle against my cheek and made a muffled nicker. No
one could have convinced me that a horse was incapable of love.

To look at him, you wouldn't think anything happened in that
blocky head. He thought about eating, and he thought about me. He
waited for me to feed him, to get on his back, to ride into the mountains or down to the bridge to watch ducks. He remembered places.

Joe's favorite place was a wild apple tree and a small stream that
ran through a mountain meadow that we discovered in late May
when we lived in the Spring Creek tent. There were deer grazing on
pale, new grass. Several spotted fawns stood near their mothers.
They stared at us. I wondered what they were thinking. To the
fawns, who had seen neither people nor horses, we must have been a
single animal with two heads. I'd heard of Indians who thought the
first horse and rider they saw were the same creature. I suspect the
deer found the concept easier to accept.

That fall the deer came back for apples, and so did we. I was standing on Joe's back, reaching for an apple—the animal with two heads had grown and changed shape. The young deer wandered into the meadow while their mothers worked the side of the tree opposite the giant two-head. I slid my legs down Joe's sides, and he turned his head for an apple. The large, luminous eyes of the young deer took the event and placed it deep into their small, excitable deer brains. Joe chomped, and I munched. We watched the fawns, and the fawns stared back.

In ways we were a single beast. We remembered things. He anticipated seeing the deer again and the ducks swimming in the steaming river. I could feel his anticipation in his breathing, the cant of his ears, the stiffness of his gait, and other, less obvious clues. We were as ignorant of receiving signals as we were of sending them, but we knew each other's mind. We shared a wordless universe. Around people my behavior was often inappropriate, but horses were another matter.

On the weekends, particularly in late fall, winter, and early spring, except for calving season, Joe and I would go up into the mountains or explore the banks of the river for signs of beaver and muskrat, for deer and bear and the unexpected. Joe remembered the impression of an owl's wings in the snow where a rabbit's tracks disappeared. I know, because he would turn his head to look when we passed that spot. He remembered that if we were slow and quiet, we would see things we'd never seen before.

I was riding Joe up Clear Creek Canyon. Hoarfrost covered the red willows on both sides of the frozen creek. The horse puffed up the trail through the red frost, his breath swirling back like dragon vapor.

A sharp sound cracked and echoed across the canyon. Joe stopped. His ears twitched and turned, following the echo. I held my breath. Joe held his. We listened. And listened.

Even though Joe had been doing all the work, I broke first—taking a deep breath and exhaling. Joe turned his head and looked at me. I sucked in, and we listened. If a horse can't see what's making a sound, he'd rather wait until he's sure there's no danger. A boy doesn't have that much sense.

We heard another sound—softer, without the echo. The first sound, that sharp crack, could have been a rifle shot or a cottonwood limb snapped off by a heavy crow. The cold air, the soft snow, and the trees on the ridgeline affected the sound.

Joe inhaled, ready to go. Now it was my turn. I leaned over and looked him in the eye. He froze, ears forward, head canted to the left. We waited until the waiting turned cold, then continued up the canyon, drawn by our curiosity.

I guessed that Helstrom had shot a deer. He worked for the Henderson Ranch and lived on the other side of Comstock Hill from us with his two skinny girls and his skinny wife. Dead deer and skinny kids are not things a horse is liable to have in mind.

I rode Joe up the side of the canyon into a stand of ancient ponderosa. These trees had strange shapes and thick, long limbs. They felt spooky, as though they were alive and watching us. The Indians who had hunted these mountains for hundreds of years knew the same trees, ran under them in elk-skin moccasins after game. Did the Indians believe these ancient pines were watching them?

We followed an elk trail over the ridge above the next canyon until we came to a place in the trees where someone had dismounted and led his horse downhill. A hundred yards below, wisps of vapor drifted up from a red stain in the snow. Farther down I saw Helstrom leading his small dappled mare through the brush along the river, a deer tied across the saddle. Hidden by thick brush and trees, the hired man could make it home without being seen from the road—not that there was a lot of traffic through the canyon in the winter. I waited until Helstrom was out of sight, then nudged Joe down through the snow toward the red stain.

He snorted at the smell of blood. I felt him tense up and patted his neck. He put his head down and sniffed where the warm blood had melted through the snow, leaving an edge of red crust. Helstrom had bled and gutted the deer and thrown it up on his horse. It takes a strong man to get a deer up on a horse and a patient horse to let him. The hired man was stronger than he looked.

From the pattern of hoof and boot prints, it appeared as though Helstrom had tracked the small herd through the trees until they dropped into the open hillside. He would have gotten off his horse, taken his shot, made a straight line to the deer, then to the brush and downriver before the game warden or a curious boy appeared.

Helstrom was the kind who could survive hard times better than good times. When possibilities opened up, his big ideas fell in on him. He was smart enough—people said he was too cagey for his own good. The hired man wanted his own place. He worked hard to get ahead. Sam said Helstrom's bad luck made him mean. I wondered if it wasn't the other way around.

We followed Helstrom's trail to the river, crossed the ice at a wide spot, climbed over the plow-packed snow to the road, then turned upriver toward the ranch.

From the bridge the main canyon spread open into a valley. Two miles later it became dark and narrow—a steep canyon of gray-blue stone that saw no sun in the winter.

Midvalley, the cabin sat above the road, across from Sam's burned-down house, the horse barn, milk barn, garage, corrals, loading chute, and machine shop. In the upper meadow, there was a long, winding feed line where clumps of cows huddled for warmth.

I put Joe in the barn, brushed him down, and gave him two double hands of oats and some hay. He tolerated a little nuzzling and went back to his oats. I wanted to stay with Joe in the barn. We'd had an exciting day. We'd had only each other to answer to. It was easy to be in the mountains. They were simple—there was no right or wrong. Things were what they were. Mother and Sam were everything the mountains were not.

I crossed the road and walked up the hill to the cabin. As I got closer to the cabin, my breathing changed. Sometimes when I came up the path I'd stumble. Once I just fell down and sat in the snow trying to breathe.

When we lived at Woodman, Mother used to threaten me with the reformatory. Whenever we drove past the huge building a half mile off the highway near Colorado Springs, she would point at it. "That's where you're goin'." I couldn't tell if she was teasing, but I decided I'd run away before they sent me to the reformatory.

Now I was thinking about running away again. I wanted to take Joe, but I'd have to cut a lot of fences to go across country. Some rancher would find us right off. Grant Willis had told me there were no fences when his father was a boy—you could just take off for the open country. Even I knew everything was fenced long before that. I'd have to follow the roads, and the sheriff would find us, but that didn't stop me from daydreaming about running away.

I ate dinner without having to say much, because Mother and Sam started in on each other before I sat down. Vicki pretended nothing was happening. It was a trick of hers, she blanked out. Sometimes she hummed and rocked her doll. As far as Vicki was concerned, Mother and Sam were not in the room.

After dinner I excused myself and slipped out with a school library book about undersea laboratories, giant squid, and adventures in foreign lands, and scrunched through the packed snow down to the horse barn. Joe greeted me with a head toss and a soft nicker.

I climbed into the loft and pushed some hay down for Joe, then I hauled two horse blankets from the grain room and arranged them in the manger. The horse ate, and I read until I fell asleep.

Every morning after the end of February, when I opened my eyes, I'd peer through the hole in the loose chinking between the logs, hoping for light. It was too early in the year for light, but I looked. It was a ritual. Some mornings I'd feel a thin layer of snow on the bedding and kick the blankets, and the snow would float down past Vicki asleep on the bottom bunk. I'd climb down the ladder, find my clothes, and get dressed. Next I'd feel the top of the warming oven for the iron handle, lift the stove lid, strike a match, try to read a few frames of comics before I stuffed the newspaper into the stove, put the match to it, tossed in some kindling, and set the lid in place. In seconds, hot pitch would start to snap and explode.

After I pulled on my galoshes, I went down the path to the barns. First I scooped molasses-rolled oats into a bucket with a Maxwell House coffee can, then at each stall I measured out oats depending on how cold it was and how hard the horses had to work. There were three teams, but in the winter a single team was used to pull the hay sled.

I was always anxious about the grain room—that someone would leave the door open and a horse would get in and eat until it foundered, which could cause its hooves to swell and split in a relatively short time. It was possible for a horse to founder so badly its hooves fell off. When that happened you shot the horse. The image of hooves falling off was fused in my mind to the grain room door.

The draft horses were considerate. They didn't trample me with their huge hooves or lean against me. They waited until I was clear, then walked into their stalls and began chewing their oats under the light of a fifty-watt bulb. The horse barn smelled of saddle soap, leather, and horse sweat. The grain boxes were worn and shiny with years of horse lips searching for the last few oats.

The harnesses were always a struggle. The pegs were too high—obviously made for a six-foot man, not a boy. I pulled each harness off its peg and heaved it up, over a horse. The harnesses were heavy. Sometimes it took a couple of tries and every bit of my strength.

After the horses were fed, harnessed, and ready to be hitched to the feed sled, I'd go to the milk shed and scoop out oats for the two milk cows, who had no manners whatsoever. They pushed and shoved each other and me to get at their oats. I started locking them out of the milk barn until I divvied up each share. When I opened the gate, they'd shove their way in. One day Ida figured she could rush into Maudie's stall and eat her oats while Maudie tried to shove past. Then Ida would back out, go to her own stall, and calmly eat her own oats. Maudie was slow at figuring things out, but after a week she went to Ida's stall first and ate her oats. Then it became a race to see who could eat fastest, run back, and reclaim her rightful oats. Ida had a big, thick skull and wild eyes. She was determined and faster. Ida was queen of the oats.

After the race for oats had settled down, I milked the cows, pressing my head against their sides for warmth. When I'd squeezed out the last drop of milk, I carried the steaming buckets back to the house, provided Ida hadn't put a foot in her bucket or shit in it. I'd put half of whatever was salvaged through the cream separator, the other half we drank.

Each morning Joe would listen to the crunch of steps from the cabin to the barn. After I fed him and went to take care of the milk cows, he would've heard Ida and Maudie shoving and skidding across the milk barn floor. After things calmed down, there would be the sound of short streams of milk hitting the side of a steel bucket, giving a metallic echo to the hard *splish, splish, splish*. Joe would've had no idea what was happening inside that shed. He didn't know about milking cows and never saw me shoot milk at cats sitting in a line with their pink mouths open and waiting. When the milking was done, the cows plodded out. Joe had no use for cows.

I ate oatmeal with brown sugar and thick milk. No one spoke. Mother was angry at Sam and too preoccupied to talk to me, which was fine. I preferred invisibility during the hostilities. Sam wasn't talking, and Mother was mad and ladling hot oatmeal from a pot. Sam decided he didn't want any, but he wasn't talking, so he covered his bowl with his hands. Mother didn't hesitate. She ladled the steaming oatmeal across his hands. Sam screamed and oatmeal flew. He bellowed at Mother, who held her ground and the pot of hot oatmeal. I got out of there.

On weekends I helped Sam feed the herd. After we had breakfast, I followed him to the barn and helped hitch the team to the hay sled. We took the sled out to the far stack. The hay was protected from hungry elk by an eight-foot fence made of long, skinny poles. It was my job to drag the tall, wobbly gates out of the way. The team followed in on their own, pulling the sled up close to the stack. They understood where to stop. Sam and I would climb the sled's front rack, barely able to reach the top of the hay, and crawl over with the help of our pitchforks. Sam always threw a fork of hay to the horses so they wouldn't fidget or try to pull hay out of the stack.

We threw hay onto the wagon until the need for stability required organization. Then one of us would go down and push hay around. One day I tossed my pitchfork onto the wagon, then slid off the stack. A tine struck my thigh when I landed. My yelp carried across the canyon through the cold air. Stupidity caused accidents, and getting hurt was frowned upon. The yelp was a mistake.

Sam glared down at me. "What's wrong?"

I said, "Nothing. I'm fine." Sam would say he was fine if he'd had a tine in his heart.

After we filled the wagon, we started the run. The cows ran along with the wagon, shoving their way in for a mouthful of hay. As more was pitched on the snow, groups of four or five cows would fall back to concentrate on individual piles. Sam liked to widen the run each day, scattering the herd in larger and larger circles, and spreading the manure path. The first year Sam ranched, he said he kept the same feed line all winter. The next spring he had a giant brown burn shaped in a figure eight. The year after that he had the largest, brightest, greenest figure eight on earth. So he widened the line each day. It was harder on the team—they had to break new trail through the snow, but manure got spread.

It took two loads of hay to feed the entire herd. Man, boy, and horses were tired. Having me to help made a difference. I had to do it alone the one time Sam got sick. Working on the ranch made me strong and determined, but I didn't like raising animals for slaughter. The notion wears on some more than others.

Late one morning working on our second load, I watched from the top of the stack as a coyote followed a rabbit through the snow. The coyote was determined and patient. He'd probably been following the rabbit for an hour. He planned on the rabbit wearing down, making a mistake, getting itself cornered. There'd be a quick flurry of feet and fur, and the rabbit would escape or be demoted to lunch.

Some thoughtful townie had abandoned a golden retriever near the ranch that winter. I named him Buddy and fed him. In return he followed us around. That morning he was rolling in horse manure, when he noticed Sam and I had stopped working. We were motionless on top of the stack, watching the drama in the meadow. Buddy stared up at us for a while, wondering why we weren't moving around up there, tossing hay onto the wagon. Finally he caught on and took out after the rabbit full tilt, barking. The coyote sat down and watched Buddy make an ass of himself. The dog quickly ran out of breath and stopped. The rabbit got away. The coyote stood up, looked at Sam and me, then trotted off the way he'd come. Disgust may not be a coyote emotion, though I don't see why not. In any case, I thought that coyote looked disgusted.

We would get back to the barn before noon. I was left to pull the harnesses off the horses. Joe would come in from the paddock, go to his stall next to the draft horses, and wait for oats. Sam would go to the cabin to make up with Mother.

I Invent Skiing

Several days after I fell in the hayloft trying on the skis, I was feeding Joe his oats. I brushed, patted, and nuzzled him. Instead of putting the saddle on, I untied him, climbed up into the loft, and slid the two long skis into the manger, crawled down, and carried them through the barn into the corral. Joe stood in the doorway and watched me work my galoshes into the straps. Then I pointed the boards toward the low end of the corral and slid a short distance, waving my arms, and fell over. Joe watched me do this four or five times, each time with the same result. After another try, I managed to go the length of the corral. My minimal progress was concluded against the corral poles. The whole business seemed pointless, particularly my futile attempt to negotiate the lumpy ice. I decided to try the pasture. At least it would soften the fall.

I shuffled along in the pasture snow for a while, wondering how old Gardner managed to ski down and back from the store. Unless he had a horse to pull him, he must've used sticks to push himself along. Sticks to push—but there were no sticks in sight. The world was under snow. I closed my eyes and mentally searched through all the ranch buildings, looking for sticks the right size. I saw them in the milk barn.

I got out of the skis, went to the barn, fetched two worn-down brooms, returned to the pasture, wiggled a foot into each ski, and pushed off with the brooms. I knew Joe was watching all of this. He stood in the doorway of the horse barn and saw me glide across the pasture, getting smaller and smaller, until I reached the slope down to the river, gradually sinking down and down, until all he could see was my head, and I was gone. With every push of the brooms, I could feel his eyes on my back. I had betrayed my horse.

The slope to the river was smooth. The water was frozen over and strong enough to carry the elk who'd made a trail across the ice. I followed near the trail to the opposite bank and tried to push uphill with the brooms. That didn't work, so I took the skis off and slid down into the elk trail.

All winter a small herd of elk had been coming down single file out of the trees, through the deep snow and along the edge of a broad, open slope that spooned out into a wide meadow. The elk followed along the far edge of the meadow to a gully, then down to the river, where they crossed the ice to make early-morning raids on our haystacks.

I carried my skis and brooms over my shoulder and followed the elk trail up the mountain and into the trees. Once I was in the fringe of trees, high up on the slope where it was steepest, I made stairs in the snow, climbed out of the trail, and slipped my galoshes into the leather loops. I pushed myself through the trees with the brooms until I found a spot that gave me a straight shot to the meadow. Straight was important. Once I had some speed, those long boards had tendencies of their own. The snow packed under my galoshes made leaning into a turn dicey. If I tried, my heels slipped off the boards, and I was in the snow. When a tree approached, falling down was the only alternative to a smashed skull. My objective was to stay upright, get up to speed in the steep drop through the trees, then shoot straight down the mountain toward the open meadow as fast as I could go. I spent a lot more time floundering in snow than shooting down the mountain. Each time I fell meant an exhausting struggle to locate the skis. Too often, one of them would sail down the slope into the meadow. This went on until dusk.

Several weekends later, I was flying, moving faster than I had on Joe, even at a dead-out run. Making sharp turns on the long skis never worked, but coming off the slope, I learned to make long, slow arcs through the meadow. At the end of my glide, I'd find the trail, take the skis off, and head up into the trees.

For several days a cold wind had blown the light powder off the slope and toward the river, leaving a soft crust on the surface. The snow was the fastest ever. My crashes were magnificent. The skis skittered over the crust and across the meadow. I had to dig around to find my brooms. The snow couldn't support my weight without skis, and I had to swim. I didn't make many runs. I spent too much time regrouping and climbing up the mountain.

After a particularly stunning crash that buried skis, brooms, and my red cap, tore two buttons off my wool coat, and packed snow down my boots, pants, and neck, I retrieved my stuff and tromped back up the trail. When I got to my exit point, I was sweating, and the snow was melting. I climbed out of the trail and took my time skiing over to the downhill run. By the time I was ready, my pants were starting to freeze and my feet ached.

I decided to cut across the hill toward the river. It would be easy. I didn't want to go fast in the cold air, and I didn't want to crash again. I just wanted to get home and get warm.

The sun was going down as I slipped over the hill. The river was right below me when I began falling through the snow. The fall took long enough for me to think about what was happening. I was sinking through fine powder, falling down and down through bright, white snow into dim, gray snow. I was immersed in powdery snow. When I stopped falling, there were no broken bones, no crunch, no sound—I didn't land, I just stopped falling. I could still breathe. I was elated.

Years before Sam owned the ranch, someone had dug into the hillside for gravel to fill log-box pylons for a bridge whose skeleton still haunted the river. Fine, blown snow had filled the dugout to the top. I had skied off the edge of the excavation and fallen through the powder all the way down to the riverbank. All I had to do was push my way forward, and there was the river.

I crossed the ice and skied home, happy and oblivious to freezing feet and stiff pants. I kicked the skis off near the barn, ran across the road and up the hill to the cabin, full of excitement, primed to tell everyone about the amazing thing. Before I got to the door, I heard Mother screaming. When I opened the door, her back was to me and Sam was sitting on the floor, his hands over his ears, staring up at her with his dead face.

My elation evaporated. Mother whirled around, her expression caught between anger and confusion. In her rage, she'd forgotten about me. For a moment I thought she was trying to figure out who I was. She said, "Where's your cap?"

I wanted to tell about falling through the snow, but this was not the time. I reached up and felt my head. I'd forgotten about the cap. I stared back at her. There wasn't much I could say. I realized my clothes were frozen, and I was cold.

Sam was still sitting on the floor. I was shivering. Mother told me to get my clothes off. One moment I'd been running, excited, oblivious. Then, except for the shivers, I could barely move my legs. Mother stoked up both fireboxes and started heating pots of water.

I sat down to pull my galoshes off. Then Sam was up and bellowing at me to take my clothes off outside. He didn't want snow on the floor. Mother picked up a pot of still-cold water and threw it at him. He was slow to duck. She soaked him, and I scrambled for the door.

Mother yelled something at Sam. After a moment the door opened, and Sam thrust a blanket at me. "Here." His voice boomed up the canyon and bounced back. "Here, here. Take it, take it, I'm freezing."

She'd soaked him from the top down. He was still wearing his long johns and socks. I started laughing. When he came after me, he couldn't get traction. I still had my boots on. We circled the house twice to Mother's pleas to stop. Sam would've caught me, but he kept falling down. He finally cooled off, stopped, and stood in the snow glaring at me. I hesitated, not knowing if he was just getting his breath or if the chase was off. Evidently the cold and the burst of oxygen let him get a grip. We all went inside. Mother stretched a line across the cabin and hung up our wet clothes.

I took a bath standing in the galvanized tub in front of the stove, which was stoked until the top turned reddish orange. You couldn't just stand there and bathe. The side away from the stove froze. The side closest burned. You had to keep turning, reaching down with a wash rag to grab some soapy water. I had to have taken several baths that winter, but that was the one I remember. In the summer, I swam in the irrigation ditch or the river.

We must have eaten dinner that night. I imagine us standing, each in his own corner—Mother silent, Vicki humming, Sam brooding, and I would've been keeping an eye on Sam.

I dreamed about wet wool coats hanging in bundles from the rafters in a large barn. It was cold, and my breath was steamy. The coats were beginning to freeze—a little crunchy on the outside and soft and wet on the inside. Sam was chasing me. I could duck under the coats, but he kept bumping against them. They made a soft thudding sound—*thush, thush, thush*—like a dog thumping his tail on plush carpet.

In the morning, I woke in the dark, felt for the right clothes hanging from the line, and got dressed. Everything was dry but the coat. I got my light jacket and an extra sweater out of the chest and went down to milk cows. I missed my cap. Dozens of critters would find it in the spring. They would sniff, paw, and peck at the wad of red wool caught in the sage. Bits of that cap would find their way into a hundred burrows and nests, and comfort generations of baby mice, moles, and chickadees.

Some weekends I skied down to the river and explored along the banks. The skis were quieter than Joe and not as threatening to animals, other than deer. Once a small white animal stood on a log near its burrow and watched. It might've been a mink. I stopped, and we studied each other.

Deer were more timid. My voice scared them, but if I whistled, wheezed, and made slight sucking and clicking sounds, they would become curious and watch and wait.

On warmer days, the soft snow absorbed sound, and the quiet allowed animals to focus their attention. They weren't distracted by a thousand little sounds, bits and pieces of light off leaves, or things moving in the shadows. Things that wanted to eat them couldn't hide as well against the snow.

Bound in my black wool coat, galoshes crammed into the leather loops attached to those ridiculously long skis, pushing myself through the snow with brooms, I must have been a comic sight. But I wasn't ashamed of my outfit. I'd never seen skiing. Mother and Sam were the only ones watching, and they never saw me shoot through the trees and come apart in several directions across the slope. It had occurred to me that a ski with sharp edges would cut into the snow and let me make turns. Of course, I'd have to find a way to bind my feet to the skis, so I could lean or twist without falling. Ski boots, shorter skis with metal edges, and aluminum poles—none of these things entered my vision. I was determined to master a sport no right-minded fellow would bother with— downhill skiing on cross-country boards without bindings, with cow-barn brooms for poles.

In a few more weekends, I would have drilled more holes through the skis to make better bindings. I'd have used leather strips from old harnesses and added buckles. I needed to screw metal brackets into the wood so I could twist the skis with my feet. I'd also have to find something better than the brooms, which packed up with snow until they were icy stumps on a pole.

I soon forgot my plans for the ultimate ski. For Christmas, I got skis with bindings, boots, and poles and a new jacket. Maybe Mother and Sam felt sorry for me or were afraid someone would see me, but most likely it was simply a moment of love. I certainly felt loved. I was nearly delirious.

Comstock Hill was near the cabin. It was much steeper than the elk run across the river and it was treacherous. A road cut diagonally across the hill down to Taylor Road near the cabin. I'd avoided Comstock because there was nowhere to stop. At the bottom there was the Comstock road, Taylor Road, a barrow pit, and a five-strand barbwire fence. I wouldn't have survived on the long boards.

Christmas morning in front of the cabin, I practiced turns and sliding stops on my new skis. It was warm, and the snow was soft and forgiving. Mother, Vicki, and Sam watched from the porch. I was showing off and paid the price several times. Vicki shouted and giggled. Mother smiled. Sam watched.

I'd made a few runs near the cabin, then moved farther up the hill and came down where there was a shallow depression left from an old ditch. Things seemed to blur for an instant, and I felt a little dizzy, then everyone was cheering, even Sam. They were shouting, "Do it again, do it again." When I asked what happened, they said I'd made a complete somersault. They thought I'd done it on purpose and were amused when I admitted I hadn't.

The air turned cold and drove them inside. For the rest of the day I settled into learning about my new skis. The sharp edges and spring-loaded bindings were great inventions. As I made a sharp turn into a stop, one thing was going through my mind—I could tackle Comstock, because I could stop before I got to the roads and the barbwire fence. My parents were unaware that they'd just handed me the implements with which to kill myself.

By the time I started up Comstock, a crust had formed on the snow. I had to kick holes through, making ladder steps all the way to the top. It was cold and clear, and I could see far up the canyon to where the cliffs closed in on the river. Below the ranch, steam rose over the bridge where the ducks swam in the open river. Near the road at the bottom of the hill, smoke drifted up from the tin chimney of our cabin. The world was silent.

I stomped a flat place in the snow, set the skis down, then stepped into the bindings and levered them down tight on the fancy boots. I'd momentarily suspended my fear of gravity and pain. No one was daring me. No peers pressuring a fragile ego. This was a boy overcome by newfangled stuff and a craving for speed. The dim voice of reason was saying, "Don't do this," but the boy wasn't listening.

I lifted one ski and pointed it down. Then the other. Within seconds, I was in free fall. The mountain dropped out from under me and shot by in a blur. The speed, the icy crust, and my lack of weight made turning impossible—I would have fallen and slid headfirst to the bottom.

The five tightly stretched strands of death waited below. There were no trees to avoid. It was a straight shot to the bottom. To survive I would have to clear the Comstock road, land on Taylor Road to straighten out, clear the barrow pit, and hit the fence absolutely upright—all five strands at once.

That is exactly what happened. It was quick. The fence knocked the wind out of me and sprang me back into the barrow pit. For a moment I couldn't breathe. I was staring up at blue sky, listening to the fence twang all the way to the bridge.

Nothing was broken. The barbs left two small tears in my new jacket. I must have come out of my boots, because I've a vague memory of looking for my skis. Staying upright was my only contribution to the accident of my survival, and even that seemed like a thought projected onto the landscape.

I never knew how Mother and Sam were able to afford skis. I never asked. They fought about money and never, ever bought anything that wasn't necessary. It was a brutal time. Buying the skis had to have been a desperate act—an attempt to undo everything that had gone bad. A lot more than me was riding on those skis. Maybe that's why I never told them about Comstock.

Spring Thaw

When the snow wasn't deep, I would ride Joe up Christie's Gulch to Hebgren Ridge and follow it to the top of Haysoos Peak. After things warmed up and the snow melted off, we discovered the white skeleton of a horse in the gulch. For some reason the skeleton hadn't been torn apart by hungry animals. Joe sniffed the bones, but didn't seem to get the idea. Mother figured the horse died from eating locoweed, which got its name because it made horses and cattle act crazy. When the ground wasn't frozen, I'd get off Joe and pull the maddening weeds out by the roots. I couldn't decide if locoweed killed the horse or if rotten horse provided a nutritious oasis for locoweed. The skeleton was undisturbed. How could such a large animal die without various critters dragging off at least a chunk or two? It was the equivalent of a dead man in a downtown parking lot with a bag of money clutched to his chest.

From the top of Haysoos we could see almost all of the ranch in the valley below. The ranch was nearly a mile above sea level, and the peak was considerably higher. Neither sound nor heat carried well in the thin air above the timberline. The treeless, stony peak was silent and distant from the valley floor below. We could see the snow line rise as spring came on, and the Indian paintbrush spotted the slopes below. The fields turned a lush pale green and water ran everywhere, flooding depressions, filling ponds, and cresting the banks of ditches. I had to squint against the sun's glare off the valley of water below.

In the spring, Sam started a new house on the foundation of the one that burned. Inside, he used something new called Sheetrock instead of plaster—four-by-eight-foot sheets of half-inch gypsum pressed between heavy paper. A farmer could, without any training, slap one up in a few minutes. You didn't need to waste hours nailing up lath either. If you were a plasterer, it was time to find other work.

The burnished plaster in the old house played tricks with the light. The walls were pale yellow, but as you walked by, soft patches of blue-green glistened and disappeared.

Plaster walls crumble and crack with age. In time, stains appear—smoke from cigarettes and woodstoves, cooking grease, condensation of generations of human breath freezing and thawing winter after winter. The insulation in those walls, if there was insulation, probably consisted of nothing more than four layers of the local newspaper from March through June. The paint peeled away, revealing other paint and wallpaper from the age of dinosaurs. You might wonder what emotions had resonated between those walls, but if we knew the language of walls, they would tell us their stories, and we would say, Get over it, grow up, stop killing each other, just stop.

We moved into the new house long before it was finished. The Sheetrock resonated with Mother's jealousy. The flat gray panels, notched for switches and outlets, absorbed Sam's brooding. Dread and gypsum dust thickened the air. The house seemed to dim as though the oily dread had left its film on the windowpanes, darkened the bare bulbs at night, forcing us to feel our way from room to room, across bare sheets of splintered plywood. We were possessed—trapped in our dark and dingy selves.

Rarick Creek and the
Secret of the Universe

After days and weeks of walking and wading and fishing Rarick Creek, falling asleep on its banks, staring into the rising, rolling water, studying the trout idling in pools amid tree roots deep underwater, it became my creek. From the point that it seeped from the ground as a mountain spring three miles up in the mountains, until it flowed into the Taylor River, it belonged to me. I became the creek in the way a malleable metal can be shaped into an object of desire. At night I dreamed its water, stones, and roots—the gold, green flashes of fish and their rust red gills. I was immersed in the motion, shape, color, and odor of the creek. It was as close as I would come to having what is referred to as a sense of self. I was the ultimate nature kid for no other reason than I got lost in its details.

I was lying on my stomach, peering over a cut bank at a large trout, when I felt a shudder run through me and I seemed to evaporate. I just went away and emerged as a thought—intangible but aware—in the middle of the universe. It was astonishing. I could understand the secret of the universe. I kept repeating, "I must remember this, I must remember this." Then I came back to the creek. All I could remember was "I must remember this."

At times I've felt that if I could stop thinking altogether, I might remember what the secret was. Whatever I understood was inexpressible, too expansive to hold as a thought, simply incomprehensible, except for that instant I was staring down at the trout and I went away.

I was ten or eleven when I saw the secret of the universe. That was about the age young Indian boys went on their vision quests, when the world talked to them and gave them definition, form, and power in the shape of an animal, an object, or a place. My place was the creek. When I became a particular bend in the creek with its stones, grasses, ripples, and roots, I stopped seeing myself. There was no me. Instead I became completely absorbed—taken over. Maybe it was a new way of being self-absorbed.

I saw a stranger fishing in Rarick Creek—a grown man. I'd never considered the possibility of trespassers. The creek was mine. No one else had rights to it. The stranger was walking along the bank, staring into the water at my fish. I came face-to-face with him in the upper meadow in a small aspen grove. I wanted to confront him, ask him what he thought he was doing, but I just stared at him. I was stunned stupid. He had no idea he'd done something wrong, even violent. Rarick Creek, my holy land, had been invaded. He went away, probably spooked by the odd stare of the mute boy in the grove.

Like most kids who grew up in the mountains or on farms and ranches, I had all of nature as a mirror through which to see myself. When I was forced out and had to move to town, I left myself behind—in the meadows, woods, water, and light of the natural world. When I lost my paradise, I lost all sense of who I was.

Socialization takes time. Instead of nature, other people became my mirror. What I thought others thought of me was a large part of who I was, but I wasn't able to read people. I didn't know how to test what they were thinking about me. Having nature for a mirror isn't the only way to become a social outcast, but it works. Evidently, I learned enough to avoid being stoned by groups of nice, right-thinking folk—maybe that's as good a definition of socialization as any.

Fishing

Father's practice was in a barren storefront on the desolate main drag of Gunnison. There was a waiting room and an office that also served as his examination room. There were two doors at the end of the narrow hallway past his office. One was to the bathroom, and the other went to a room I was told to avoid.

I doubt if I understood what a terrible humiliation the move to Gunnison was for my father. At the Woodman sanatorium, he had been a lord living in his manor on a hill overlooking a grand estate that served all his needs and pleasures. In the hospital on the valley floor, he would sit in his beautiful, sunlit office, surrounded by glass cases filled with serious books and lung tissue suspended in jars. He made his rounds and prescribed. He saved lives. He was as elegant as the reflected light.

During the spring and summer, when I visited my father in his dusty office, he didn't want me wandering around, so I read *Life* magazine until he had time for me. We'd visit. There were no more beatings. The morphine must have been doing its job. He'd ask about Mother and Vicki and what I wanted to be. He wanted me to be important—the twisted wish of every parent whose life trajectory has taken a plunge. Successful children are a breath of self-esteem for failing parents, but it's a pricey indulgence. Parents' dreams are nightmare dragons to a child.

I visited Father alone. Vicki and Mother went to the general store to stock up on groceries, oats, and sundries. He had expectations for me. Because of the incident with the egg, there were no expectations for Vicki. Mother decided she didn't want him to think about Vicki. She pictured herself through my father's eyes and hated him for what she imagined he saw. She had a good imagination.

It must have been the middle of August. It'd been hot for weeks. Everyone was waiting for rain. Conversations started with a reference to the temperature in hell and ended with prayers for rain. I sat in the waiting room, sticky and sweaty, reading about a plane that flew faster than sound, wondering if the pilot could hear himself talk, when I got a whiff of a strange stench. My search for the source led me to the forbidden door. Father was occupied with a patient, so I was free to explore. Something was buzzing behind the door. The door opened into a large space that went far back to a garage door on the alley. Flies filled the air. The room was empty except for the line of shelves and countertops against the walls and the buzz bombing flies. On one counter a line of boxes and bags ran halfway to the alley. I held my breath long enough to discover a horde of rotting meat and vegetables. I ran back, closed the door, and sat in the waiting room wondering what that was all about.

Father had picked a bad town for a medical practice. Patients brought him food in lieu of cash. He was gracious and took their offerings, but he had no refrigeration, and he didn't cook. The accumulative result was roasts, steaks, and every vegetable in season, rapidly decomposing in his back room. It was a rotten arrangement. No other business in town accepted food. They said things like, "Cash money on the barrel head." But the citizen farmers of Gunnison County were taking advantage of a weakened and disillusioned man. Probably a few came in and offered food because that was all they had to give. Then the word got out, and Father was deluged with edibles.

My father died broke and alone in Salida, Colorado, at the age of forty-six. He'd left Gunnison and gone there to set up a practice. I don't know why he left—probably creditors and new beginnings—the usual painful reasons. It was one of a thousand things I never got around to asking.

Sam and I went to Salida after Father died to get his things. His mattress blew off the truck on the way back, because Sam hadn't bothered to tie it down. We backtracked several miles, but no luck. It was typical of Sam not to tie anything down—let the wind take it, let it rust in the rain.

Sam threw Father's things into an old shed that lacked doors or windows. I remember walking across a meadow in the July sun toward that shed, stepping through the doorway, and staring at the boxes, books, and clothes strewn over the floor. It was what was left of my father. In his medical books were pictures of bacteria, blood cells, and really bad skin. I tried to look through the microscope, but couldn't make sense of it.

My father had overcome the odds that were dealt him. He had escaped the brutality of a working-class life, outlived the expectations of his damaged heart, and saved lives. Mother once referred to him as a good man, and long after she stopped hating him, she said she'd been proud of him. She told me that before we'd gone to Woodman, he'd resigned his job at the Denver General Hospital because the administration decided doctors would not be allowed to care for women who'd had botched abortions. He'd done that in the Depression. Jobs were scarce, and he had a wife and child to care for. He was a brave daddy. And there were his things in that shed—scattered helter-skelter, destroyed by rats and rain. I was never able to make a difference in his life, and had he lived, I would not have fulfilled his dreams.

The one thing I kept from the floor of that shed was a short bamboo brush rod for fishing streambanks. Father had never mentioned that he fished. The rod came with a reel—black with several holes drilled through its sides to make it light. The reel made a beautiful and solid clicking sound when I turned the ivory knob. Fine brass screws and four brass spacer pins held the rims in place. There was a brass slide button to let the reel spin free when I pulled the line off and floated it out over the stream.

I had fished with worms. I kept them in a Prince Albert tobacco can with a hinged lid. Worm fishing had its own earthy, writhing, odiferous world of slime and rusty hooks. The most disgusting smell I remember was opening the lid on a Prince Albert tobacco can full of worms that I'd left on a rock in the sun the day before. Slimy, stinko, sun-cooked worms.

I learned to tie flies with fur, feathers, silk thread, willow cotton, and yellow lichen. I lacquered the filaments of decomposed leaves to make tiny gossamer wings. The Almont store stocked only bait hooks, so I made fly hooks from wire. I hammered points and left long shanks on which to tie my fantastical experiments. Sam taught me to heat and quench the hooks to hold their shape. My first flies were an attempt to improve on nature—red-green bugger bugs, fuzzies, yellow bombers, and blue zingers. All scared the trout, except blue zingers, which they ignored. After many luckless hours, I was forced to admit that fish were not interested in the beautiful, irresistible flies tied by my own hand. I was mad that they rejected my creations. If I'd had to depend on what I caught on those flies, I'd have starved to death eating my ego. I succumbed to figuring out what interested fish. I caught several delicate, freshly hatched bugs and used them as models.

After a lot of trial and failure, I began to catch fish with my hand-tied flies and suddenly discovered that little boys with stinky worms in Prince Albert cans were the scum of the earth. Worms were separated from the lowest depths of fishing hell only by salmon egg chummers. At the age of ten, I became a fly-fishing snob.

Bovine Bigotry

When the grass greened up in the late spring, we moved the herd into the high-mountain pasture to graze on government land. Several ranchers went together on the lease. It took two or three days to drive the cattle up the road to the cow camp. In the fall, after the hay was up, we'd round up the herds, brand the late calves, and bring them back down.

There were corrals, a holding pen, and a bunkhouse with a cookstove and a cook. There was a clear creek nearby for water and bathing.

All that enthusiasm—bawling cows and calves, bellowing bulls with nut sacks the size of handbags, cowboys chasing half-grown calves through campfires, scattering orange-hot branding irons, horses bucking, notched ears, bleeding wattles, calf nuts in buckets, blood, shit, singed hair, the stench of burned flesh, and old, thick-chested Sandy Dunbar, riding his wide-eyed mare between charging bulls, cracking a rawhide whip, and bellowing louder than the bulls. I don't think that happens anymore. When ranching went big-time, all that enthusiasm had the life sucked out of it by holding companies and feed lots.

Mother missed the power and status that she'd earned as the administrator of the Woodman sanatorium. She was proud of her dairy herd, but the Gunnison locals were put off by her stories. The women were leery. She was too young, pretty, and smart. Besides, she'd come from Colorado Springs, divorced that doctor husband of hers, and snapped up the county's most eligible bachelor. Either none of them figured out that Grant Willis, that mulatto horse packer of hers, possessed a prowess that extended beyond horses, or they were too scandalized to allow such evil to pass their lips. The cowboys just leered, snorted a little, and generally acted like boys.

Mother's breeding advice went unheeded. Ranchers weren't big on brood lines—they put bulls with cows and got calves. Anyone hearing her stories about the prize Holstein herd and imported bulls or her theories of breeding would've been pretty generous to take it all in, much less believe it. Gunnison was the center of things that mattered, and Colorado Springs was city people.

Sandy Dunbar was one of the few who took Mother seriously. They became friends. Sam depended on Sandy for advice. The three of them would ride for hours talking horses, cows, and grass. Unfortunately for Mother, Sandy wasn't her champion to the locals, not because he didn't like her, he just didn't talk about people.

Mother came up with brass ear tags for a line of heifers artificially inseminated with the sperm from a prize Hereford bull for hire. No doubt, the idea of upgrading the herd was hers. We had our own homegrown breeding program, and the tags to prove it. The cowboys must've had an entire litany about those tags—rancher ritzy—two-inch brass plates with routed numbers painted black. Tags were only used to identify that pricey prize bull's purebred Hereford heifers—no runts, crosses, Black Angus, longhorns, or other lesser breeds.

Hereford bulls produced big calves. Every year a few first-calf heifers died trying to give birth to one of those big calves. Sam liked to give me the job of pulling calves out of the cows that were having trouble. This involved sitting in the mud behind the heifer, who was already down, reaching in up to my elbow, finding the calf's front feet, and pulling. Sometimes I'd have to plant a foot on either side of the heifer's rump and pull as hard as I could. Once, we had to use a fence stretcher—the calf died, but the mother lived. Another time a calf died and rotted inside the womb. It came apart as I pulled. That was bad, and it stunk. To everyone's surprise the heifer survived.

What was wonderful was to see a healthy calf, encased in placenta, slide out into the bright world. It wouldn't have survived if it hadn't been pulled. Knowing that made sitting in cold mud and shit worth the trip. If the mother died, I'd towel the calf off and bring it into the house. During calving season, we took the table out of the dining nook, put a fence up, put straw down, and had a calf corral. We had to feed them with a bottle. If a cow lost a calf, we'd try to match her up with an orphan.

We started using a smaller Angus bull for the young heifers. No one in the area was using an Angus-Hereford cross at the time. I doubt if that was an original idea, but it was another of Mother's innovations that set the locals atwirl. The mixed-breed calves never killed their mothers. On the other hand, as steers they didn't bring as much per pound at auction as the Herefords—pure bovine bigotry. Angus-Hereford steaks looked and tasted the same as purebred. Evidently, the taint came off with the hide.

The Outsiders

Sam and I went to visit Gardner, the strange little man with the underground cabin and the can-covered shed. We parked in the weeds, and Sam disappeared down the hole into the cabin. I waited in the truck. Sam said I could come in, but there was no way I was going down into Gardner's rabbit den. Hours went by. I couldn't imagine what they talked about for so long. Gardner had to have been unusually interesting and smart to hold Sam's attention. I wish I'd gone. Gardner was in his nineties then, so he was born in the 1850s. That hunkered-over, arthritic runt had seen and understood things I'll never imagine. He was a sage in a rabbit hole. And I sat in the damn truck.

Maybe missing out on Gardner made me pay attention to Lee Steen. Decades later, in the early seventies, I met Steen in Roundup, Montana. Both Lee and Gardner were hunched over and short, with intense, beady dark eyes and shiny skin with black pores. Both made things from junk and were considered crazy by the locals.

Lee made trips into the woods in search of dead branches and logs with some human characteristics. He dragged them home and added whatever was needed to finish them off—arms, a head, buttons, a hat, a mouth, or eyes—then painted them many colors and gave them a story. He had three acres of guys of all sizes and shapes, maybe thousands of them, and each one had a story. He stashed the penis guys and the fucking dolls in his root cellar, so as not to offend the offendable.

He never said anything about art. He called the figures he made his "guys." Art seemed the farthest thing from his mind. Lee was the holy man of make-believe. I made pilgrimages to see him and listen to the stories about his guys.

Lee had a brother, Dee, who died before I came around. Dee made jokes with cars. He'd taken two 1948 Studebakers—the ones that had a back that looked like a front—cut them in half, and welded the two fronts together, back to back. You could tell which was the real front only by the steering wheel. On the front that was the back, he welded four chrome nymphs chased by a winged chrome Mercury.

Maybe Gardner was making jokes with his cans, and I was too young to get it, or the humor was too personal.

The kids in Roundup broke the lusty Mercury and the fleeing nymphs off the Studebaker and busted out the windows. The juveniles had acquired their attitudes from their parents, who, if there is a God, will pan-fry in hell.

Lee Steen had a spark, a keen sense of humor, and a sweetness and generosity that deserved the town's respect. They thought he was mental, that his guys made of wood in human shapes and painted up and given stories were ridiculous. Maybe the folks in Roundup were scared of Lee, the way I'd been scared of Gardner.

Had those nice folks known Lee was rich, they would've robbed him. One day he showed me his money. He had a dresser drawer filled with neat piles of fifty-dollar bills. Lee had vivid memories of the Depression in the thirties, and he didn't trust banks. He'd been selling his guys to tourists for decades and changing his take into fifties. He had over a hundred thousand dollars in that dresser. I don't know who found the money, but after he went to the rest home, various collectors, dealers, and museum staffers—some by their own account—pirated his work. A few dozen pieces too big to stuff in the trunk of a car ended up in the Paris Gibson Museum of Art in Great Falls, Montana. But the majority of his guys were no larger than a foot or two high, and about three hundred were ten inches or less.

When the looting began, people from across the state gleefully made off with the joy and radiance of two lifetimes. The Steen brothers were Montana's greatest artists, whose humor and insights still make me smile. If every one of Lee's guys were to make their way to Paris Gibson's Museum, perhaps the shock of seeing all those faces would give people a glimmer of his sense of humanity, but the stories would be missing.

The last time I visited Lee was on a bitter-cold day, a few months before he went to the rest home to die. He lived in a tiny shack—a chicken coop without chickens—just boards and tar paper, no insulation. He was sitting in the green overstuffed chair in front of his potbellied coal stove in which he burned wood. Smoke leaked from the stove, which was why his skin was dark and shiny and his pores were black like Gardner's. His two dogs were on the floor next to him.

I was mystified by the pile of boards on his bed. We didn't say anything for a while, just listened to the wind howl. After twenty minutes or so, I asked about the boards. He'd been sitting with his back to the bed, and I think he'd forgotten about them. He had to remember the boards before he could explain why they were on the bed. After a few minutes he said, "I put the boards up to keep the dogs off."

I was confused. "Where do you sleep?"

"In the chair." I'd irritated him. It was obvious there wasn't anywhere else he was likely to be sleeping since the space was taken up by the dresser, a washbasin, the bed, two dogs, a stove, and one green overstuffed chair occupied by a cranky old man.

Two of his guys lay near the stove. I asked what he was using for firewood.

"I couldn't get out for wood this winter. I'm burnin' my guys." Knowing it would be useless, I didn't bother to suggest he use one of his fifty-dollar bills to buy a few cords of wood.

The thought of him burning his guys made me sick. When I got home, I called the county attorney in Roundup and explained that Steen was crippled and couldn't get out to find firewood.

"Not my problem," was the man's quick, practical answer. After some gentle persuasion, Lee got his firewood, and his guys were saved for later looting.

I was too young to appreciate Gardner, but I got a second chance. When Steen appeared, I paid attention.

The End of an Era

When human beings decided to raise crops for cattle feed, their lives took a turn. In a relatively short time in human terms, machines became part of our thinking. The number of cows, horses, sheep, pigs, and human beings made a great leap—and no more picking up camp and wandering off to warmer winter climes—you stayed put. Draft horses and oxen became objects of irrational pride. Contests were held at fairs. Losers of the great pull went home long-faced wretched, comforted only by the possibility that there's always next year.

With the arrival of steam-, gas-, and diesel-powered engines, the fundamental competition was in the machinery. The contests were held at the bank, not the fair, and you bet the farm, every time.

The transition from horses to engines took over a century and will never be completed. Crops, markets, money, politics, regions, personalities, and devotion to the different faces of God determined when and where the change would come, if at all. The engine-powered machines crept across the country from region to region, valley to valley, and farm to farm, displacing draft horses one mortgage at a time. The horses were demoted to "canners and cutters" and turned into dog food. A lucky few went to pasture.

I saw the end of one era—the moment before the internal-combustion engine replaced horses on the Taylor River Ranch. The lap-over was both exciting and amusing. I missed horses. If you had men who were good with horses and horses that were good with men, they seemed to merge, moving over the land, plowing, planting, cutting, raking, and stacking.

With a little guidance from Sam, I learned to operate every horse-drawn machine we had. The horses knew how to keep me out of trouble. As a rule, they wouldn't drag a machine too close to rocks or a ditch and bust up a wheel or cutter bar—something their driver was supposed to pay attention to, but didn't always. I must have been a curiosity to them.

Haying season, like branding, had its peculiar sounds, smells, and images. We cut and stacked hay in two large fields separated by the lane that ran from the house and barns down to the river.

I started on the sulky rake, the least hazardous of the haying jobs. I worked my way up to operating the buck rake, then the mower. Sam didn't want to let me mow, but I pestered him. Even Sam had to be nervous about letting a kid operate a horse-drawn mower. You could stop a tractor by throttling back, but if a team got buggy, you had your hands full. On my left was the sickle blade, skimming along the ground, slicing everything in its path—hay, weeds, bunnies, birds, snakes—or me, if I fell off. With the aid of a gopher hole or a diversion ditch, those sprung seats could launch a full-grown man into the air. Boys bounced higher. My physical memory of haying with horses involved an ongoing balancing act.

The sulky rake sported a line of twenty curved tines on a long bar. I was perched up on an iron seat bolted to the tongue. The rake skimmed just over the ground, gathering the mowed hay into its elongated basket of steel tines. Just before we got to a row of hay, I pulled a lever that dropped a cog in the gear on the right wheel. The wheel gear turned the bar, the tines arched up, and the hay dropped in line at the end of the row. With every pass the rows grew longer and longer, stretching across the field until they merged in the distance. Each row was ten to fifteen feet apart, depending on the thickness of the hay.

There was a natural speed limit. After the tines lifted up and dumped their hay, it took a moment for them to drop to the ground and start raking again. This left a little hay on the ground on the away side of the row. The faster I raked the more hay passed under the rake before the tines came down. I liked to go fast. So did the horses. We were having a grand time racing across the meadow, snapping the tines up and down. That I was missing three feet of hay at a whack hadn't crossed my mind. We were flying, and it felt great to see the horses stepping out over the mowed hay beneath their feet and hear the *chunk-athunk* of the rake. Sam wasn't happy with what he referred to as my antics. He walked out into the meadow and waited for the next pass. Though my enthusiasm must have impressed him, he quietly explained it was a bad idea to think of the hay rake as a racing sulky. Stately was better than racy. That was the end of antic haying.

I liked the shape and configuration of horse-drawn machines. Most were simple, functional, and elegant. The sulky, or hay rake, with its arched tines, tall steel-spoked wheels, and high-sprung, cast-iron seat was an exquisite machine drawn by two Percherons the color of straw stubble dusted with snow. Of all machines designed to separate the earth from its bounty, only the incomparable hand scythe brandished by a muscular set of arms was more elegant than the horse-drawn hay rake.

If we were lucky and it didn't rain for a few days, the mowed hay cured in the sun before we bucked it up and stacked it. Curing hay was a matter of letting it dry so it wouldn't rot in the stack and smolder all winter. *Curing* was one of those words that described a variety of everyday activities. Everything got cured—sides of beef, leather, sourdough, bacon, colds, and little bastards.

The buck rake was used to gather up the long rows of cured hay.

The team was hitched behind the rake, and the driver sat on a sprung seat behind the horses. A buck rake was elongated and un-wieldy, with a battle wagon demeanor—definitely a contraption. It had a set of eight wood pikes or forks that faced forward. They were about eight feet long, thick as a man's forearm, and tapered to a point. The butt end of each pike was bolted to a brace bar that also supported a backstop of stakes. The rake was driven down a row and bunched the hay onto the forks.

After I'd gathered a full load and canted the forks back, I had to back up the team to make a turn. In forward mode, it took half an acre to turn a horse-drawn buck rake. Horses were made to go for-ward. They're graceful going forward, but awkward in reverse. On their own, they'll back out of a water hole or back up to a post to rub their rumps, but they look comical. We only made horses back up when we needed to get a piece of machinery out of a tight spot or when we roped calves. Sandy Dunbar, Sam's rancher friend, had a mare that was so bad at backing up she'd just sit down. Sandy thought she was stubborn and sold her to a summer dude, who had no need of reverse.

When I finally got the buck rake turned around and bumped across the field to the stack, I'd lower the rake forks between the forks on the stacker, which lifted the hay up and back and threw it onto the stack.

That kind of stacker was called an overshot. Attached to the overshot's forks was a long cable that ran up to a pulley on the back-stop of the stacker, then down to another pulley at the base and out to the buggy. The stacker buggy was a bare bones Model A Ford without the body—no fenders, cab, or hood—which made it easy to see what we were about to run over. It ran backward. We used re-verse gear going out and the brakes coming in. The buggy would pull the cable back about thirty feet until the hay forks hit the stop bar and the load was thrown back onto the stack.

Haying was a season of delights. There weren't a lot of dramatic events, perhaps because everyone was working hard and focused. Our minds didn't wander around looking for trouble. Except for the weather and broken machinery, there was a predictable pattern to our lives, and for a few weeks, Mother and Sam were distracted from their epic struggle.

Other than the warm air, men laughing, and the odor of horses and fresh-cut hay—a secure cocoon for a boy—there were only three images that stayed with me.

On a warm afternoon when the air was heavy and the sky overcast, a fellow named Dave Hollingshead had the buck rake. He brought in a load of hay and dropped it on the stacker forks. I was running the overshot buggy and Sam was on the stack. He liked pushing hay around. He called down that he wanted more hay far back on the stack, so I took the load up fast and jammed the brakes just before the forks hit the uprights. Something long and dark leaped from the flying hay, twisting and turning against the gray sky. Somebody yelled "snake," and we did what you do when snakes fly. One of the stackers jumped and twisted his ankle, Dave sprang off the back of the buck rake and landed running backward so he could keep an eye on the snake, and I sat on the buggy, mouth open, watching the rattler strangle the air.

Sam followed the snake's arc as it dropped out of the sky, caught it in the curve of his hay fork, and calmly tossed it over the side. Except for Mother's rants, nothing seemed to get him worked up. I liked to spy on snakes, catch them, let them curl around my arm, yet the glimpse of a twisted branch in the hay would scare the bejesus out of me.

Late one afternoon, a lightning storm caught three of us and our teams in the open. The thunder and lightning came at the same time, striking trees just across the river. All of us headed for the stack.

The stackers and the buggy driver were already burrowed in. The stack may have been the riskiest place to wait out a storm. The overshot was the highest thing in the field, and the lift cable was the closest thing to a lightning rod on the ranch. Obviously, lightning wasn't our only concern. A black cloud was headed our way, and we wanted out of the rain. We hunkered down on the side away from the storm and waited. What came wasn't rain, but half-inch hail.

We unhitched the horses and brought them back to the stack. The hail stung their rumps and the thunder made them jittery. A big gelding's skin rippled like he was shaking off flies. He put his head down and leaned into the stack. One of the mares put her big nose near my face and snorted. Her black nostrils quivered. I was her protector. She expected me to stop the hail.

I sat on my haunches and watched the lightning through the horse's steaming legs. Between flashes, white hail bounced off the dark field, and the air smelled of wet, musty horses, fresh hay, and electricity.

There was a young man, seventeen or eighteen, who said his name was Ben, that he was a cowboy, and he wanted a job that involved riding a horse. He wore a white, Western shirt with pearly snaps, tight jeans with bleached-white deerskin gloves in his back pocket, tooled boots, and a wide-brimmed cowboy hat. He didn't look like anything I'd ever seen. He'd hitchhiked to the ranch to ask for a job. Sam said we were haying and there were no jobs that involved riding a horse, but we needed a driver for the stacker buggy. Ben sulked long enough to let us know it wasn't his sort of thing, then accepted the offer.

The next morning he went out with the crew. After several tries and excessive grinding, he mangled the transmission into reverse, jerked the forks up, lurched the hay onto the stack, killed the engine, and popped the gearshift into neutral. For a brief moment everything was still. Then the weight of the forks began pulling the buggy toward the stack. The leverage increased as the forks reached a forty-five-degree angle. The faster they dropped the faster they pulled the buggy toward the stack. Ben panicked. He forgot there were brakes. We were all staring at Ben, at his white face and his bleached-white deerskin gloves clutching the steering wheel, pulling with all his might, yelling, "Whoa. Whoa. Whoa, you son of a bitch."

The forks bounced when the stacker hit the ground and the Model A hurtled into the stack. For a brief moment after Ben extracted himself from the hay, we were all relieved, then we were all falling down laughing, gasping in our glee of tears and snot. Ben's face wasn't white anymore. I'd never seen a person's face turn that shade of red. I think he walked back to the road and hitched a ride to town, but we were laughing too hard to take in the full measure of his misery. He was just gone when we got back to work.

The cowboys who came around the ranch were boys. If they weren't too timid to talk, they bragged. They rarely had a girl, a car that ran, or money to get through the winter. They were so lonely it was painful to watch. I don't remember one who had a horse of his own. Ranchers were poor, hired men were impoverished, and cowboys were a notch above slaves. But the young cowboys stood out in their distinctive style of glitter and fringe—the pearly buttons and those white deerskin gloves. A few wore pointy-toed, sorely worn snakeskin boots. Like carriers of a disfiguring disease, they transmitted fashion from the horse operas on the movie screen to the open range. The part of their paychecks that didn't go to altering their brains in bars went to altering their bodies in Hansen's Western Wear. What a young, lonely cowboy wore and how he wore it was a talisman—a magic garment meant to vanquish fear and ignorance. For many, those tight outfits were who they were—no room for metaphor.

What most cowboys saw on the surface was pretty much all they saw. Charles Marion Russell, a painter and sculptor of cows and cowboys, knew a man called Pretty Shadows. Russell said Pretty Shadows sounded like an Indian name, but it wasn't. The moniker came from the fact that the man was a fancy dresser—he liked fringe and lots of it. The tapaderas on his stirrups, the edges of his chaps, and the arms of his jacket were heavily tasseled. On top of it all he wore a large, swooping hat. When he rode, he liked to watch his shadow moving through the prairie grass and over boulders, cut banks, and the face of cliffs.

Most of the cowboys I knew as a boy were as vain and image-conscious as movie actors. Grandmothers called them "sweet," but the boys, when out of grandmother range, cursed, told improbable tales and probable lies, and killed things, especially things they never intended to eat—snakes, birds, bugs, rabbits, coyotes, racoons, black bears, or pretty much anything that moved. If you asked why they'd shot a chipmunk out of a tree, they'd say practice. They could never get enough practice.

Maybe the most defining characteristic of the cowboy mind-set was the desire to do only one thing. That one thing was to be on a horse. Weather didn't matter. Anything that could be done from the back of a horse was honest work to a cowboy. I've seen cowboys roll Bull Durham in the wind, pick up grain sacks and calves, open gates and barn doors, fix fence, and kiss girls without getting off their horse. Mostly they pushed cows around. If there were enough cows, noise, and dust, they'd tolerate cows, but they dreamed of driving wild horses across the plains at a dead run.

On Sundays, they went to town and lined up outside the Rialto for the afternoon matinee, which depicted the heroics of a resolute parade of rising and falling cowboy stars.

The cowboy hero lived out yonder, at the end of the mythic trail with his cowboy helper, because they were too righteous to be tolerated for extended periods. The hero's role was to come to town, do the stinking job—kill bad guys, humiliate the cowardly townfolk for being spineless, sniveling wimps—and leave. Heroic purity was as unbearable as a double shot of Clorox. We needed them pure, but not next door. And if they weren't pure, we didn't want to know about it. Maybe the Lone Ranger and Tonto hoed beets to survive and pleasured themselves in unmentionable ways. What happened at the end of the trail was their business.

I never met a cowboy hero devotee. The cowboys who watched the flickers never fessed up. Among the matinee gaggle of small children, the cowboys stuck out like cacti with hats, but their inner needs, whatever they may have been, overcame their chagrin. At least they were killing time instead of small animals and horses.

Then one Sunday, Superman was up there, a thick-waisted, thick-jawed Midwesterner in baseball pajamas and a cretin's cape, flying across the Sunday screen on wires, screwing with the cowboy paradigm. That stodgy Superman drove the cowboy heroes and their cowboy helpers off the marquee and down the alley—*Hi-ho, Silver, away!* The cowboys didn't much like Superman.

No matter what I felt or said about cowboys, in my secret heart, I wanted to be one. The idea of riding the range, driving wild horses across the plains, sleeping out under the stars, and braving the elements had great appeal. The idea of just doing one thing was a definite draw, but independence was the clincher.

Before long, I'd acquired a pair of deerskin gloves and a cowboy hat. It was straw, but it was a cowboy hat, which I painted with cobalt blue, brick red, and yellow-orange designs. The gloves were as fragile as lady's gloves and tore the first time they touched barbwire. A rainstorm put an end to both hat and gloves.

My attempt at fashion may have been inspired by hormones. I'd fallen in love with two girls in their twenties from New York who'd rented one of the river cabins. I enticed them with a pet chipmunk that would climb into my shirt pocket, then poke his head up while he ate a peanut. They'd charmed me, because they were pretty, sassy, smart, and they were so bored after a week in "net-ture," they paid attention to me. They gave me butterfly kisses with their eyelashes and fixed me sandwiches. Their laughter made me laugh— like the Mexican waitresses, only this laughter was tinged with something extra. It had electricity in it. All I wanted was to be around those girls.

Bucktoothed

I had buckteeth. Grown-ups considered it cute, but my school-
mates and the hired men set me straight. I was a freak. Mother convinced Sam to pay for braces. Looking back, that seems totally
improbable. She never explained how she did that. They drove me
all the way to Denver, where I was sorely braced with screws, wire,
and nasty little hooks—punishment for imperfection. We subject
ourselves to endless pain and sleepless nights so we can bulge out in
some places and not others. Deciding where the bulges go and don't
is everyone else's job but ours, and they can never make up their
minds.

After a couple of trips over the mountains for the initial installa-
tion, Mother and Sam arranged for me to stay with relatives in Denver for the rest of the summer and have my braces tweaked weekly.
I stayed with one of my father's sisters, Ann, and her husband, Gordon, who'd been a war hero. "Gordon" sounded heroic—a huge
warrior covered in leather armor, swinging a thick sword. But the
war had left a dark cloud in Gordon's mind, and he wasn't very
heroic by the time I came to stay. Ann said, "Gordon keeps to himself." He had a small room that was referred to as the study, but he

never studied. Sometimes he sat in the little room all day, stared out the window, and kept to himself.

Their daughter, Ellen, the cousin who would later write to me about Vicki and the egg, was beautiful and smart and played the piano. She played the theme from *The Third Man* a lot. It was a movie I'd never seen. Eventually, I tired of *The Third Man* and gloomy Gordon, the brooding war hero. Ellen had a cousin who played high school football and ran with a gang. He was a good guy. At least he got me into the gang even though I was a lot younger. Somehow it wasn't like a real gang. We went all summer without having to fight anybody, and I didn't have to prove I was tough.

On weekends we went down to watch the real gangs on Larimer Street. Those were older guys who'd fought in the war or pretended they had. Some let you think they'd been in the thick of it when they'd been riding a swivel chair and cooking the army's books for the black-market guys. They weren't spit-and-polish types. They were angry and sulky and ragtag. They rode army-surplus motorcycles, wore surplus boots and jackets, and smoked Lucky Strikes. They drank stink whiskey and the local piss beer. No one talked, but a lot got said. They stood around checking things out. They were waiting. They were prepared to wait for a long time. There was a fight one night outside a movie house—three on one. Even that was quiet. Just the *thud-thud* of fists. The guy went down. Then it was the *thud-thud* of boots. The fight stopped, and blood was seeping out of his nose. The marquee lights reflected off the blood, turning it different shades of red. We were hypnotized. A little trickle of blood pushed its way out of the puddle and came in my direction. Then the guy let out a groan. The groan broke the spell, and we took off. I don't know what the others had in their heads, but I was running from a river of blood.

After that we started going to the amusement park at Lakeside. The most memorable thing about the gang was running. We ran through other gangs' territories to get to places. As long as we showed respect by running, they didn't bother us, at least that's what I was told. We never had to test the theory. I like to think we were a make-believe gang running from imaginary gangs.

That summer, we showed a lot of respect—we had to run through three different territories to get to Lakeside where the roller coaster shot out over the lake. They said one time the roller coaster went off the track into the lake and everybody drowned. Of course, somebody had to say that. Somebody said a kid jumped so high off the swimming pool diving board that he grabbed a high-voltage line and got electrocuted, and they left the hands on the line to teach other kids a lesson. Being in a gang makes you believe all kinds of silly crap—a basic requirement for people in groups.

On the ranch I could perfect the illusion that I wasn't lacking in native savvy. There was time to think, anyway. There was time to get an idea about someone. In the city I had to deal with lots of strangers. You were expected to figure people out without knowing them. I had to think faster about everything—at least I had to decide faster. In the beginning, the brooding quiet of gang life drew me in. The gang seemed to run in opposition to city life. There were gang rules and gang time. The gang felt slow, something like cowboys, but it wasn't like that at all. In a gang there was a storm under the surface. No one talked. It was more a language of gestures, glances, silences, and slang grunts that compressed everything into small wads of condemnation. I learned that everything was loaded, and most guys had a hair trigger. Every little thing had consequences. You didn't talk, because anything you said could come back on you. If just looking at someone could be taken the wrong way, why screw with words?

At the end of the summer I went home. Ranch life had changed. The hired hands, the other ranchers who dropped in, even my parents talked too much. I couldn't tell if someone was being sarcastic or joking. I got suspicious when people were cheery. I wondered what the cows were thinking. It took a couple of weeks to get a grip on cowboy time and ranch life, where a cow was just a cow.

I was able to disappear back into nature, into that world where I didn't have to think about who I was all the time, or what others thought of me.

Slide Rock

Not long after I got home, I was confronted by another difference between nature and the city. In the mountains I didn't have the luxury of blaming my bad luck and poor judgment on others. My mistakes were my own.

Mother wanted to be alone one day. She pointedly suggested I take Vicki for a ride. We saddled up and started out in the early afternoon. I don't remember where we went, but much of the landscape has stayed in my mind. The ride was uneventful. I was a little annoyed at having to watch out for my sister. She wasn't a bad rider, but she didn't pay attention to things like tree limbs, so she was a worry.

We rode until she wanted to head home. I decided to take a ridgeline I'd never been on before. We found a deer path and followed it for a good hour. The ridge started to drop off sharply on both sides, where it turned to loose shale. The trail narrowed until it felt as if we were riding on the edge of a giant stone knife. Then the trail disappeared as though the deer had taken wing. The horses started to balk. There wasn't enough room on the ridge to turn around, and they couldn't back out. We were stuck. I was staring down at the shale slide, wondering what to do, when I noticed a shadow spreading across the valley floor, moving in our direction. Some huge thing was descending upon us. The sun was setting— night was falling. Now there was real reason to panic.

We were in such a fix that even if Mother and Sam could get to us, there wasn't a thing they could do to help. When the horses stopped, Vicki got scared. She started to cry. I said, "Don't cry, Vicki. We'll be okay." And she stopped crying. She really believed her big brother could save her.

Because of the work I've done and the places I've been, I've come so close to being killed so many times that I've stopped counting. But I can remember twice when I almost killed someone else, and this was one.

I told Vicki to tie her reins loose, then put her hands around her horse's neck and slip off the saddle. If she held on tight, she'd land on her feet in front of the horse. If she let loose, she'd tumble down the mountain. She held on. Then I did the same. We stood for a moment, getting our nerve, and watched the shadow move up the mountain toward us. There was only one thing I could think to do, and that was to slide the shale to the bottom. The problem was the horses. I told Vicki to wait until her horse was clear, then to sit down and slide to the bottom using her feet as brakes. It'll be like sledding, I told her. Then I took Joe's reins, stepped off the trail, and started to slide standing up. I didn't want to sit down, because I was afraid Joe would crush me. If I could stay on my feet, I had a chance of getting out of the way.

Joe's head came around, then he pivoted on his hind legs and came down behind me. His rump was on the shale and his front feet were braced in front of him. Vicki's horse followed and managed to catch up with Joe. The two horses put their muzzles in the middle of my back and we slid clear to the bottom. We all got down without a scratch.

Had I really thought about our chances, I would have been too terrified to slide down that mountain. My naivete had been our savior. We felt terrific. Really full of ourselves. Vicki was laughing. The horses were tossing their heads and snorting. They knew they'd done something extraordinary.

We were in the bottom of a canyon. The sky was still light, and we weren't more than four miles from home. We'd be on the road before dark. The first thing I noticed was that there didn't seem to be a trail. There was always a trail in these canyons. We got on our horses and started down. It wasn't long before we figured out why there wasn't a trail. Dense patches of downed lodgepole pine covered the bottom of the canyon. A twister had come through and knocked down every tree in its path. Getting a horse over a single log two feet off the ground takes patience. Just moving through that mat of timber with my sister seemed overwhelming—with the horses it seemed impossible. The slide had been the easy part.

I'd start with one log, then the next, but soon I'd trapped myself. The horses had to be turned around, sometimes backed out. I would try another route. If I were charged with designing hell, it wouldn't be a hot bath and brimstone, it would be the endless struggle of coaxing panicky horses through wind-fallen timber at night, followed by a terrified, whimpering little sister. It was so agonizing, I don't remember a lot of detail. It just went on and on. All of us were cut up and scraped. The horses, being heavy and thin-skinned, got the worst of it. Their legs were nearly stripped. We stopped to rest once, but the hopelessness of what I'd gotten us into overwhelmed me. We didn't stop again.

We persisted, and we got out. Long after dark we reached the road. It was a black, moonless night, and we were so tired we felt dead.

Looking back, the smart thing to do would have been to walk out and leave the horses and come back for them in the daylight. They might have figured it out on their own. But I didn't do that, so I'll never know.

Killings

A slingshot is a simple weapon, just a forked branch and a strip of inner tube. I probably invented slingshots, too. I found a branch off a willow that looked about right, cut it down to size, stripped the bark off, and notched the fork ends for the strip of inner-tube rubber. There were a dozen ways to attach the rubber to the fork. The most successful method I'd found was to cut a slot on the end of each fork and tie knots at the ends of the rubber to keep it from slipping through the slots. That way the tension was even on the release.

I shot at dozens of birds in flight but always missed. I shot at bats from the barn loft in the evening. They came in close and fast but always dodged my stones. I had to be the worst shot in the world, but bats were phenomenal dodgers. One day in frustration I took a shot at a bird on a pole fence. I got lucky. It was a beautiful bird, maybe a bunting. It had a dusty blue chest and some reddish markings near its small black beak. I'd killed something—stopped it in its tracks. One minute it was alive and spectacular, its head bopping around scanning for bugs, just full of itself, then zap, it was dead. I felt stupid and sick.

Killing for food was a simple, matter-of-fact thing, but I found killing for the fun of killing wasn't fun. It bordered on horrible. I'd destroyed something I wasn't prepared to lose. My empathy wasn't for the dead bird, it was for the loss of something I thought was beautiful. The bird was dead—I was the one in pain. If it wasn't for self-pity, would we feel pity at all?

I was still standing in the yard, feeling bad about killing the bird, when its mate flew down and sat in the same place on the fence. She was alone and confused. She didn't know what to do. I felt terrible for the bird and for myself. I put another stone in my slingshot and fired. To my surprise, I hit her. I never wanted to kill anything again.

Henderson's hired hand, Helstrom, and his skinny wife had a fight outside the Almont store. Before it was over, he gave her a black eye and broke a tooth. I heard about that later. I was on the school bus, and Mother had come to pick me up. Usually she got me at the store, which was across the bridge from where the bus stopped, but she was early, so she drove over the bridge and waited. The ruckus started in front of the store and ended before the bus came. Mother picked me up and asked the Helstrom girls if they wanted a ride across the bridge, but they were shy and looked at the road and shook their heads. When we crossed the bridge, Mrs. Helstrom was sitting on the steps, hunched over and shaking. I guessed what'd happened and thought about the girls seeing their mother like that.

We didn't stop, because there were a lot of people around her by then, and we had to get home to get ready for the roundup. Both our ranch and Henderson's were part of the grazing association that leased summer pasture from the Forest Service. We were going up early the next morning to start the herds down. The Helstroms had their horses in a trailer, because they were headed up to bring Henderson's cows down with the rest.

After he'd tired of beating his wife, Helstrom had taken his wife's roan mare out of the trailer, tied it to the frame with the halter rope, and started the pickup. As his wife watched, he gunned the engine, jerked the mare off balance, and dragged her up the road.

Mother and I didn't understand what had happened at first. I was thinking about the Helstrom girls when I heard Mother swearing. There was a dark red streak down the middle of the road. It was obvious that something was being dragged. Mother had put everything together and knew what was happening. She was swearing and crying. I watched the streak widen, then there was a gush of red. Helstrom had dragged the mare until her hide tore open and her insides spilled out.

He must have driven back down the canyon that night. The next morning we had to start Henderson's cows down ourselves. It was a good thing we never saw Helstrom again. I wanted to kill him. Mother and Sandy Dunbar would have. There was speculation that he'd run off with another woman. No one knew much about him. He'd kept to himself and raised hell with his family if they talked to anybody. His wife said she was going back to her parents' place, which was in Nebraska or Kansas. I wonder what happened to the skinny girls whose father dragged their mother's roan mare to death.

Our Bank Robbers

A couple of weeks after hunting season, some cowboys drove up the road and stopped outside the gate. I was carrying a pail of milk from the barn to the house when I saw them. They sat in their car looking things over. I stood in the yard and watched until my arm ached, then went in to run the milk through the separator. They pulled up near the house, and one of them got out and came to the front door. They'd heard we had cabins to rent. Sam said it was the first time anyone rented a cabin after the end of hunting season.

They didn't say what they were doing, and Sam didn't ask. For whatever reason, they'd come to hole up. I decided they were bank robbers. Once a week they'd go to Almont for groceries. There were four of them—all thin and dirty. The only way to wash was in a tub, and you had to heat water on the wood cookstove. Once you washed, you had to rinse in your dirty water unless you wanted to start all over, so once you got real dirty there wasn't much point in bathing. Some people went all fall and winter without looking at more than a glass full of water at a time. Gardner never bathed. He did fall off his mule in the middle of Spring Creek the summer we lived in the tent, but soap wasn't involved. There's a limit to dirty, after which dirt won't stick to you. That's when your skin gets shiny. The cowboy bank robbers reached their limit before they found us, but they liked new outfits. The woman who ran the Almont store said they lived on eggs and Spam and bought new clothes every week—shirts, underwear, socks, and Levi's—and left their old ones in the trash. She'd never seen anything like it. She was suspicious from the first.

I was always on the watch for them. Even though I couldn't see the cabins from the house, I could see the smoke from their stove curl and twist up through the cottonwoods along the river. I'd never seen smoke near the river in the late fall when the trees trunks were black. The air currents that skimmed the foot of the mountain had been invisible until those cowboys fired up the stove. Some days their smoke went straight up and disappeared. Other days it curled and snapped through the tall, black branches, and sometimes it lay low, spreading up and down the river like a mist.

I wasn't just curious, I had cowboy bank robbers on the mind night and day. Had they killed anyone? Where did they stash their loot? One day they went to town—all four slouching in their gray '38 Plymouth. I walked down the lane to their cabin and peered in through a window. It was dim and grimy inside. There was a table and four chairs. The only thing on that table was a heap of cigarette butts in a pie pan.

Four grown men, sitting at an empty table, chain-smoking all day and half the night, had to be on the run. Mother called them "our bank robbers," but it was hard to believe outlaws were hiding out in our cabin.

That night I lay awake thinking about that pie pan of crushed cigarette butts and how scared those guys were. I didn't want the cowboys to get caught, but I knew they would. I was going to turn out just like them. Someday, I'd end up on the lam.

In fact, they had robbed a bank, drawn guns and pointed them at people, taken a bag of bills, and fled in their Plymouth across the mountains. The sheriff arrested them outside the Almont store. The arrest sounded simple and uneventful. If shots had been fired, people would still be talking about it.

The cowboy bank robbers probably came home from fighting Nazis, expecting a little respect and a job. After two or three years the opportunity train hadn't stopped at their door. They decided to make their own luck, but they were too desperate and they lacked that essential ingredient—a firm belief that banks needed robbing.

When they came to the end of their plan or ran out of courage, they rented a cabin on the river and waited for the sheriff. If Sam suspected, he never turned them in, either because he didn't like to mess in other people's business or he just didn't give a damn. Maybe he felt sorry for them.

Every time I read about a bank robbery, I wonder what happened to our desperados. If they're alive today, they'd be in their mideighties.

The Elk

Every winter the ranchers had big problems with elk. One morning we woke up and counted three different herds in the field—150 elk. Mostly we were plagued by small herds. They'd wait in the trees until dark, then come down and break through the stack fences, eat their fill, and leave. Then the cows would come in, pull hay from the stack, and trample more than they ate. We tried to scare off the elk, but shouting and firing the shotgun into the air didn't affect them. The state Fish and Game gave us fireworks. We shot a bunch off, but the elk didn't budge. Nothing deterred elk. Sam had had enough of a small herd that came down every night, crossed the river, and raided the stacks. He decided to follow their trail into the mountains and kill as many as he could. For reasons I've forgotten, he took me with him.

Finding the elk was the easy part. They aren't like deer, who spook and bound away—elk stand around wondering what to do next. It turned out that this particular herd made the trail I climbed for skiing, so I'd thought about them a lot, but never gone far enough up the trail to spot them. They'd done me a big favor. Without that trail, I'd never have made it up the mountain to ski. Sam and I had to climb the same trail to kill them. We passed the place where I always climbed out of the trail and kept going until we were well up into the trees.

Sam spotted them first. They were less than fifty yards above us, lying under some big pines. When they saw us they started to get up, rumps first, then their front legs. Sam stood straight as a pole and started firing. He was nervous. What he was doing was illegal. Killing a bunch of elk and leaving them to rot could put him in jail. His shots were wild. He managed to down five of the six. Two died, the others were partially paralyzed. One elk with a big rack walked into the dense trees, one careful step at a time. Sam kept shooting and missing. The sound of each shot ricocheted across the valley. He was a bad shot that day. Had he believed it was his right to kill those elk, his focus would've been sharp and his hand steady. Believers are sure shots.

Sam ran out of bullets with three downed elk still to be killed. They lay there and watched us come up the trail toward them. It must have been steep at that point, because their trail zigzagged up the hill into the trees. I walked up to one whose back legs were paralyzed, intent on cutting his throat with my hunting knife. He struck out with a front hoof, clipped the knife, and knocked it into the air. The knife disappeared in the snow.

Sam didn't have a knife. For a moment he stood in the midst of his little massacre, traumatized and motionless. He had a look in his eyes I'd never seen before. When he saw me staring at him, he turned to the task at hand. He grabbed his rifle by the barrel, lifted it over his head, and brought it down on the neck of a young bull elk.

I waded through the snow to a dead pine, broke off a sap-heavy branch, and waded back. Up close, my elk had a huge rack. He seemed impossibly large and prehistoric—he was down, but I was swinging up at his head. For some reason he never used his horns, just stared at me from the corner of his eye, waiting for the impact as though he knew he was dying and wanted it to be over with. I dazed him with a solid blow behind the ear, then kept swinging until he was dead.

Killing can be a simple business. My hands were steady, and there were no second thoughts darting around in my head. I was focused on the job of killing that elk. On a ranch you hear the phrase "put it out of its misery" several times in a year. It's a practical, necessary thing, an act of mercy—something you can believe in. It's when you have doubts that killing gets messy.

The Hole in the Wall

By Christmas, the pressure in the house felt ominous. I didn't want to touch anything. The walls seemed charged and brittle. Sam and I came in from feeding the cows. He'd stopped speaking two weeks before. We had worked next to each other in total silence all morning. He stood in the doorway between the kitchen and the living room, his arms limp at his sides, and glared at the Christmas tree that Mother, Vicki, and I had put up the week before. Then he turned back to face the door jamb, spread his legs to brace himself, and began pounding his fists into the wall on either side until he'd pounded a hole clear through. His fists were bloody. Saliva drooled over his lip and down his chin.

He gripped the holes in the broken Sheetrock and began slamming his head into the door jamb. Blood splattered several feet each time his head smacked against the jamb. *Smack, smack, smack.* He stopped when he got woozy. Head wounds really bleed. Blood poured down his face, soaked his undershirt, streaked the jamb, and sprayed the Sheetrock. He turned and stared in our direction—the whites of his eyes shining through the dripping-red mask. It was one hell of an impressive sight.

For a moment, for the first time ever, maybe, we felt something in common—like a family, all feeling the same thing at the same time. Except what we were feeling was a heady mix of terror and bewilderment.

Neither Mother nor Sam would clean up the blood or repair the hole in the wall. For each of them, the refusal to erase the blackened blood was a message. I tried wiping the blood off, but it'd soaked into the bare wood and unpainted Sheetrock. Vicki would stand in the doorway and stare at the stain. I don't know what she was thinking. It's probably there today, under several layers of paint that will peel away and people will wonder. Evidence of past lives.

The Big Snow

That winter there were places where the depth of the snow seems inconceivable now. Some places in Crested Butte had double-decker outhouses. At some point, you stopped digging down to ground level and started climbing up to the second story. One old man slipped off his hard-packed, icy path into the soft snow. He was discovered days later frozen solid, his arms clinging to the ice path. When I heard the story, I wondered if he slipped going or returning, but further information was not forthcoming. Perhaps it was a rural legend. Not many die clutching their path.

We were snowed in for most of February and had to consume an entire case of canned spinach. A big case. Having to work through a case of spinach isn't a terrible thing, but my bad memories focused on those endless cans of spinach. People who lived on ranches had a survivalist strain, and they tended toward irrational behavior in the winter months. How else do you account for canned spinach?

After fifteen days with snow to the eaves and no human contact beyond the fear spawned by Sam's bellowing and Mother's screaming, my only escapes were milking, lunging the team through the snow to feed the cows, and taking care of Joe and the draft horses. The rest of the time I hid with my books—either in Joe's manger or in the outhouse with a lantern. Our house in February might have been a diabolical experiment in human nature. In any case, I got the feeling we were being fiddled with.

The grown-ups were ready to reach for the guns, when far down the canyon, below the bridge, we heard the high pitch of a wound-out diesel engine. The county was coming to dig us out.

The plow had a giant rotary fan in front that ate its way through the snow and blew a huge plume, up and away from the road. Long after the snow melted off the pastures, the road would be defined by a barrier of ice on either side. The melt would run down the middle, leaving muddy ruts long into spring.

It was a cold day with no wind, and we could see the plume move up the canyon. After what seemed hours, it ate its way past the house and up the valley toward Spring Creek, leaving a ridge of snow eight feet high. We had to dig through to get to the road, but we were free. At least I was free, I could go to school. I hated school.

Joe had a habit of making new paths through the snow in the corral. From time to time he stopped to check out the gate. Where did he think he was going? Where did he want to go? The other horses stood in the center of the corral watching the steam rise from their collective nostrils.

The day I went back to school, Mother and I crunched down the road to the adobe garage that housed the Ford. We left the chains on from first snow until the mud dried in the spring.

The piston rings on that car were so badly worn that compression was a wish—the windshield wipers worked only when you took your foot off the gas. The sudden pressure on the cylinders helped beat the lead babbitt bearings out of the crankshaft and made that nice knocking sound. When the temperature dropped below zero, the car wouldn't start. By lighting a kerosene burner under the oil pan an hour before we were ready to go, we could heat the block enough to start the engine. Risking car, garage, and ourselves to fire was necessary only in cold weather, otherwise that Ford car started right up, every time.

Joe would have followed the sound of our footsteps to the garage and the muffled crunch of tires through the cold snow. He couldn't see me, but he knew I was in the car. After a while, the car returned. Then Joe waited all day for the car to leave again. When it returned, I'd come to feed him oats and hay. Joe never saw the Almont store, where Mother bought groceries, or where she crossed the bridge over the Gunnison River to meet the school bus. Joe must have thought about the car. It was rounded and dark. I doubt that he liked the car.

Bighorn Sheep

Several dozen bighorn sheep were bedded down on a hillside near the bridge, waiting for the first thaw before they made their way into the high country. Mother was driving me down to Almont to the school bus. We were on the lookout for the bighorns, because we'd seen them in one of the few places where the wind had blown the snow clear of the meadow and the road. We spotted a big ram lying in the pasture, facing away from the road, apparently asleep. Mother said, "I hope that big bastard doesn't decide to jump the fence." As though her words were a command, the ram sprang backward, turned in the air, cleared the fence, and landed directly in front of the car. His hoof left a nick in the fender as he bounded away.

A few weeks later, I was crossing the yard with my milk buckets on the way to the house. The sun was out, and it was warmer than it'd been since fall, but each step made a sharp crunch that echoed off the barn. Then a crunch came from the road. I stopped. Another crunch. Something was on the road, hidden behind the snowbank near the cut into our driveway. I waited and listened. The thing on the road wasn't moving. Mother saw me and opened the door. I pointed toward the road. Everything was still.

Then there was a series of rapid crunches and the big ram

lunged past the driveway. He stopped just out of sight, and everything was quiet. Then another ram lunged past and stopped. Silence. Three more made the lunge, then a dam of mountain sheep broke loose and stampeded by in a blur. Mother and I walked to the road and stood between the high banks of snow and watched the herd, maybe twenty or thirty. They ran for a couple hundred feet, stopped, and looked back. They kept an eye on us until they were sure we were harmless and continued on their annual trek to the high country.

Final Spring

Joe and I were following an elk trail along the river in the early spring when the ice cracked down the length of the river. I'd heard dynamite before. The breaking ice sounded like an explosion, but it was sharper than dynamite and the echo was long, all the way up and down the canyon. Joe jumped, and I fumbled to stay on, grabbing his mane and the saddlehorn. The edges of the ice along the riverbanks lifted, letting the center where the ice cracked sink slowly under the water. We could see air bubbles trapped in the submerged ice.

In the spring, needing a last-ditch diversion, Mother and Sam decided to move the house a mile and a half farther up the valley at the mouth of Rarick Creek. No doubt Sam enjoyed the challenge, but a ranch gets busy in the spring—he had to have been determined to please Mother. Things between them were the worst ever. We were all wretched. Changing where we lived was the only thing we could change, but I doubt it occurred to us that moving the house was an act of desperation.

They chose a spot on a hillside overlooking the creek and the little meadow. Mother loved that spot. It had another advantage. It
was clean. There were no corrals around to provide a perpetual supply of cow shit to the well.

For reasons that have eluded me, every other ranch house in
Colorado and Montana was built down-grade from the corrals.
That time-honored motif has provided generations of ranching
families with a history of dysentery and dead babies.

I'd never heard of moving a house. It seemed a little crazy and
magical and very exciting. We jacked the house up high enough to
get two long beams and four double sets of wheels underneath. Just
getting the house up there on the wheels took a while, in part because a ranch needs constant attention, and in part because Sam was
figuring it out as he went along. For two weeks, the house sat
perched in the air with its pipes and wires dangling down. From
time to time, Sandy Dunbar, Sam, and the hired man would crawl
around in the soft dirt underneath, murmuring and pointing. When
they emerged, they would squat on their haunches and draw lines in
the dirt or gently stroke the air with their hands, solving puzzles of
pressure, stress, and inertia.

One evening, Mother and I were coming back from the Almont
store. From the bridge we could see the house drifting above the
newly green meadow. The image reinforced what it felt like to be
inside the house—a curious, floating sensation. The house seemed
weightless, on the verge of gliding away, but the air inside was
leaden.

We towed the house behind Sandy's big stock truck up the road
toward the meadow. The house hung over both sides of the road.
Anyone coming down that road would not have been pleased. We'd
gone about a mile when a nasty odor and a lot of smoke billowed
out from under the truck. The clutch was slipping. Mother and I had
to go to Gunnison for another clutch while Sam and Sandy took the
old one out. That night, with me holding a flashlight, they put in the
new clutch. In the early-morning dark, Mother and Sam walked

along in the barrow pits on either side of the house, watching the wheels as the operation crept up the road. I fell asleep in the truck while Sandy drove. We got to the lane by first light. Making the turn off the road was a primitive piece of trickery. The wheels under the house were fixed to I-beam axles under the long support timbers. To make a sharp turn, the axles had to slide back on one side and forward on the other with the encouragement of sledgehammers and grease. Pythagoras said that with enough grease, wedges, jacks, and a good clutch, you can move anything.

Sam and I dug a basement under the house and poured a foundation. It would have been easier to dig the basement with a backhoe before the house was in place, but we didn't have a backhoe—we had shovels and a wheelbarrow, so it didn't matter that much if the digging came later. We left columns of dirt where we'd put blocks to hold the house; then we put in posts and dug out the columns. We went back to using an outhouse for a while, until we hooked up the plumbing.

The foundation took two or three weeks, because we mixed small batches of concrete with a hoe in a tin trough and poured them into the forms with buckets. Our daily progress was marked by diagonal gravel lines where the concrete dried from the day before. We framed in spaces in the west wall for a door and windows. We weren't optimists. Human families build shelters. We were playing make-believe.

I was fishing in the woods above our newly located house when I saw a beautiful snake partially hidden under a log. I caught him to show his bright colors to Mother. He was about two feet long and had a bulge in the middle. I continued fishing, flicking four or five feet of line into the water as I walked along. The snake stopped struggling. He was watching the line. He seemed curious about what I was doing. While I was watching the snake watching the line, I caught a small cutthroat and flipped it up on the bank. I was kneeling in the grass, trying to hold the snake and work the hook free from the fish at the same time, when the snake started to convulse. The bulge in his middle began moving toward his head. He was trying to regurgitate something. I laid him in the grass and watched his jaw unhinge and a small trout emerge. He thought I wanted his supper. I decided he'd been through enough, and I let him go. When Mother heard the story, she said I'd probably made the snake sick to its stomach and I was damn lucky I didn't get bit, because I'd be dead. Probably not, but I was uninformed about snakes. I'd never even seen one throw up.

Mother and Sam no doubt hoped that moving the house to Rarick Creek would change our lives—it was Christmas skis, only bigger. But Mother's life didn't change, so no one's changed. We were stuck in Mother's big jail, and everyone, including Mother, was planning an escape. Vicki seemed to disappear without leaving the house.

I figured Sam wanted to kill himself and maybe us. I just wanted to go into the mountains and never come back. I thought Mother intended to take Vicki and me and make a run for it, but Mother's plan was never clear.

It was late spring. The river was still rising and cold from snowmelt in the high country. Down where we were, things had started to green up. Mother told Vicki and me to get in the car. Sam was gone, probably down in his shop, hammering scrap iron into a long, thin blade.

The car was a silver-gray Buick with a grille full of big teeth, donated by Sam's parents to replace the Ford. We drove up the road for miles. Mother was quiet and sullen, and it scared me. Usually she tried to find ways to distract us when things were bad. She was fascinated by nature and normally acted as tour guide to the world.

She leaned forward slightly, hanging on to the steering wheel

and staring down the road. It felt like we were going to die. Vicki
had stopped singing to her doll. Mother just drove. We went up and
up into the high country to an old ghost town called Tin Cup. There
wasn't much left, a few cabins with the glass broken out and three
stores in the same condition. I think three or four cabins had cur-
tains, but no people appeared.

We got out and walked down the muddy streets. Mother was
wearing her long wool coat. It was red. I remember because the
town and the sky were gray.

She looked at me, then Vicki, then back to me. Vicki started to
cry. Mother acted as though she didn't know who we were. She was
stroking the spot between her eyebrows with her left hand, just
touching lightly and rubbing the same place. The other hand was in
her pocket, and I was holding on to her arm. Vicki had a grip on
Mother's coat.

We walked and walked. I didn't want anything to change. If we
just kept walking and nothing changed, it would be okay. It seemed
important that we didn't stop. We walked in a big circle around Tin
Cup and back to the car. Mother stared at the car for a long time.
Vicki and I stood on either side of her and waited. I was still holding
her arm. Everything depended on holding on to her arm.

We hadn't eaten since the night before, and Vicki was pleading
with her to take us home. Mother was gray and blank. She said we
should get in the car. It would be all right, just get in the car—as
though we better go before she changed her mind. She drove fast
without speaking. All the way home my entire body was trying to
keep that car on the road.

Fifty-five years later as she was dying, she began talking about
the trip to Tin Cup—the gray sky, the way the ruts jerked the Buick
from side to side, and the abandoned buildings. Then she looked
over toward the side table where she kept her snub-nosed thirty-
eight revolver. She said, "You better get that out of here." I wondered if it was the same one she had in the pocket of that red coat.

It was dusk when we got back to the house. Sam was sitting on

the fender of the pickup waiting for us. The yard light made his face
yellow against the gray sky. Mother parked in the gravel cut and
turned the engine off. Sam looked down at his bare feet and didn't
move for a long time. We sat in the car and waited. He was still staring at his feet when he slid off the fender and started toward the
house. He was slow and clumsy as though his feet were lumps.

Vicki and I didn't move until Mother took a deep breath and
opened her door. We climbed out into the glare of the yard light and
followed close through the piles of sand and gravel and lumber
scraps. Things weren't finished. There were no steps to the front
door, so the only way into the house was by a dirt path around the
back, beyond the yard light, and up a stepladder to the kitchen.

It must have drizzled when we were in Tin Cup, because the path
was damp and slick. Mother took Vicki's hand, and they went
ahead—large and small, dark gray figures beyond the rim of yellow
light. I resisted, but the house was pulling at me as it had pulled
Mother and Vicki up the ladder and through the door.

Inside, it was quiet and dark. The three of us stood in the kitchen,
listening for Sam. For reasons I don't understand, we couldn't turn on
the lights. All we had to do was reach up and flick a switch, but we
couldn't lift our arms. We couldn't move our legs either. I guess we
were scared stiff, but I didn't feel stiff. I felt heavy and thick and needed
to pee. I braved the living room. The yard light lit the floor in patches,
making the darkness deep black. I went from light patch to black patch
until I found the bathroom door. I tapped, but there was no response.
When I tried the knob it was locked. He was in there. I wished I could
have locked the door from my side and kept him in there.

I couldn't hold the pee any longer and ran to the front door,
pulled it open, and let go into the blinding light. It was the best I'd
felt all day. I wanted to pee forever.

Mother was standing in the dark asking what I was doing. I
whispered that Sam was in the bathroom, and I had to go. She said it
was bedtime.

I lay in my bunk and listened until I fell asleep. I had a vivid dream. Vicki and I were in our bunks. Sam came through the door, went to the closet, took out a rifle, and started to leave when Mother came in.

I woke up and lay there. My thoughts were flying around. I climbed down and crossed the room to the closet. I stood in the dark in my pajamas and listened. The house was silent. I felt around for the two rifles and the shotgun, took them out, one at a time, and tried to unload them without making any noise. The shotgun was empty, but the others were loaded. For their size, guns are made of heavy stuff. They make thick, rich sounds—nice sounds, except when you're scared of being heard. I laid the bullets on the floor, and I got the rifles back in the closet without waking anyone. The boxes of bullets and shells were on a high shelf. I had to carry the chair over, climb up, and find the boxes.

I sat on the floor in the dark feeling around for the loose bullets. Each time I found one I slipped it into the box. Then I hid them under the foot of Vicki's mattress, and climbed back into my bunk. I felt foolish and scared at the same time. I listened for an hour before I fell asleep.

The lights were on and Sam was in the room. He was moving toward the closet, just as he had in the dream. He took out a rifle and started to leave. Mother came in. She was yelling at him to put the rifle down, then she made a grab for it. Mother had both hands on the rifle, one on the butt and the other on the end of the barrel. Sam was holding on, and they were pulling back and forth—he was silent, and she was yelling. He pushed her back past the bunks. For a moment I couldn't see them. I heard the rifle hit the floor.

Mother fell backward into the bedroom. She didn't move. I jumped off my bunk and bent over her to see if she was alive. I couldn't tell. Her eyes were closed. She was very still, then blood gushed from her nose, down her cheek, into her hair. It soaked into the plywood, seeping into the pattern, making bright red lines in the pale grain.

Vicki saw Mother and the blood and let out a wail that climbed higher and higher then fell back into a convulsive gasp. Sam was somewhere in the dark house, maybe watching us, certainly listening. He had to have heard the madwoman wail that erupted from his stepdaughter's little mouth. My sister's shrill wail with its backdraft gasp was one of the most terrified sounds I've ever heard.

I was staring at my dead mother. Blood bubbled out of her mouth. Vicki's wailing was whirling the blood around and around in my head. Then Mother's lips moved under the red foam, and I put my ear close to her mouth until I could feel the bubbles break against my ear, as though I were listening for her last words trapped in bubbles of blood. Then she was talking. Her voice was hoarse and faraway. She was telling me to get Vicki to the car. I didn't think Mother could get up. A moment before I didn't think she was alive, but she rolled over onto her knees, braced against the door jamb, stood up—blood still streaming from her nose—and staggered into the dark living room.

When Vicki realized Mother was alive, the wail subsided to sobbing. I took all the guns, including the one on the floor, and hid them under my mattress. I got a coat on Vicki, boosted her through the window, and held her hand until she could almost touch the ground. Our room was on the upward side of the house, against the hill, so she didn't have far to drop. I crawled out and led her up the hillside away from the house and into the sagebrush. Then we were above the gravel cut, where we could see the car and its gleaming grille in the yard light.

Mother was in the car. Sam was pounding his fists on the roof and bellowing for her to open the door. At that moment, bellowing seemed like a good thing. He hadn't said anything for a week, and the silence had us terrified. I said something to him, I don't remember what. He looked up at me and said, "It's all right. I'm not going to hurt you kids." I grabbed Vicki's hand and we slid down the gravel and ran to the car. Mother reached over and pulled the lock up on the passenger side. We crawled in and locked the door.

Our run to the car must have confused Sam. He backed away, then turned and lurched through the piles of gravel and sand toward the house. I assumed he was going back for the rifle. Mother started the car, swung it around, and gunned down the lane toward the road.

Sam started after us. I kneeled backward on the seat and watched. He was running, silhouetted against the yard light. Mother asked if I could get the gate open before he caught us. I looked at the gate and back at Sam. The gate was coming up fast, and Sam wasn't far behind. I said no, and Mother put her foot on the gas. The gate loomed up in the headlights—five horizontal pine boards and two diagonal boards. We hit dead center. It bowed, split, flew out and up in the headlights, and disappeared above the car.

We were through the gate in a flash. Yet the two halves seemed to hover in the air like wings—a single image, fixed in my memory. It was the moment we escaped death. We were free.

The Buick swung across the road and almost rolled in the barrow pit, but by the forces of mass and motion and the illusions of time and space, we made the turn onto the road. I looked back for Sam. I couldn't see him. I was so focused on Sam that I didn't realize Mother was driving too fast until we nearly skidded off the road near the bridge. The car thundered across the wood planks, scaring Vicki and me and waking the ducks. The headlights blurred the timbers. I asked Mother to slow down. I said, "He can't catch us now."

Mother was focused. "The hell he can't. He's got the goddamned pickup."

I'd forgotten about the pickup. Mother drove like a race car driver. I watched the road behind us for headlights. We did that for the sixteen miles to Gunnison. There were no headlights behind us—Sam had forgotten the pickup. She drove straight through town to the county jail, woke Sheriff Cope, and told him Sam was trying to kill us.

Cope hid the Buick in the jail's garage and took us upstairs to the apartment, where his wife made us something to eat. Mother and

Vicki slept in the guest room. I slept on the couch, but I wanted to sleep in a jail cell.

The next morning Mother had two shiners and a swollen nose. She said Sam hit her between the eyes with the rifle butt and knocked her out. I told her about hiding the bullets and the guns under the mattress.

We knew Sam would find the guns. He'd be after us, and we had to stay out of sight. We stayed in the jail apartment for a week. Mother made arrangements to go to Montana to be near her father and brother. We got reports that Sam was driving around looking for us. He'd even driven to Colorado Springs, where Mother had friends.

One evening after dinner, Cope got a call that a fisherman had found a body in the river. The sheriff got his deep waders out of the closet and didn't come back until late that night. He said the body had been there for weeks, trapped under logs. When Cope tugged at the body it came apart. The sheriff got most everything but the head, the right arm, and the left hand. There was no way to tell who it was.

Cope took a bottle of whiskey into the shower and stood under the spray trying to wash the smell off until long after the hot water was gone. He was so drunk he couldn't smell or feel a thing. His wife dried him off and got him to the dinner table.

Cope sat in front of his pork chops and mashed potatoes and sniffed at his hands for any hint of decay. When he was sure the odor was gone, he reached for the salt and pepper, but he was so drunk he couldn't see the difference. First he shook salt on the back of his hand then brought his face down to his hand and licked it. He did the same with the pepper. He'd pickled his taste buds and couldn't taste anything.

Mother asked if he wanted salt. Cope nodded. She salted his dinner, he mumbled thanks, and passed out.

We had to clean the potatoes out of his hair before we eased him onto the floor and dragged him into the living room. Mrs. Cope put a pillow under his head and covered him with a blanket. He slept till noon the next day.

I was sure Sam would find us. He'd kill the sheriff, then come for us. I spent the days in a chair by the window with Cope's green army binoculars and watched the street. One night I got the jitters and couldn't sleep. I hid in the bathroom and tried to sharpen Sheriff Cope's straight razor on his leather strop. The strop was made of two pieces of leather connected to a ring on one end that hooked to the wall next to the basin. The other end had a handle you held while you brushed the blade back and forth. One side of the strop was smoother than the other. I kept nicking the leather. I couldn't stop, I couldn't help myself. It was just nick, nick, nick. The strop looked like rats had gnawed it. Now I was afraid of the sheriff. Cope never mentioned the strop, but when he looked at me, I knew what he was thinking. I stopped eating. Vicki ate and asked for more.

Mother wore thick-rimmed dark glasses even though she stayed inside the whole time we were there. I only saw the bruises when she took the glasses off at bedtime and asked me to look. She spent the days helping the sheriff's wife do laundry, clean, and fix meals for the prisoners. The dark saucers around her eyes turned an iridescent purple, then green, yellow, and gradually faded away.

When Sheriff Cope figured Sam had a chance to cool off, he drove up to the ranch, and they had a talk. Cope came back by dinnertime and said everything would be all right. Sam was distraught and apologetic. He wanted us back. Mother called him, and they talked. He said it would be okay if we came back and got our things, but I didn't go. I never saw Joe or the Taylor River Ranch again.

She asked if I wanted to go to Montana. We could spend the summer at Uncle Bud's cabin on Flathead Lake. I could fish and swim. Bud had a small wooden motorboat he said I could use, and he would teach me to water-ski behind his big outboard. Everything would be okay. I didn't really believe I'd get to water-ski, but the lake sounded pretty good. We would be together and away from Sam. Then she said Sam wanted to drive us to Montana.

My heart sank. *Would that be okay with me?* I went along with it because that's what she wanted, but I knew, sooner or later, he was going to kill us.

I was too naive to understand their obsession. During those long winters, their minds intertwined, coiled and clung, and struggled to escape. Close your eyes and imagine a mass of squirmy, grasping tentacles. They were desperate characters.

PART THREE

Monkey Town

Leaving Colorado

Sam drove us from the Gunnison jail to Monkey Town, Montana. That was Bud's pet name for Missoula, which he claimed was run by a bunch of monkeys.

After spending the night in Jackson Hole, Wyoming, we ate breakfast in a big log café with heavy round tables. At the table next to ours, several local ranchers were talking about cattle and the weather. When Sam finished his French toast and sausages, he went over to the ranchers and introduced himself. Would they mind if he asked a few questions? Ranchers are easy. They invited him to join them. He asked questions about the price of land, how many acres you needed to run four to five hundred head, how water was allotted, about government grazing rights, and where was the closest railhead for loading cattle. They were an unusually well-spoken bunch. Their answers were slow coming, but thoughtful. Sam fit right in. Everybody was at ease, having a good time. Sam asked if they had trouble with elk. They looked around the table. No, there didn't seem to be a problem with elk. Sam nodded. He was surprised and pleased, of course. A man with a mustache and a dark-tanned face that turned white at his hat line looked off in the distance and shook his head. "But those goddamned moose." Sam seemed to rise up out of his chair, said thanks for your time, and we got out of Jackson Hole.

On the way up the valley we saw a cow moose and a calf in the pasture along the road. They were running parallel to the car and keeping up. I'd never seen animals so graceful. They seemed to glide above the ground. Then they came to a jackleg fence about six feet high. Both the cow and her calf sailed above the poles. I closed my eyes and watched them jump that fence over and over.

My Uncle's Crowd

Sam didn't kill us. He went back to Colorado, and I forgot about him, or at least put his memory in suspended animation. Maybe that was why the summer was so idyllic. We were rejoicing in our freedom.

Mother, Vicki, and I stayed on Flathead Lake in a motel room Uncle Bud rented for us. It was a place to sleep and eat. The summer was spent on the water, the dock, and sometimes walking down the road to Dairy Boy and coming back with top-heavy cones of gloppy imitation ice cream. The days were free-floating and wonderful but not particularly memorable, except when I made a sharp turn in the small motorboat and the engine shot straight up off the transom and plunged into the lake. After that, I rowed.

I saved a little boy from drowning, which made me a big hero for a day. All I'd done was reach into the water and pull the kid onto the dock. He weighed nothing. He gagged a little, then started breathing. I carried him over to his mother, who thought he was dead. She was screaming and pulling her hair. I'd seen Mother hysterical, but nothing like that.

Uncle Bud and his best friends, Soapy Russell and Eddy Bracket, came up on the weekends. Their names suited them. I don't know if

Soapy was a nickname or not. I never heard him called anything else. Neither he nor Eddy was a match for Bud, but they had that small-town savvy. The liquor made them quick. Mostly they were Bud's loyal, devoted, lifelong friends—buddies who would've helped bury the bodies if there were bodies to bury.

At first, they hung around Mother. I didn't like them, probably because they weren't paying attention to me. Mother said they nauseated her. After the second weekend, they gave up and got Bud to take them out in his aluminum outboard so they could chase around the lake all day. They went to bars in Big Fork and Somers to drink. They drank in the boat, then they came back in the evening and drank on the beach.

A variety of Bud's acquaintances appeared in the evening. Most came up from Missoula after work. They'd build a bonfire on the beach. Eddy would drive his big Chrysler onto the sand and turn the radio up. I don't remember the music, but it would have been Sinatra, Dorsey, Krupa, and the swing bands. It wasn't my music. I was waiting for rock and roll.

There were hot dogs, burgers, beer, and whiskey, and there were lots of women in their twenties and early thirties who acted like young girls. Mother called them loose women. She said Bud and his friends made passes at them, which was true, but Mother seemed a little too obsessed. She had fantasized that Sam chased loose women. Sooner or later, all men chased, and all women were loose.

In the evening, Vicki and I were confined to the cabin—a stand-alone motel room paneled in knotty pine with a kitchenette. Each era has a defining fancy—that persistent, repetitive thing. In the fifties we fancied knotty pine.

I listened to the music and laughter and watched people dancing in the firelight. I didn't mind that the women were loose or that Bud and his friends chased them. They laughed and told stories and teased each other. There was nowhere on earth I'd rather have been.

When Mother thought Vicki and I were asleep, she'd go down to the bonfire, sit on a log, drink a beer and smoke a cigarette. I don't remember her dancing. She just drank her beer and watched. People must have wondered what she was thinking. I bet she made them nervous.

There were other fires lined out along the edge of the lake. I'd slip out of the motel and walk from fire to fire, standing back in the shadows, watching and listening. Every fire was different, but usually it would be a weekend family gathering. They'd be all ages. I don't remember teenagers. Maybe they stayed in town.

I was sitting on a piece of driftwood, mesmerized by the sound of the lake washing the sand, intermingled with voices of a family by their bonfire. They were horsing around and laughing. The air was warm and smelled of hot dogs and pine smoke. I thought I was out of sight, but a girl about my age spotted me and came over. She invited me to join them and asked if I wanted something to eat, just like a woman. I was too embarrassed to accept her offer, but I walked back to the motel room thinking how wonderful girls were, and how good they made me feel.

The rowdiest fire was always Bud's and his friends'. The whiskey made them funny and edgy. There was grabbing, shrieking, and dirty jokes, but not much kissing and no making out. Bud tested new guys, made passes at their girlfriends and wives, challenged them to contests, bet on prizefights and baseball, wrestled them into the sand, outran them, outswam them, outdrank them, and outbluffed them. Nobody knew whether he was crazy or not, so he won at speedboat chicken. At three o'clock on Monday morning everyone raced back to town, boats in tow. No one got killed. They drank and drove big cars fast.

Alcohol had replaced going to church as the primary social lubricant for a particular group of postwar types. Drinking brought them together. They drank to make love, deals, and money. They drank to loosen up, hitch up, and break up. Most of all, drinking defined the arc of friendship and love. Drinking was just too damn good to be true.

━━━

For a few weeks, Bud had a sleek 1930s mahogany boat with a sloping back and an inboard motor. The twin exhaust pipes at the waterline made a throaty bubbling sound—deep and warm and somehow safe. Even today, if I catch a whiff of hot manifold mixed with oil, steam, and gasoline, I get a glimpse of that boat streaking across the smooth, blue lake. Some weekends we water-skied all day. It was the summer Mother had promised.

The boat became a problem. Bud began bringing it in too fast, slamming the dock, and acting like the boat was disposable junk. I didn't understand what Bud had against his beautiful boat, but he'd decided it stood for something he didn't want to be a part of. Perhaps he thought it was pretentious. Grandfather would have liked that boat.

Maybe it was that simple—the boat may have reminded Bud of his father's pomposity, which he detested. On the other hand, my mother's sense of style, composure, and high-horse attitude were, to some degree, seeded in her father's need to escape his class.

The boat seemed to take on a personality. Late one evening, Bud walked down to the shore near the dock and started swearing at her. He threatened to take her out the next morning, run her into the rocks, and tear her bottom out. Bud's friend, Eddy, never got into arguments with my uncle, but he loved that boat. Years later, Eddy told me he'd gone down to the dock that night and crimped the fuel line. The next morning the boat wouldn't start.

Bud glared at her for a while, then walked up to his car and peeled out of the motel's gravel parking lot. Before dark, he came back with a new fiberglass Gull with a big engine. It was so fast you could water-ski on the bottoms of your feet. After fifteen tries, I managed about ten yards. It stung like hell, but I impressed Bud and a couple of girls. I think Eddy ended up with the mahogany boat.

Soapy Russell was a dark force in my kid life. He was nothing like Sam, but he was large, moody, and sometimes scary. One day Soapy was assigned to take me waterskiing behind the Gull while Bud was off chasing the neighbors' wives. We went far out into the lake, like a shot across the water. Then he started turning the boat in tighter and tighter circles. I was laughing. I was going faster and faster, then my arms were being sucked out of my shoulders. I quit laughing, but I knew Soapy couldn't throw me, no matter how tight he spun that boat. At high speeds, water is hard as concrete. I hit, skipped like a stone, and came up naked and dazed. Soapy took his time fishing me out, and he wasn't smiling. He wanted to be with Bud, but he'd been assigned to entertain a hyper brat who didn't know his place—and Bud was off with some woman.

Soapy wanted to be Bud. They acted like high school buddies, drinking hard and driving fast. Soapy came for the fireworks and stayed too long.

Town

Leaving the mountains and Rarick Creek was leaving everything good I understood about the world. It was leaving myself. For several years, I'd been like a trout in a stream. Except for a few disruptions by my parents, I knew instinctively how to negotiate the water.

In Montana I felt like one of those white plastic balls blowing around inside a Bingo bubble, bouncing off a hundred other plastic balls. There was no sense, no rhythm, no pattern to anything. The majority of people living in Western towns after the second war had been raised on farms and ranches. They were as rattled by the experience of town as I was and didn't know how to behave around one another. Even our friends were strangers.

Bud was one of the smartest men I've known. His animal instincts were well tuned. He was also a logician who understood human motivation. He could make men feel transparent, and that made them afraid of him. Women, it seemed, wanted to be seen through and accepted. In any case, women liked Bud.

He got his clothes at the Mercantile, the big department store on the corner of Higgins and Front. The fabrics were good. The basic men's styles were on the prewar side. Fifties styles had that nice California sheen—a bit too slick for Bud. He had a tough, lean, forties look, defined by Montana's perpetual economic depression. He liked his sleeves rolled up, a loose tie, and scuffed blood oxfords. He went to the office in the same clothes he drank, fished, and fucked in.

His insurance company became the largest in the state. The girls in the office took care of the walk-in trade while Bud went after the big accounts—mines, lumber, timber, and heavy-equipment companies. Intelligence helped, but his main business skill was staying clearheaded while drinking from midafternoon into the night. Money focused him.

Young businessmen in the fifties were exceptional at good-old-boy. It's an elaborate, convoluted game with a lineage that goes back to apes, maybe ants. Its rules are constantly evolving, with changes inside the changes. Good-old-boy takes time, money, food, liquor, memory, and a healthy reserve of counterfeit empathy. Anyone who wants to build and maintain a substantial career has to play. Decades of good-old-boy eventually bring the meaning of life into question.

Bud once believed he would spend his life painting, but that didn't work out. It didn't bring in enough cash to support his family, so he started the insurance brokerage—fire, casualty, and liability. He didn't just dislike business—he hated business. It was a slow death, and it meant dealing with businessmen.

Only politicians and university professors disgusted him more. He said politicians were like hot dogs, all lips and assholes. His attitude about the university was common to small college towns. Professors and their wives were seen as devious hypocrites and bad tippers. I doubt they were more devious than average. What really got the town down on them was that we bought into the professors' view of themselves as aristocracy. They acted as if they were better than the townies, but they didn't behave better.

■■■

Two primary rivers, the Bitterroot and the Clark Fork, meet in the Missoula Valley. Missoula was called the Garden City for the many truck farms that originally supplied Butte and other mining towns with fruit and vegetables. Several drainages had flooded the valley over the centuries, leaving the soil unusually rich and fertile.

In the early days, the town fathers tried to get the legislature to build the state prison in Missoula. Prisons were known moneymakers. Deer Lodge got the prison, because the robber baron William A. Clark wanted it there. Missoula got a liberal arts college. It was pretty humiliating.

In the fifties, Missoula's economy was a mix of lumber mills, truck farming, the railroads, and a pulp mill that made thick brown paper for sacks and cardboard boxes.

Waste water from the mines and the smelter a hundred miles to the east killed off the fish in the Clark Fork River, which runs though the middle of town. Tons of wood scrap from the lumber mills were burned in giant metal cones called teepee burners, emitting a constant plume of smoke. Thousands of gallons of chemicals that the mills used to treat wood were disposed of in holes in the ground and contaminated downstream wells. Sulfur dioxide from the pulp mill and water vapor in the air made sulfuric acid, which combined with smoke from teepee burners, turning the sky into a stagnant smog. Waste water from the pulp mill flowed directly into the Clark Fork River. The city sewer was the river.

It took citizen groups twenty years of constant battle with judges, politicians, corporations, the rich, and the unions to get things partially cleaned up. Then people came and saw a town without sewage in the river or sulfuric acid in the sky. They said, "Oh, what a nice clean little place. Let's build something here."

I haven't heard the phrase "Garden City" for several years. Maybe the chamber of commerce still uses it, but the truck farms and the fertile soil were paved and built over as Missoula recently went from a town to a city.

City is a legal description. You can't just say you're a city. A government official has to inspect your books and see that you have enough concrete, cars, asphalt, big box stores, toxic waste, rapes, murders, and missing children to qualify as city material. He probably gave the mayor a plaque.

In the fifties, Missoula was just beginning to see better times. That was relative, of course. Mother claimed the economic depression of the thirties had no noticeable effect on Montana. The state had bottomed out long before.

The railroad had conned the immigrant farmers—the honyockers—with free transportation and promises of cheap, bountiful land. It was a dream come true. After a few years, the homesteaders, like their crops, dried up and blew away. A lucky few migrated west, drawn by visions of a little fruit farm in Oregon.

Grandfather had suspected farming was a fool's bargain. From the beginning, he was planning a different future—he'd built his homesteader's cabin out of cottonwood logs, which quickly rotted into the ground. After years spent as a traveling salesman for Standard Oil, he settled in Missoula and sold real estate.

He was bent on punishing me for an endless list of minor or imaginary transgressions, so I only got to know him well enough to hate him but not enough to understand him. My only glimpse into his mind was a photograph he kept in his den of a honyocker's wagon with the words *Oregon or Bust* painted on its canvas side. Most of those who escaped Montana took their horses and left the cars and trucks. They couldn't afford gasoline.

After World War II, Montana still languished near the bottom of the nation's economic scorecard, but in the western part of the state, timber was our golden goose. Half the families in the country were building their dream home. A little money dribbled in and with the money came a trickle of people.

Rupert Morgan trickled from Brockton, Massachusetts, settled in Missoula, and put some of his family's shoe factory wartime profits into a men's clothing and shoe store—the finest in the state.

Rupert brought along a beautiful wife and a grand attitude. When he and his wife were introduced to Bud, Rupert fingered the fabric of my uncle's Missoula Mercantile jacket and made a slight dismissive shrug. Bud didn't seem to mind. He looked Rupert dead in the eye and nodded, then turned to Mrs. Morgan and smiled.

Missoula was a provincial little valley town that depended primarily on reducing prehistoric trees to narrow boards. To the locals, stylish clothing was one more reminder of their shabby lives. They didn't like reminders.

Rupert's haberdashery foundered. Early one morning, it burned to the ground. People walked past the blackened shell of his once-bright palace of fashion and smiled at Rupert's misfortune. He had it coming, that snazzy dresser.

Rupert Morgan had wanted to change them, to make them look swell. That was his big sin. Most of his detractors were hypocrites. It was Sinatra time—they wanted to look swell, they just didn't want to be rushed into it.

One of Bud's friends was a mechanic named Stanley, a war hero who was full of bravado. Stanley was okay, but his wife glittered. Everybody called her Sparky. Stanley fell in love with her and stayed behind when his unit shipped out to the States. They spent one winter in a tent before they made enough to get them to Missoula, where they opened a car repair shop. Bud sold them an insurance policy and threw in an invitation to the endless party.

One night, they were up at Bud's house, which was fifties modern with big bay windows. It was perched up on a hill called Farviews, so named because you could see above Missoula's smog to the mountains on the far side of the valley. The mix of acid mist, wood smoke, and streetlights created a pleasant glow. In the valley below, the toxic vapor smelled like sewer gas and damaged people's lungs and throats and increased the death rate. The Monkey Town boosters jabbered, "Smell the money. Smell the money." The smell was as close as most people got to the money.

About two in the morning, Sparky got mad at Stanley and asked if anyone was ready to leave. Bob Rothweiler offered to give her a lift. Rothweiler owned a prefab house factory. He'd lost both legs in World War II and wore prosthetics, but got around pretty well.

He left with Sparky and a bottle for the road. Instead of taking her home, he drove way out of town to his prefab factory and turned off the road into a field behind the plant. That field was about where Costco is today. They sat there for an hour, drinking in the dark. Then Rothweiler started pawing her. He was strong, and she knew he could rape her, so she agreed to let him have some, but only if he removed his prosthetics. That must have been a struggle in the front seat, negotiating the steering wheel and the gear shift. Sparky smoked a cigarette and took a few sips from the bottle while she waited. When he had a free hand, she gave Rothweiler the bottle, grabbed his legs, and hopped out of the car. He lunged for her, but Sparky was quick. She flung the prosthetics far out into the dark field and told Rothweiler he could have all he wanted, but he had to catch her first. She walked back to town while he crawled around in the weeds looking for his legs.

The last I saw Soapy Russell was in the early seventies. He was the night clerk at the ancient Priest Hotel. The long, narrow halls were coated with layers of a whitish oil-based enamel seasoned with nicotine. When the hotel caught fire, the walls exploded, killing an old, whiskey-soaked cowboy who had proclaimed he was the grandson, and at times, the reincarnation of the Sundance Kid.

Eddy Bracket sold siding. He was an easygoing guy. Ethel married him because he was the best her bait could catch. He was a decent man who made a decent living. That's what Ethel wanted before she discovered her vibrant self was shackled to a sinking bore. She rebelled. Her dismissive gestures and inflections said, "I've heard this all a thousand times before." These trivial humiliations alleviated her boredom. She took one thin cut, then another, and another to mask the taste of her despair. When she had him down to the size of a toad, he slipped away in search of happiness, which, of course, he found in a younger woman.

When a man looks to another woman for comfort, his traditional line—"My wife doesn't understand me"—is either a lie or delusional nonsense. The wife understands too damn well. The other woman's appeal is her naivete—the main reason she's often young. His best hope is that it will be years not months before she sees him for what he is and makes prosciutto of his soul.

Grandfather's generation talked a lot about character. Character was supposed to involve honesty, dependability, and honor, but I discovered that too many of the people held up as having character, including Grandfather, didn't.

Belonging to lots of organizations was supposed to be an indication of character. Grandfather had a wall of plaques and drawers of pins, ribbons, and memorabilia from a dozen organizations. He was the grand overlord of the Masonic Lodge for a while and wore one of those hats and a black cape with a red satin lining. After he died, I was presented with the cape and a secret Masonic book on how to rule the world. The lady at Mr. Higgins's Second Hand Clothing and Costumes got the cape. I kept the book.

I only know of one of Grandfather's deals. He was a member of the chamber of commerce, of course. At a chamber luncheon the decision was made to buy Widow Simms's old house on Broadway next to the post office. The chamber intended to tear it down and put up their own building. They set a figure for their high bid and instructed the secretary to make the widow an offer.

Promptly after lunch, Grandfather, who was not the secretary, paid Mrs. Simms a visit. When the secretary showed up later that afternoon, Mrs. Simms informed him that he'd have to speak to Grandfather, who'd just purchased an option to buy the property.

Over the years, several upstanding people went out of their way to say what an honorable fellow my grandfather had been. Most of them I considered about as honorable as Grandfather. Usually, I just nodded. Sometimes I told them about Mrs. Simms.

Whatever drove my grandfather, and whatever his flaws, Mother loved him. She was his defender to the end and helped take care of him when he died. You can't ask for more than that.

I thought Bud had more character than most. A lot of people disagreed, and they had their reasons. At least he was honest, and there was no posturing. He unnerved the phonies by flinging the truth at them, though often as not, his candor was fortified by booze.

When Bud was old and all the buzz was gone, he said that the most disheartening thing about business was everyone became a mark. If you spent your life trying to get money out of people, your chances of becoming a deeply cynical, isolated drunk were about eight in ten. With odds like that, he couldn't refuse.

In 1981, the year my uncle was dying, we talked several times. He'd turned old. He was only sixty-three, but in the cliché of the day, he'd been rode hard and put away wet. As we talked, it became obvious he believed he had failed, because he'd gone after the money instead of what he cared about and loved. He forgot he'd given up painting not to get rich, but to make a living for an extraordinary woman and their talented children.

He'd quit painting forty years before, but continued to see the stories, shapes, light, and colors in the ordinary—things a painter saw that completely escaped most people. I liked and admired Bud, and I wonder, if he'd stayed a painter, what his life would've been like. My guess is, he would have disappeared from our lives, unable to tolerate any of us, and taken up residence in a distant land where time never ran out, where the natives spoke in soft, sweet voices, where the grace and beauty of the women needed painting.

He had legendary qualities. He'd made and lost fortunes, taken big risks, and played for high stakes. He once built a lumber mill in the Amazon, but Indians with blowguns and poisoned darts scared off the workers and the foreman. The jungle did its part by reducing steel to rust. Later, more determined, meaner men than Bud killed the Indians, brought in portable Swedish mills, and cut the jungle down.

Our last discussion was about Paul Gauguin, one of the painters he and Mother had talked about when Bud was at Woodman. My uncle was particularly fascinated by Gauguin's nun with the sensually haunting face, who couldn't avert her eyes from the sight of Jacob wrestling the devil.

I said, "It was an angel Jacob wrestled, not the devil." Bud insisted. "Why," he asked, "would an angel have a tail wrapped around its thigh, and why would Jacob wrestle an angel, anyway?" Angel or devil, it was his favorite painting. Both Bud and Gauguin were unnaturally passionate for that nun.

Almost Sex and
High School

In the fall of 1953, after summer on the lake, Mother, Vicki, and I lived in a shack on South Avenue. The floor in my closet-size room rotted out, and the bed fell through to the ground. I started in the seventh grade at Washington School. We were close to broke, and the only footwear I had was a pair of cowboy boots, so from the first day I was a marked man. They called me the Wyoming Cowboy. When I explained I was from Colorado, they called me the Wyoming Cowboy From Colorado. Things went straight to hell from there.

I did manage to make friends with two girls, Rhonda and Janice. They asked me to go to a movie at the Campus Theater. Mother said no, I was too young. I went to bed early, waited until she was asleep, then crawled through the window and met up with the girls at the theater. The next week, Mother relented. She'd read that boys deprived of female companionship were more likely to become homosexuals. It was an innocent age. Fags and commies were the scourge.

The next summer, when I wasn't working odd jobs, I spent my time with Rhonda. She had horses. We'd take them down to the river and coax them into the water, then we'd slide off their rumps and hold on to their tails as they swam the river. We rode up into the mountains and spent hours sitting side by side in a meadow, so close the hair on our arms almost touched, and not saying a word for fear of sounding dumb. We wrestled in a hay barn at the fairgrounds. It was incredibly exciting, but I don't remember even holding hands or, God forbid, kissing. I never knew what went on in Rhonda's head, but I had the sex shakes so bad I'd get dizzy.

After the summer with Rhonda, it was as though I blacked out for a few years. During that period a lot happened. Sam sold the ranch in Colorado and got back together with Mother. They purchased a house on Farviews and had two children of their own, James and Carolyn. Sam bought a ranch on Butler Creek, which didn't have enough water for good irrigation, and sold it. He tried fixing furniture, but people had already started throwing out their old furniture instead of having it repaired, so that didn't pan out. He bought a bunch of equipment and manufactured wrought-iron framed copper planters. That failed because he didn't know how to market them. Then he managed to start a trucking business. All he had to do was drive night and day and he could make money, so he was on the road most of the time.

Mother opened a riding stable, which actually supported itself and brought in a little money. They both worked all the time, which was great for me, because they were hardly ever home at the same time. Fortunately for everyone, the basement had an outside door so I could come and go without disturbing whatever was simmering upstairs.

When I was fifteen, I got to know Mike Geary, Rick Goldsby, and Jerry Hoff—an odd mix of recluse, genius types. We would stay up late at night, working on cars, drinking beer, and talking engines, racing fuel, tires, and ignition systems. I don't remember any of us talking about girls. Being youngest, I mostly asked questions. They liked that, because they got to argue over the answers.

They drag-raced on a strip of two-lane blacktop that ran through a cornfield from a road on the south of town to an old army barracks. It was long enough to make a quarter-mile run and stop on the straightaway. One night the cops waited until about a dozen cars were on the strip and set up roadblocks on both ends. They thought they had us trapped, but we killed our lights and took off in a dozen different directions into the corn. It was actually easier to see in the dark instead of being blinded by the lights bouncing off cornstalks. We could get oriented by the haze from town. The cops didn't have enough sense to turn their lights off, and they couldn't see a thing.

My friends were building up the biggest V8 engines they could get their hands on. I didn't have the money for a big engine, so I decided to soup up a '31 Model A Ford. The older guys were amused, but it was a challenge. They loaned me parts and helped put the engine together. It had a milled aluminum head with eight-and-a-half-to-one compression, a milled flywheel, dual Stromberg carbs, an Emerson ignition, and overbored pistons. The engine had so much compression it was always blowing head gaskets. The car was very light. It was fast when it ran, but I spent more time tearing it down and putting it back together than I did driving.

The flaw in the Model A project was that I wasn't old enough to own a car, so the only way I could get it licensed was to put the title in Sam's name. That was his ace in the hole for keeping me in line.

My friends and I were misfits. For various reasons, we couldn't get a grip near the gravitational center of the high school hierarchy, so we drifted off to the far edge of the social galaxy. Eventually we each created our own center of gravity and lived off the residual heat.

At the time it never occurred to me that the role of the misfit was to reorganize and reshape society. Every once in a great while, a gravitational outlier invents something that fucks with the force. Assault rifles, fashion design, the http, and theoretical physics are the weapons of misfits. They will rearrange everything from hemlines to paradigms, or just shoot you for your shoes, because someone—probably a really nice guy like Tommy-football-star—wouldn't let Johnny-picks-nose-in-class join Power Club.

The functional alcohol high of my uncle's crowd spilled over into my generation. We didn't drink to get drunk. The alcohol ramped us up. At least that's how I remember it. Maybe it blotted out most of my memories of high school, but I think high school blotted itself out.

I remember flashes, like stealing gas and tires with a kid named Jack. One night, a city cop, Bear Tracks Lockridge, spotted us. We escaped, but not before he shot two holes in the trunk of Jack's '41 Chevy coupe. We stayed up the rest of the night patching and re-painting the holes.

Another night, we encountered Sheriff Joe Day. We'd just si-phoned five gallons of gas, which was in a jerry can on the floor of the backseat. Sheriff Day, a six-foot-six giant, stopped us because Jack's taillights had blue glass in their centers. We called them snake eyes. It was a beautiful effect, but illegal. Sheriff Day decided the car was a little loud so he got in and revved the engine. Jack had straight pipes on a Chevy V8. They made a wonderful, deep-throated *raaaappp*. The sheriff looked over at me and said we should get that fixed, then he sniffed. The car reeked of gas. I don't know why, but he didn't bother to look in the back. Get rid of the snake eyes and get a muffler, and that was it.

Soon afterward, I went on a date with a girl named Jane. She turned out to be Sheriff Day's daughter. He remembered me when I came to pick her up, but he decided I was all right. Several weeks later, Jane and I went on a double date with Rick and his girlfriend Jean. We promised to be back by midnight, but stayed out until two or three in the morning. When we got Jane home, her mother ran out and told us Joe had the highway, police, and sheriff's departments out looking for us. "You'd better lay low for a couple of weeks, 'cause Joe'll kill you if he finds you."

I laid low. A week later, Jane called and said her father had cooled down and I could come over. Joe answered the door, looked down at me, and said, "You're lucky I didn't catch you, 'cause I was gonna kill you. Would ja like a beer? I just made a fresh batch."

Joe claimed that in terms of sheer manpower, for one hour I was the object of the biggest manhunt in the history of Montana. I didn't know whether to believe him or not, but it sounded good.

There was a girl whose name I can't remember, but I think of her as Inez, because of the street where she lived. She was shy. I doubt she had girlfriends even though the girls in high school seemed generally decent, generous, and practical. I've been told I have an unusually naive view of girls. Lucky me.

Inez lived in a tar-paper shack in an area of town called the Cabbage Patch. Her father built his shack supported by twelve stones set on the ground. The walls were rough-cut one-inch boards reclaimed from concrete forms and covered on the outside with scavenged tar paper. The place sat on an unclaimed piece of land on the corner of Second and Inez streets—gumbo-clay roads without signs, a block off California Street. Across California, Hart's oil refinery had spewed a fine petroleum mist over the Cabbage Patch for twenty-five years before it went bust. It left its legacy in the gardens, wells, and people who lived there.

Although I was awkward and out of sync, I managed to ask Inez to a dance, maybe a prom. I don't know if she'd ever been on a date. I picked her up in a 1941 torpedo-backed Pontiac I'd bought for one hundred bucks from Ricky Tabish's dad, who'd given me a job repairing truck tires and pumping gas.

Inez came out of her father's tar-paper shack in a white gown and glided over planks laid on the mud. I handed her a gardenia. I wanted to pin it on her gown, but was afraid her father would see me fumbling over his daughter's divine anatomy. As she pinned the gardenia on her breast, her eyes glistened. She looked as though a boy had never given her a flower.

I don't remember the dance, only coming back to the Cabbage Patch and walking her along the ditch past the defunct refinery. A trace of petroleum from the well water lingered under the gardenia scent rising from the untouchable breast.

I wonder what happened to the girl I called Inez. I went to a high school reunion and looked through the yearbook, trying to find her. She must have been a year ahead or behind. On the other hand, no one remembered the Cabbage Patch. When we were in high school, Missoula's population was about fifteen thousand. Everyone had known about that impoverished neighborhood of blackened shacks. Maybe it's natural it would be forgotten. If not for Inez, I doubt I'd remember.

Long after the refinery shut down, and the children of the Cabbage Patch had escaped to promised lands they'd conceived while drinking in cars, the landscape changed. Modular condos and ministorage replaced the tar-paper shacks. No one from the Cabbage Patch made it to the reunion.

Tuffy was the basketball coach's wife. When I was a freshman in high school, she was involved in community theater when I had a small part in a play, which I'd been trapped into by my mother. I don't remember the play, but I have a photograph of me upside down in the air looking surprised or horrified. The man responsible for my levitation is twisting my arm and looking equally surprised or horrified. I had a crew cut.

Tuffy gave me a ride home one night. She liked to talk, and we became friends. We went for drives in her convertible, once to the top of Pattee Canyon. I had a crush on her, because she was beautiful and sophisticated and she paid attention to me. I don't think she knew what effect she had on me. If she did, she would've laughed.

Our paths hadn't crossed for several months. I was walking past the Missoula Club on a Saturday night when I saw her at the far end of the bar. I went in to say hello. She was pleased to see me, and we talked for a few minutes, until her intoxicated, basketball-coach husband came through the back door. He asked what the hell I was doing and told me to get out. I didn't dawdle.

Monday morning, the homeroom speaker called me to the principal's office. I was off the freshman football squad and permanently excluded from all sports. Why? I'd been drinking in the Mo Club. But I hadn't been drinking. "Yes, you were, a reliable source saw you." It was a terrible and devastating injustice.

I'd had high expectations. I had good hands. I could catch anything. Even though the coach had only used me as a tackle dummy, I knew I was going to get my chance. I never did. My chances of being a football star were spit on a grill.

Thirty years later, I was at a fund-raising event and went to the bar for a beer. There was Tuffy, popping tops and filling cups. I asked if she remembered me. She looked at me for a moment then smiled and said, "Sweetheart, I saved you from a life of football."

Some Jobs

For years I'd gone to the same barber in the basement of the Florence Hotel. His name was George, and he was better educated than I'd ever be. He'd read deeply and played the violin beautifully. One spring afternoon, as he was cutting my hair, I described some plan I had with considerable enthusiasm. He listened carefully, then gently said he didn't understand me, but hoped I got what I wanted. He removed the sheet and carefully brushed around my neck. I got out of the chair and looked at him. He was near retirement, and I was a kid, so it was brash when I said I didn't understand him either. Then I went way out past the boundary of civility. I asked how a man so accomplished and educated was content to spend six days a week cutting hair. He looked as solid and sure as a prophet and said, "It's my duty." It was years before I understood what he meant. I also developed an appreciation for the fact that failure has its uses, and too often success is a dead end.

I had lots of little jobs. Early on summer mornings, I picked up trash at a drive-in theater and at several hamburger stands. It felt great to be out in the world when the town was asleep. Sometimes a breeze came through the Hellgate Canyon in the night and blew the pulp-mill stench out of the valley.

One of my perennial jobs was selling tickets for shows, mostly cat shows, dog shows, and horse shows. People who obsessed over animals were their own breed. My rule of thumb at the time was, the smaller the animal, the stranger the people, and the larger the animal, the meaner the people. There might have been some truth to that, but I doubt it. Horse show people had the most money, exhibited a lot of faith in their intelligence and good taste, and walked around with their shoulders back and their heads up. They strutted their stuff. Most cat show people seemed mentally unstable, at least about cats, but later I came by a cat. The dog show people were by far the gentlest breed. They took everything in stride and had the most fun. I still go to dog shows, not to see the dogs as much as to listen to their owners carry on.

For two years, between the twenty-fifth of June and the fifth of July, I had a fireworks stand that made grocery bags of money. Competition from big outfits and the need for permits brought that little scheme to an end, but it was great fun to be in the midst of a cash blizzard.

I knew several people who had tremendous ingenuity and believed they could do damn near anything. It was an irrationally optimistic time, which made it a great time to be a teenager.

Bob Anderson started a fiberglass-boat factory with nothing but a handful of drawings, some plywood, and a big steel building. It might've been a military-surplus Quonset hut. Fiberglass saturated with plastic resin was postwar miracle stuff. You could make things out of it without hydraulic presses, casting furnaces, or milling machines. Anderson made molds from which he made boats. I wanted to learn about mold making. The problem was, I'd heard that Anderson wasn't hiring.

I walked four miles in the rain, from the house on the hill out past the edge of town to the Gull boat plant—the same place that made Bud's speedy boat. I was soaked through. That was the real reason I got the job as apprentice mold maker.

Bill, the master molder, was in his early forties, handsome, smart, and driven. He wanted to start his own company and had been acquiring the next generation of fiberglass equipment. A thousand things were waiting to be made out of fiberglass. He'd already built a shop at his place outside town. I met his wife once when she picked him up after work. She was direct and intense and the sexiest woman I'd ever seen—not made-up, magazine sexy, but smart-sexy to her core, and she had all the faith in the world in Bill. A woman like that doesn't pick an average Joe out of the lineup.

We worked hard and fast. Every twenty minutes we'd be overcome with acetone fumes and have to take a break. We'd go out back, smoke cigarettes, and go back to work. For the first two weeks my whole body itched from the fiberglass.

When we weren't making molds, I did lay-up on the boat line. Anderson's boats were made by spraying a coat of finish resin into a mold, letting it dry, then layering in fiberglass cloth of varying thicknesses and weaves and saturating them with a two-part resin. The cloth had to be built up a layer at a time and the air bubbles worked out before the resin set up. Corners and edges were always touchy, because the fiberglass cloth had a mind of its own and tended to pull away from a curve. It took patience and a lot of acetone fumes to build a boat.

Water and speed and beautiful boats were Anderson's desires. He'd made wooden boats since he was a boy. When fiberglass came along, he realized he could make a living building boats out of it. After a few years, the corporations got in the act and the small manufacturers were on the way out. Not only did the big companies have national marketing campaigns, they were spraying a mix of chopped fiberglass and resin directly into their molds instead of laying cloth up a piece at a time and brushing in resin. Anderson discovered he could buy boats cheaper than he could make them. He closed his plant and started retailing nationally known brands. I don't know if he felt defeated, but it didn't seem right to me.

One winter evening I was cruising around the fairgrounds looking for an abandoned twelve-cylinder, overhead-cam, 1938 LaSalle coupe that I'd heard about. The search had a mythical, holy grail feel to it. No one was sure such a car even existed, but I knew if I could find it, life would be splendid.

After an hour of slow driving, the LaSalle appeared out of the falling snow, snugged up next to a long, one-story building that'd been a county storage shed. There was a light on inside the shed. Through a fogged window I could see a man pulling a lever on an enormous press. Every time the lever came down it made a deep, satisfying *whir*. He repeated the same action over and over.

I wanted to know what he was doing, and I needed to ask about the LaSalle, so I knocked on the door. He was irritated at the intrusion until I asked about the car. He wouldn't sell it, but we talked engines for a while—it had a cracked block and eight not twelve cylinders—then he invited me in to see his operation.

His name was Lester. He was making what he called self-release ski bindings. I'd never heard of such a thing. He said it was his own invention. To my knowledge he designed and manufactured the world's first safety binding—though knowing how that kind of thing works, there were probably several hundred guys in shops around the world inventing the same thing at the same moment.

Lester had designed a binding with a tension-adjustable, spring-loaded ball that fit into an accessory socket on the toe of the boot. A lever clamp forced the heel forward and held the boot in place. It was simple and elegant.

He started showing me how the various machines on his assembly line worked. Then he was asking what time I got out of school and how many hours a week was I willing to put in. Before I could ask, I had a job. After school I'd punch and rivet bindings and listen to his stories. He'd skied in the Olympics one year, but crashed. During the war he was in the U.S. Army's 10th Mountain Division in Italy. One morning on patrol, he skied out of the trees and saw a line of German soldiers crossing the slope below. Since they'd already seen him, he decided to ski straight down through the middle of their line. He was into the trees again before they got their rifles free and started shooting.

During the forest fire season, Lester contracted with the Forest Service to drop borate from a military surplus Hellcat fighter bomber. Borate was used as a fire retardant, because it robbed the flames of oxygen. It was mixed with water and dropped as a slurry, low over the trees. Dropping borate was probably the most perilous day-to-day flying ever undertaken in peacetime. Lester complained about his competition. Johnson Flying Service was a big outfit and had lots of leverage. Lester said Johnson and the Forest Service, also known as the Forest Circus, were in cahoots. Eventually the government just gave everything to Johnson, and Lester was out of luck.

I went to his house once. It wasn't finished. When I drove up, all I could see was an enclosed stairway on a concrete slab. The roof of the stairway slanted at the angle of the stairs. It looked like a wedge on a slab. He'd built the basement and hadn't gotten any further. He wasn't the only one. A lot of people started houses after the war and ran out of money or time or both. About two dozen slab-wedge structures were scattered around the valley—testimony to intentions and dreams put on hold. Lester put his house on hold and pursued his dreams.

The Main Spot was a bar on Main Street, which was actually a side street. The bar was in a thick, stone-walled building that might have been the jail in the late 1800s. On one side there was a grill and the bar, on the other were linoleum-topped tables, chrome-tube chairs with red plastic seats, a popcorn machine coated in brown, baked-on butter, a pool table, and two pinball machines that worked. Like most bars, the lighting was minimal. The only window had never been washed.

When I was sixteen, I started going there for a beer and a burger and to play the pinball machines. I got to know Al, the owner. One night after closing, he unburdened himself. He was overworked, hadn't had a vacation for five years, and the business was making him buggy. He said he needed to get away for a few days, but he didn't have anyone to run the place. I offered, and without a pause or asking my age, he started showing me how to run the bar and flip burgers. The next day, Al was gone. I was Missoula's youngest bartender.

The seven days I worked the bar and grill were uneventful. The customers came in and ordered their usual. I took care of business, and when things were slow, I read. Al came back refreshed and his humor restored. Bartending seemed pretty easy, and I asked if I could work part-time. He said he'd think about it.

The next day he fired me. He said, "The customers didn't like you. Actually, they hated you. Bartenders don't read books. They listen to drunks. A good bartender can make them believe what they're saying not only makes sense, but that it matters. You don't want that job, do you?" He grinned, paid me, gave me a small bonus, and told me to come back after closing.

At two-thirty in the morning, Al drove us south of town a mile outside the city limits, near where Kmart is today. It was the end of July, and the air was warm and agitated. He turned off the highway and drove up to an old one-story house surrounded by tall cotton-wood trees. Several cars were parked in the dirt driveway, but the windows were dark. When Al turned the engine off, I could hear a deep-throated kind of wailing music I'd never heard before. I didn't know this place. There were no signs. It was completely off my map.

When we got inside, I think Al handed me a beer, but I don't re-member drinking. I just watched. I had stepped out of Missoula into a world, unknown to my uncle's crowd or my friends, where Frank Sinatra and Dean Martin were strangers. This was a dark, smoky world of Mexican marijuana, bootlegged whiskey, and Nevada prostitutes. Men whom I'd never met but later learned owned bars, ran games and girls, loaned money, and fenced stolen goods sat at small black tables with leggy blond women and listened to three Negroes and a big white guy play that music. A Negro with a long, thin face, large, flat lips, and eyelids closed over sockets the size of half-dollars was making that mournful wail by sliding a bottleneck over the strings of a guitar that lay on his lap. It would be four or five years before I heard music like that again, when a tough, independent-minded professor named Leslie Fiedler sat me down in his living room, pulled out a precious album of seventy-eights, and played Robert Johnson's "Crossroads."

I never went back to the house on the edge of town. I couldn't go by myself, and Al wasn't offering, probably for my own good. There were men there who took advantage of the naive and innocent, because somebody had to pay.

Running Away to
California

I don't remember what precipitated it, but in my junior year, Sam and I had a fight, and I left home. I had to leave the Model A behind. For one thing, Sam had the title; for another, it wouldn't go more than fifty miles before it blew a gasket.

My father left an inheritance of fifteen hundred dollars after the Hudson and his interest in the plane were sold. Half went to Vicki and half to me. Mother gave me my share to get me out of the house. In January I took off for California, hitchhiked to the foot of the Sierra Nevadas, then caught a bus over Donner Pass.

Halfway up, we slid off the road in a snowstorm. The road must have closed behind us, because there was no traffic. We were on our own. It was so cold the guys on the bus took turns helping the driver get the chains on. It took us a long time, and a prim Christian lady, who'd read about the Donner cannibals, knew we were in for an event of tragic proportions. She pleaded with the girls behind her to sing something to take her mind off the terrible things that were destined to happen. The girls were happy to oblige, but all they knew were raunchy ski songs. The Christian lady was so scared she bit her lip. Finally she turned around and said, "I don't care if your songs are raunchy, just sing." Before we crested Donner Pass, she was whispering a chorus as though it were a prayer. By the time we got down the other side, she was so happy to have escaped being eaten by her fellow passengers, she was singing the dirty ditty full out with the rest of us. I wondered if the part about Santa's big red wand made it into her prayers that night.

I ended up in Sonora, California, sharing a room with a guy named Ray, who was avoiding Los Angeles for a while. Ray was incredibly nice to me, almost as though I were some kind of experiment. He took me cruising with some of his buddies when they drove up from L.A. one weekend. They belonged to a gang called the *pachucos*. I didn't say more than five words all afternoon. Later, Ray said his friends thought I talked too much. They didn't ask me to cruise with them again. I'd heard about L.A.'s *pachucos*. They'd end up killing me for sure.

I decided to go to high school in Sonora, because they had a real art department in a glass-enclosed penthouse on top of the main building. The art teacher's name was Leno Borelli. He was a tough, stringy guy who didn't take crap from anyone. A big kid mouthed off at him one day, and Borelli threw him down the stairs.

On Fridays, Borelli's wife took over for him, and he drove to Stockton to take classes at the College of the Pacific. I don't remember how it happened, but he started pink-slipping me out of school on Fridays, and I would ride in with him. He liked to drive fast. My job was to keep an eye out for cops. He talked about Picasso, Kandinsky, and Kline, and quoted the beat poets.

You could sit in on any class at the college. I followed him from class to class the first Friday. He was taking philosophy courses, and soon I ventured off on my own. In the campus bookstore I met two girls who looked alike. They turned out to be sisters, and they invited me over for dinner and promised to get me home. I found Borelli and told him I had a ride back. They fed me, gave me a place to sleep, and took me back to Sonora late Sunday night. The girls were sweet and funny. They asked a lot of questions about what I thought of things—not what I liked, but what I thought: "What do you think about coffee?" It was a kind of game.

I waited all week so I could go to Stockton to visit the sisters. The college was an excuse, but I wasn't fooling Borelli. He'd seen those girls. He was merciless.

Sonora was an unlikely place for a town. The old part was built in a narrow canyon. The main street was the bottom of the draw. At either end the town fanned out where it could. The post office was way up on one hillside. From there you could see the entire town from top to bottom. I'd gone up to the post office to check for mail and was standing outside opening a letter from my mother when I heard a low roar. Far down at the bottom of the gully a stream of motorcycles, two abreast, began snaking its way up the draw through town and out the top. There had to be hundreds of them. The roar from the engines shook the hills for twenty minutes. They were the Hells Angels on their way to Angels' Camp, where they supposedly terrified the town for several days.

I opened Mother's letter. It was short. There was a five-dollar bill in the envelope and a note that said, "The five dollars is from the sale of your car. Mother." Not only was the car dear to me, but the engine parts belonged to my friends, and I didn't want to welsh out on them.

I don't think my parents were all that bad. Like most people, I always managed to justify my behavior, so at the time, I wasn't conscious of being an intolerable, out-of-control teenager with a nasty attitude, but I was. They must've been thrilled to see me go.

When school was out, I went to Stockton to say good-bye to the sisters. Leaving California was a relief. I was homesick. I knew I'd miss the sisters, but I missed Montana more. They dropped me off at the intersection of two highways on the outskirts of Stockton, and I started hitching home.

I waited for four hours without a ride. When a tanker truck stopped at the intersection, I jumped up on the running board, opened the door, and asked for a ride before the driver could shoot me. He said he hadn't slept for two days and needed the company. An hour later, he fell asleep and started to drift off the road toward a gas storage tank. I had to hit him to wake him up. He overcorrected and nearly jackknifed the truck before we stopped.

The next ride was with a guy who had one of those small, overpowered Studebaker sports cars. His girlfriend was scrunched up next to him with her hand in his crotch. They were evidently working on some kind of sex-thrill-death fetish. Going over the mountains between Oregon and California, he started passing cars and trucks on blind curves. It was definitely thrilling. I didn't stay for the climax. I found another ride at the next truck stop.

In Idaho a guy picked me up in the evening. I fell asleep. When I woke up, there was a full moon and nothing but black, jagged lava for as far as I could see. He said it was called the Valley of the Moon. It was spooky and beautiful. After a while he said, "This is the end of the line," in a voice that sounded flat and final. I thought he was going to kill me. He waited until I got out, then turned off at a construction site hidden in the lava across the road.

An hour later a car slowed down, went about a hundred feet past me, and stopped. I ran up, grateful not to be abandoned on the Moon. There were two rough-looking guys inside. One rolled the window down and looked me over. There was a long silence before he asked if I knew how to drive. I said I could. He explained they'd been working on a gas rig in Arizona, made a pile of money, had too much to drink, too little sleep, and wanted to make it home, which was Polson, Montana. I said I was headed to Missoula. He said, "We'll be sober by Missoula," crawled in the back, and fell asleep.

I drove into Montana over Lost Trail Pass. As I dropped into the Sula Valley, the sagebrush blurred past in the headlights and the smell of rain on stone welcomed me home. I drove down the Bitterroot Valley to Missoula. It was just getting light when I stopped in front of my parents' house on the hill and woke up the riggers. I offered to drive them to Polson and hitch back, but they insisted they were sober enough to take it from there. They waved and drove off. Going right into the house didn't seem like a good idea, so I walked over to Uncle Bud's, let myself in through the garage, and fell asleep on a couch.

Later that morning, I called Mother. When she realized I was in town, she asked, "Why'd you come back?" I couldn't say anything for a moment, then I asked if she knew who'd bought my Model A. She found a receipt and an address. I borrowed Bud's station wagon and drove over to a place on Stoddard Street. The Model A was sitting in the backyard, and three kids were leaning over the engine. When I got up close, I realized it was a different engine. I asked where the other one was, and they pointed to a patch of weeds. They said I could have it. It wasn't any good. They couldn't get it to run.

I broke the engine down and gave the parts back to my friends. None of them ever souped up a Model A again, but they could put those parts on the walls of their shops and admire them, and I wasn't a welsher.

Vicki

I know a few things about my sister, Vicki, but there are large gaps. She was a con artist, a vixen, and a Lady Godiva. She had at least four children, maybe five.

At thirteen she ran away and joined a circus in St. Louis. She rode a white stallion with a flowing mane and covered her budding, bare breasts with her long blond hair. When her tender age was revealed, the police sent her home to Mother. Hanging out with the circus crowd was probably one of the best things Vicki ever got to do—better than Mommy prison in Missoula.

When she was fourteen, a Missoula potter who preyed on confused, lonely girls got her pregnant, drove her to Seattle, gave her a hundred dollars, and abandoned her in the Pike Street Market. Being abandoned in Seattle was tough on Vicki. She lacked the good sense and skill needed to navigate Missoula, much less a city. I was sent to find her and walked the city for five days, not knowing where to look or how. I was four years older than Vicki, and I felt intimidated.

She called Mother, said she had a new boyfriend, a sailor, and hung up. Bremerton was where the sailors were. I went down to the docks and found the right terminal. As the crowd surged onto the

Bremerton Ferry, I turned and watched the departing mass of human bodies disappear down a long enclosed gangway. I wasn't expecting to see my sister, but a half block away, head hanging, was a girl with a funny walk. An aunt of ours once described Vicki as having a slight hitch in her get-along. When Vicki heard me call, she ran back in a stream of tears, happy to have been tracked down, to have been saved from loneliness and the street, to have even her marginal family's marginal love. Her sailor was shipping out the next day. She wanted me to meet him, so we got on the ferry and went back to Bremerton. He was nice. He wrote a few times. She never saw him again.

I took Vicki back to Missoula on the train. She had a baby girl and gave her up for adoption. Twenty-five years later I tried to find my niece, but that door was shut.

We had hidden Vicki in the family's mental attic. It isn't normal to ignore your little sister for half her life. She was dysfunctional and careless, which made her a danger to herself and others. The family wanted to avoid her, and she returned the favor. She disappeared from awareness early on and did not reemerge for several years. When she did, it was dramatic and brief.

My sister's conflicted and terrifying life was ended in Sacramento at the age of thirty-eight by someone who raised a double-barreled shotgun close to her lips and blew her face off.

I stood on the cool linoleum tile of the Sacramento Police Station listening to a competent young detective quietly advise me not to look at Vicki's body, by which he meant face, because there was no face. I stared back, nodded, then turned and walked out the door into the blazing California sun. I didn't know how to respond to the detective, having temporarily misplaced the standard manual of human emotional responses. Not until I was standing on the sidewalk, shivering in the intense, three o'clock heat, did I realize how cold the station had been. Was imagining what was left of Vicki going to be more terrible than actually seeing my headless sister's fluorescent white body on a steel table in a hollow room cold as a slaughterhouse? I decided to stay in the heat of the sun and live with my imagination.

Mother said that two days before the murder, Vicki called and said someone was stalking her and intended to kill her. Mother hung up on her. Vicki had been manipulating Mother for years. Several times she'd threatened to kidnap Carolyn, her half sister. To Mother, Vicki's call was just one more manipulation. Mother had to tell me about hanging up on Vicki. She needed to be reassured that Vicki's stalker was imaginary, that her daughter was the victim of a random killing. I wanted to believe that, too.

The last time I saw my sister was on a crowded street in San Francisco the day after I returned from Sacramento. When I saw her, she had her face back. We stared at each other for a moment, then she turned and disappeared into the crowd. As I walked along the sidewalk, I kept seeing pictures of her in shop windows.

It took me the entire afternoon to get back to Pier Three, where I was staying with my friend Pete, who was the watchman on a decommissioned ferry boat waiting to be transformed into law offices. Pete lived in a trailer parked on the main deck.

When I got back to the sanctuary of the ferry boat, I didn't want to talk to anyone, so I began exploring. After an hour of poking around, I'd made my way up to the pilothouse on the top deck. The door was locked, and I peered in through the window. There was a framed photo of the ferry docked in Seattle. Beneath the photo was the legend: *Bremerton–Seattle Ferry*. It was the same ferry where I'd found my sister, twenty-four years before.

Seven years later, that nice cop from Sacramento called to tell me a serial killer, who'd murdered twelve other women in California, Arizona, Texas, and Minnesota, confessed to Vicki's murder. He'd used the same shotgun on all of them. He'd found Vicki wandering along the freeway the day he killed her.

Decades later, as I watched my Mother dying, I wondered if she'd kept that portrait of herself, pregnant with Vicki, on the wall of the bedroom, as a reminder of the daughter who should have been.

Even if cousin Ellen's letter told the real story, who was at fault? No one living knows. Mother felt guilty for the rest of her life, but that didn't mean she wanted to kill or damage her daughter. Whatever happened, my sister's reaction to an egg continues to reverberate through the family pond.

An Education, Sort Of

There was and is a place on the corner of Higgins Avenue and Pine Street in Missoula called the Oxford. It isn't what it used to be, but what is? You could order brains and eggs and the counter-man would shout to the cook, "He needs 'em." If you asked for a roast beef sandwich, he shouted, "One Married Man." If you ordered a Married Man, he looked you in the eye and called back, "One-beef-san."

In the back room of the Ox, there was a running day-and-night poker game, which could be seen through the open door on Pine Street. The cops drove by all the time, but to my amazement they never happened to look in. Maybe the Oxford was the only place in the entire state where poker was legal. I never asked.

Just down from the Ox on Higgins was a magazine shop—Rudy's News. Everyone called the guy who ran the place Rudy. I used to go in there in the evenings. In the back was a cubbyhole with a low ceiling and a bare sixty-watt bulb where he kept the strange stuff. That's where I discovered Bukowski, Burroughs, William Carlos Williams, Pound, Rexroth, Bateson, and a dozen others who made a difference. "Rudy" didn't look like the type who read William Burroughs. He was squat, had short, curly salt-and-pepper hair, a slightly squarish face, and smoked cigars. He made his nut selling girlies, sports, *Time, Life,* and the two local rags.

The selection he kept in the cubbyhole didn't fit with the rest of his shop. I never remember anyone else going back there, so I didn't understand why he bothered to stock those books. We never talked, mostly because I read a lot and didn't buy, so I felt guilty. One night as I was leaving and had the door half open, I mumbled, "Good night." His reply was, "Better contrarian than Rotarian."

It must've been a cold night, because I remember holding that freezing brass handle, turning, and smiling back at the little square-headed, cigar-smoking magazine man.

His name was Art Evans, and he became a primary force in my education. Art introduced me to several books, including Camus's *The Stranger* and Jean Paul Sartre's trilogy, *The Age of Reason.* Sartre, an existential Frenchman with a wandering glass eye, found a clause in the social contract that read, "Hell is other people." Which I took to mean, if we allow ourselves to be defined by others, they will gladly design our own private hell. Watch out for peer review.

Besides the books, Art introduced me to a number of the town's literate ghosts—those who'd chosen to ignore the town and the trends. One of those ghosts was Albert Partol, a freelance anthropologist who'd spent most of his life among the Salish Indians on the Flathead Reservation. He'd written their stories and collected their stuff for close to fifty years, but he wouldn't publish anything. He was extremely paranoid that someone would take his life's work and twist it around or steal it. One night, Partol took me to his house after Art closed up. I wasn't a threat, and he needed to talk to someone, so we stayed up all night. He told stories and showed me two hundred accumulated years of Salish magic wrapped in animal skins. He was a rational man, but he seemed to put stock in what the Indians referred to as powers. He told me of a man who, it was claimed, had the ability to know where the elk would be when the tribe needed elk. The man who knew the elk wouldn't talk about it, but several of the tribe said it was true. He had elk power. That was the way they explained it. I wasn't convinced. I wanted to know how it worked.

It was just daylight when I walked home in the cool summer air with a head full of stories. Over the years Al and I talked in Art's and on the street, but that was the only time I got to see the inside of Partol's overstuffed museum. He had stories and theories for everything, but he never explained elk power to my satisfaction.

Bert Pfeiffer used to go into Art's place for some left-wing publication. He was a commie—no apologies. He was also a dedicated scientist, and his work exposed the extent of the damage from radioactive fallout from aboveground atomic tests in Nevada. Bert's work, perhaps more than any one thing, put an end to those tests. Bert never caved in to the National Science Foundation, the Board of Regents, or the scientists who were afraid their association with him would put an end to their federal grants. Bert became one of my best friends, and we argued about communism for years.

Lee Nye, a local photographer and lay philosopher, was another influence. He had a storefront near the high school, where he displayed his work. In back he had a studio and darkroom. I'd walked past his place for several weeks, stopping to look in the window at the unusual black-and-white photographs. One day I went in. I was a kid with bad skin, a crew cut, and a lime green leather bomber jacket. Lee was arty and cool. I must have said something that salvaged the moment. We talked for an hour. He said drop in anytime, and I did. After two months of drop-ins and hours of talk, he said, "Come and work for me, and I'll make you a genius." I asked how much he paid. He was pissed—I should be paying him—but he left the offer open. I don't know why I didn't let Lee make me a genius. No one else ever offered, so I missed my chance.

I still came around. For three months, we spent at least one night a week going from one pinball machine to the next in every bar in town. We were pinball zealots. We always ended up at the Main Spot, where I'd done my stint as Missoula's youngest bartender.

The Campus Theater was owned by Warren and Gertrude Gavin. When they moved to Dillon, they turned the theater over to their son Douglas. An arbitrary collection of individuals, including Douglas, known simply as Gavin, along with Charles, Neville, Arginald, me, and half a dozen others, put on concerts, light shows, plays, and kept our cars functional. Arginald observed that our lives revolved around the wheel and its attachments.

Gavin discovered an enormous, thirties-vintage theater speaker shaped like a cornucopia. It weighed about a hundred pounds. We gave it a coat of yellow paint, hung it off the marquee over the sidewalk, and renamed the theater the Golden Horn. Inside he built the best sound system in town. There was one spot in the theater where you could stand and the sound would come from inside your head. It was a little addicting.

Gavin was generous. He juggled the regular movie fare, which paid the mortgage, gas, and lights, with our not-for-profit ventures. He created a place for us to play, experiment, and conjure our own world. Gavin was the innkeeper of fantasies, and without him our lives would have been smaller.

Commies and Moralists

The Missoula of the 1950s was not a great place for adult misfits. Joseph McCarthy, the FBI, the House Un-American Activities Committee—or HUAC—and local anticommunist vigilantes snooped out every possible threat to the American Way. I might not have known any of this, except I hung out with Kurt, a swell guy I considered my best friend, whose father, Leslie Fiedler, came home from the university every day and listened to the news, read the newspapers, and talked to us about the commies, McCarthy, and HUAC.

The lonely neighbor who called the mayor to complain about weeds, dogs, and kids became a spy. People were put on watch lists. Some had their jobs threatened. Teachers turned in teachers. A zealous principal questioned certain children about their parents. The fifties were an ice age of thought.

There were those, on both the left and right, who really wanted a totalitarian American state. The reason this country doesn't have a director of morals, or our own version of Stalin and the KGB, in spite of Joseph McCarthy and J. Edgar Hoover, is that all over the country, tough, no-nonsense types like Leslie Fiedler, Art Evans, Lee Nye, Doug Gavin, and Bert Pfeiffer weren't afraid to stand up to the would-be tyrants and give them a reasoned explanation of why they should go fuck themselves.

Those same people encouraged Missoula to become a safe haven for aberrant behavior. From the early sixties to the mideighties, all the "isms" exposed themselves with impunity. The citizenry was tolerant—in part because we'd had enough of moralists and anti-commie hysteria—and equally important, rents were dirt cheap. It was the perfect fertilizer for invention. The place became a mecca for a generation of writers, painters, potters, sculptors, musicians, and dancers.

PART FOUR

Work

The Fours

Before we were permanently impaired by our search for truth and fast cars, we had to get real jobs. That was sobering.

I worked nights in a sawmill. It was outside, and the temperature could get down to thirty-five below zero. Things break when it gets that cold. During downtime, we'd stand around a fifty-gallon drum fed by an endless supply of wood scraps and forced air. The drum stayed cherry red and roared day and night all winter.

I'd talked my way into a job at the sawmill when I was fifteen, but they needed my "federal number." Today you get a social security number at birth, but then you had to be sixteen. That was supposed to stop child labor, but saner souls understood that child labor was a fact of life and some families would starve if their kids didn't work, so a birth certificate wasn't required to get a social security number. You just went in, said you were old enough, and they gave you a number.

The sawmill was actually a planing mill where rough-cut boards were run through a long, screaming machine and turned into smooth, uniform, finished lumber. The mill planed pine, fir, and larch—local trees from local mills. Only a few years before, planed lumber was a novelty.

When lath, plaster, and rough-cut studs were replaced by Sheet-rock and planed studs, our homes lost their distinctive feel. The interior surfaces of prewar America reflected a subtle, elusive light. By the midfifties, the walls of newly built houses were made flat and uniform along with the mass production of our expectations.

I was lazy, but I would work hard until I figured out how to make the job easy. That's what got me on the number-four boards. Boards from the planers were laid out on three heavy chains driven by a long shaft with cogs, which engaged the chains and moved the finished lumber along for fifty feet. It was a wide conveyor. In the planing mill this was known as the dry chain. A grader marked the boards for quality—ones, twos, threes, or fours. The chains conveyed the boards from the building that housed the planers and the graders to the chain crew outside. We pulled the boards off according to their grade and slid them onto stacks.

The stacks sat on bunks that could be picked up by an under-slung lift. The lift buggy was driven over the stack, and a steel lip on either side slid under the edges of the bunks, lifted the stack off the ground, and took the bunks out back to the dry sheds. The lift buggy reminded me of a giant insect that slipped over its prey, grabbed on, and skittered away.

If you worked the chain, you worked cold in the winter and hot in the summer. The planed boards were thinner, lighter, not as wet—hence the dry chain—and easier to handle than rough-cut or green boards. Number-one boards were the best grade. Four were the worst—they had knots, splinters, and stains. Most stains were minerals sucked up through the roots. Some were mildew.

None of the crew liked the fours. Even with thick steel staple-covered mitts, slivers could get in under a mitt and jam into your wrist or the palm of your hand. They told me about a fellow who had a board splinter that went through his wrist, pierced the palm, and came out between his fingers. It was every man's duty to make a job suited to morons sound as deadly as possible. If a job didn't pay, at least it could be dangerous.

The mill was as low as you could go, and the four pile was as low as you could go in the mill. It was such a despicable job the foreman had to rotate the men on the chain through the different grades to keep them from getting even more surly about their lives, their work, and their wives. After the first week, I riveted straps to my mitts to keep them tight on my wrists. I offered to do the fours and let the rest of the crew rotate on the ones, twos, and threes, which they were happy to do, but they were not happy with me. My little trick with the strap was show-offy. What annoyed them most was that I liked the fours. You were not allowed to enjoy a lousy job.

I made things worse by talking on breaks about Mike Geery's rail dragster he'd built up from a '49 Olds V8 engine retrieved from the Clark Fork River. When it was finished, he had the pistons and crank from a '54 Olds that jumped displacement from 303 to 324 cubic inches, heads milled ninety-thousandths and seated for '50 Chevy intakes and Hudson Hornet exhaust, a full race cam, modified solid Buick lifters and Caddy rockers, a high-volume Stromberg 48, and a reconfigured Lincoln Zephyr distributor, which made a hellish hot spark.

Mike's inventiveness infected his friends. We knew we could do damn near anything, but Mike's rail job and my optimism were a lot of crap to millworkers, most of whom had neither the time nor the money to fix their pickups. A millworker took home $1.15 an hour.

Beside the fact that I wasn't cool, they had good reason to hate me. Most of them hated anything outside their circle of experience, which wasn't a bad policy—it let them know where they stood with the rest of the world.

There were nine or ten men on the night shift. They all had wives and two to five kids. At least six had four or five hundred acres in the Bitterroot Valley—known to some as down the Root and to others as up the Root. They all had a mortgage. They raised cows, sheep, or hogs. They all had chickens and dogs and two or three horses. They grazed their cows on what land they had, which was never enough for the number of cows they grazed. In the winter, they tried to get by without buying much hay. They lost calves to underfed cows, and they lost cows. They wanted to be ranchers, but they had to work the night shift in Delaney's mill.

During a lunch break, a fellow who worked the planer and had recently moved down the Root told me about a neighbor who'd committed the perfect Bitterroot crime. The neighbor got mad at his wife and clobbered her so hard he killed her. He was afraid to turn himself in, and he couldn't figure out how to get rid of her body without looking suspicious. He sat on the porch, drinking a beer, trying to come up with a solution, when the hogs started a ruckus. His wife usually fed them, and it was past feeding time. He got up and walked over to the hog pen. There was the answer. Hogs would eat damn near anything. He'd seen a hog catch a squawking chicken and chomp it down to the feet. On the last bite the feet dropped off either side of the hog's jaws and fell into the mud. There was no doubt that the hogs would make quick work of the wife.

He went back to the house and picked up her body and the slops bucket. He wanted it to look like she slipped and fell while slopping the hogs, and they'd eaten her. He dropped her facedown in the pen and went to Stevensville, so he'd be in the bar drinking while the hogs finished her off—that was his alibi. It was perfect, except for two things.

First, since she always fed the hogs, they were fond of her. In fact, they all got around and nuzzled her, out of affection, no doubt. They also wanted her to wake up and feed them. Since her husband had need of hungry hogs, he'd left the slops bucket empty.

Second, she wasn't dead. All that hog nuzzling brought her around. She walked the ten miles to town and reported the incident to the sheriff. But the strange part of the story was that she dropped the charges and went back to the bastard.

The fellow telling the story stared up at the sparks flying out of the teepee burner, shook his head, and said, "Jesus, Bitterrooters."

Little outfits under five hundred acres, like those owned by the night-shift guys, were going for taxes. The twenty-acre-ranchette craze hadn't hit, because California was still the golden land. Montana wasn't worth spit. Within a year or two, the millworkers would be lucky to have a night job. Their wives would take the children and leave, and the men would advance the joy of weekend drinking to nightly vigils in one of several derelict Missoula hotels.

The crew was suspicious of me down there at the end of the chain. They were baffled by my obsession with the fours. They wouldn't ask, but they knew there was a secret to it.

To me it was a mystery—the fours set off an electrical storm in my memory. In the months I worked the fours, I relived my entire childhood in their reddish stains, hard dark knots, and mildewed blue-green hues. Each board was a separate painting, and each painting caught a flicker of memory, sliding past into the stack.

As a board slid through my hands, its pattern of knots and colors matched a code in my mind that sparked a memory from my childhood. A pattern would fly past, and I would remember the glint off the brass gun shell in the wet grass. In the next pattern I would remember the goldfish in the greenhouse pool; in the next, the wire basket that protected the light in the tunnel; in the next, a key in a pack rat's nest; in the next, the little fox and the flopping fish; and next, my hand held Mother's red coat; and the next and the next. For eight hours every night, I lived in the flow of images and memories. The process embodied the inner workings of memory. I've tried for years to understand it but can't. Maybe that trace of something between the image and the memory was like seeing the secret of the universe. The fours revealed my childhood. Things I'd forgotten since the moment they'd happened flashed by in the fours.

The fours were laid in stacks. The stacks were dried in kilns the size of train stations and sold cheap to ranchers for sheds and fences. The boards that carried my memories were used to reshape landscapes, define boundaries, and keep cows from wandering.

The Fire

After high school, which I never finished, life became a series of jobs. I didn't last long at any one of them, but I rarely quit or got fired for the same reason twice—the money ran out, the contract ended, the season ended, the foreman couldn't stand me, I couldn't stand him, I went a little nuts and jumped ship, and there were others, including the fact that I could be a real son of a bitch. Being lazy never got me fired that I remember.

The summer I was twenty, I was living in a tent on Flathead Lake. I had a construction job in a plywood plant in Polson, about ten miles away. Another fellow and I were hired to build a steam room for the incoming logs. The idea was that steam would loosen the bark before the logs went to the peeler. The challenge was to build a long, high, insulated room as cheaply as possible. The contractor found a thousand creosote-saturated railroad ties and had us stack them like brick and periodically drive three-quarter-inch rebar through three or four at a time with a sledge. We carried the ties on our shoulders, walking up the wall of ties from one end, tipping the ties forward, then backing out and setting them in place. We worked ten-hour days in the July sun. The creosote soaked into our shoulders, and the wear from the ties left thick calluses. It was the only time I've had calluses on my shoulders. Nothing I could do made that job interesting, fun, or easy.

The night after we finished with the steam room, I was lying in my tent listening to the radio. A news bulletin came on about a large fire in the Jocko Canyon southeast of the town of Ravalli. They were in need of firefighters at the Bureau of Indian Affairs office in Dixon. I packed some extra clothes and drove to Dixon. There were about a hundred men milling around in the parking lot of the BIA warehouses. I spotted an official-looking fellow with a clipboard, and I went up and asked for a job. He took down my name and social security number, and said, "Go find yourself a crew boss."

I pushed my way through the throng in search of a crew boss who didn't have a full crew, which was fifteen plus the boss. Everyone was full up, so I went back to the clipboard man and said all the crews were full. He said, "Shit, I'll have to find another crew boss." I told him I'd be a crew boss. I was joking, of course. I was a kid, and I'd never fought a fire. He told me to wait. I thought I'd pissed him off, but I waited. He returned shortly, handed me a clipboard, and said, "Okay, you have crew number eleven." It was dark, he couldn't see how young I was, and he didn't bother to ask if I'd had any experience. Suddenly I was a crew boss. I stood near the dock while a crew formed around me, and I wrote down names and numbers.

Several trucks came into the staging area, and we were told to load up. I had a sawyer on the crew who was too drunk to climb into the truck. I said, "I think I have to fire you." I told him to sober up and find us the next day.

When the trucks came over the hill north of Ravalli, we got a full view of the fire in the Jocko. It was the first inkling I had that I was in over my head. The sky was bright orange for several hundred feet above the canyon. We didn't know it then, but the fire went back into the wilderness for forty miles to White Horse Lake, where it had forced two crews into the water. We were going into one of the state's worst fires in several decades. Figuring out how I could get out of the crew boss job, if necessary, was suddenly a priority. I started talking to the men in my crew, sorting the smart and experienced from the average guys. I found two I could turn the job over to. Two out of fifteen wasn't bad.

The next morning we went out on a small fire that had been started by embers dropping out of the sky from the updraft of the main fire. One of the two men I'd picked the night before had a lot of experience and common sense. He'd be the one I'd go to and say, "I don't know what I'm doing, it's all yours."

I didn't want to be a boss, but I wanted to see if I could figure it out, to see if I could do it. I just didn't want to get anyone killed.

The BIA was different from the U.S. Forest Service. Whatever else I might have thought about the USFS, they'd put more thought into fighting forest fires than anyone in the world. The BIA's firefighting capability barely existed. It wasn't well organized, which would give me a chance to learn something before I got fired. I became extremely attentive in the midst of total chaos.

There were trucks, D-8 Cats, front loaders, giant water pumps, radios, food supply trucks, cooks, piles of paper, sleeping bags, hundreds of men, and a tent city. Above all this were spotter planes and borate bombers. For not being well organized, the BIA had a lot of equipment.

That night we were sent into an area where they thought the fire was spreading. The smoke was so dense that from the air it was impossible to tell what was happening on the ground. They paired us up with another crew that was mostly Indian, except for the crew boss, who was a nervous little white guy. Maybe it was his first fire, too. Most of my crew were migrant Mexicans who came up from Brownsville, Texas, every year to pick cherries on the east shore of Flathead Lake. That year they got up before the crop was ready. They were happy to land the firefighting gig. It sounded to me as though they led terribly hard lives. I later learned the Mexicans thought cherry picking and hoeing beets in Montana was a vacation.

To get to the fire, we had to hike into the base of some cliffs and find our way to the top in the dark. It wasn't sheer, but it was steep, and if you went off in the wrong places, you could fall into the canyon. After a couple of hours, we managed to get to the top. We walked in about a quarter mile to get a look at what was under all that smoke. What we saw scared every one of us. The fire had been burning in eighteen inches of pine needles, twigs, and dead branches on the forest floor. Not long before we'd topped the cliffs, the fire had caught a breeze that lifted it into the treetops, where it crowned. We were standing under a firestorm. It was both spectacular and terrifying. The trees were old-growth ponderosa, some four feet in diameter and over 150 feet high.

The other crew boss just said, "I'm gettin' outa here," and started running toward the cliffs. His crew didn't move. They turned and stared at me. The Mexicans were more nervous than the Indians. We all needed the job, so we weren't going to run unless we absolutely had to.

I decided to stay because the breeze was to our backs, which meant the fire wasn't going to move in our direction unless the wind changed. That wasn't too likely, because warm air was still rising off the cliffs and creating a buffer zone. If the wind from the south didn't pick up until morning, the buffer would hold until the cliffs cooled. The Indians probably knew this, because they said they'd stay if I did. I said, "I guess you have a new crew boss." The Indians nodded and waited for the white boy to tell them what to do. The only thing I knew to do was to start digging a fire line to prevent the fire in the groundcover from creeping toward the cliffs, so I sent the crews in opposite directions digging a fire line.

The fire in the treetops was another matter. I was staring up at the fireworks, assuming all we could do was hope the wind held until the borate bombers came in the morning. If the wind changed, the crown would leap over us, and we'd be trapped. As it was, we were trapped between the fire and the cliffs.

Between the two crews I had three sawyers. The one I'd fired two nights before came up and asked if I wanted them to go in and start felling trees into the burn. Obviously that was how you stopped a crown, but it didn't seem possible. For one thing, the tinder was smoldering under the trees nearest us. How could you fell a tree while the ground was on fire? I looked at the sawyer and nodded. He said he'd need someone to drive wedges for him. I set the other two sawyers up with wedge drivers, and I went in with my guy. It became immediately apparent how this worked.

The sawyer made an initial cut, ran out, stomped his feet to cool them off, and ran back in. After he had a deep cut on the side away from the fire, he started on the other side. The wedge driver drove wedges on the away side. I spent most of the first night running back and forth between driving wedges and stomping my feet. I discovered that a good sawyer with a wedge driver can drop an awful lot of timber in a short time.

After a few hours of pounding wedges, I decided to check on my crews, found myself a replacement, and started down the fire line. What both crews had done, having no direction from me, was to dig their lines along the burn, resulting in a very crooked fire line, because fires burn crooked. I never questioned this method. The line was there, and it was stopping the fire. What else would anyone want? It took me three or four days to figure out this didn't make much sense. What made sense was digging a straight line between two points and letting the fire burn down to it. It also took about a fourth as much time to dig the line.

So I was learning, no one had been killed yet, everyone was too tired to pick a fight, and the fire hadn't crowned over us. My crews were impressed when I radioed the controller and demanded they start feeding us steaks. When we came in that morning, we had steak and eggs.

There were some bad spots. My best sawyer got his calf sliced open by a kid with an ax.

I inherited another crew that I put out during the day to maintain our line. One morning after I'd just fallen asleep, someone came in and said one of my day crew guys had died of a heart attack. I went up to help bring him out and found he was still alive. In fact, he seemed pretty healthy. We made a stretcher with poles and blankets and got him down the cliffs to the road. I was so relieved, it didn't occur to me that he might've faked it.

The longer I was out on the mountain with that radio, ordering steaks and borate drops, the cockier I got. One day I asked for a drop in a particularly hazardous ravine. The pilot came in on a low pass, saw I had the radio, came back, caught me with the tail end of the drop, and knocked me ass over teakettle. I don't know if he wanted to kill me, but he took the bravado out of me. It was a very long while before I wanted to stand up.

After about a week on the fire, I noticed I could tell when and where the fire would burn. It was as though the timing and strength of the wind changes, odors, sounds, humidity, temperature, barometric pressure, electrical charges, moisture in the floor, and elements I was unaware of had all come together, creating a pattern that told me what was going to happen within the next eight to ten hours. That sounds far-fetched. Perhaps it was all a coincidence—a series of lucky guesses—but I was under tremendous pressure to get things right. All my sensors were working overtime. I didn't feel like I was rolling dice. I just seemed to know.

Humans were designed, not unlike animals, to read the natural world unconsciously. To early hunters, that kind of direct knowledge, in contrast to rational thought, had to seem magical and informed by animal spirits that would warn, protect, and feed them. Standing on the ridge at night above the cliffs, watching the fires burn, I had a glimmer of what Al Partol, the anthropologist, was saying about the man who could find the elk.

We intuitively understand that we lack the direct knowledge necessary to live in cities. We scramble to make up for the loss with laws, police, cameras, DNA, and databanks. We need more of everything, and we need it faster. Unfortunately for us, the faster we go, the farther ahead we have to see.

One day I worked up the courage to run deep into the fire where it had already burned. It was relatively cool, but the smoke was thick. I stood and listened for a while and watched the smoke surge and twist through the blackened trunks of the giant ponderosa. About fifty feet away, where the smoke had momentarily cleared, I saw the shape of a bear. I couldn't tell if it was a black bear or a grizzly. It was standing up, looking around, as if it was trying to figure out where it was. I stood still and waited until it disappeared into the smoke. I was curious about what it would've done, under the circumstances, had I walked toward it. I was curious but not foolish enough to find out.

We could have stayed and done mop-up, the cushy job, but everyone, including me, wanted to get home. The Mexicans wanted to get back to their real job, picking cherries. As for me and the Indians, we just wanted out of the smoke. The fire had been our own little war, and we wanted to disappear for a few days. Several of us stopped off at the bar in Arlee. We'd been walking on eighteen inches of pine needles for weeks. When our feet first hit that concrete floor, we wobbled like a bunch of drunks.

I sat in a booth with three of the crew, including the fellow I'd picked to take over if I lost my nerve or wised up. When the other two went to the john, I asked if it was obvious I'd never worked a fire before. He said, "Yeah, I knew, but they don't, and better not tell 'em." Then he grinned. I was just happy I didn't get anyone killed. I was lucky.

The Woods

One fall, I worked for Jerzy Corkran, who had a salvage logging contract on several hundred acres of the Lolo Forest previously logged by the Anaconda Copper Mining Company. The ACM originally got in the logging business to supply their underground mining operations in Butte with lumber and timber. They went in big and fast, tore up mountainsides, trashed the watershed, and got out. The Forest Circus contracted with small outfits to scavenge what the big guys had left in their rush to high-grade the best and easiest timber off one mountain and move on to the next.

Corkran owned a piece of land in a canyon southeast of Missoula, a trailer house, and three acres of early American logging equipment. He was antisocial, brutish, and potentially dangerous. He had a brittle relationship with a manly woman, who made table lamps from sagebrush—lacquered and burnished to a soft yellow glow. She had her own trailer, parked parallel to Corkran's. A narrow, enclosed walkway connected their sheet-metal shacks.

One morning, she poked her head out a window and invited me into her side of their arrangement to show off her sagebrush lamps. She saw me looking through the walkway that connected the two trailers and decided to explain how she and Corkran had maintained for nine years. It was rumored he had a thick dick, but it didn't make up for being a short-fused SOB. She took me outside and pointed to the bottom of Corkran's trailer. Like most trailers that stayed put, it was up on blocks, the wheels and tires long gone. Then she pointed to the inflated tires on her trailer. It was ready to go. "If the old bastard gives me grief, I can be outa here in five minutes." Every few months those tires had to be reinflated with a hand pump. No doubt she made sure he was around to watch. The two of them had been aligned for nine years in their parallel tin shacks of burnished sagebrush, diesel fumes, and sexual ecstasy, balanced above the threat of the wheel.

Independent logging operators were known as gypos. They were a tenacious bunch. Most were deep in debt—unless they managed to team up with a smart woman who could read contracts and manage the books. The work required big machines, expensive repairs, expensive downtime, and speed to catch up for lost time. They had to employ truck drivers, boom operators, cat skinners, sawyers, hookers, and choke setters. When someone was too hungover to work, the boss had to fill in. Gypos worked fourteen to seventeen hours a day until they went tits up, which all did, eventually.

The truckers tore down mountain switchbacks as though they were one-way streets, air horns blaring as they approached blind corners. They drove fourteen hours, went home, started on a six-pack of piss beer, worked on their trucks, ate cold steak, and went to bed next to a cold woman who had no other place she could go.

The gypos ran full out. If something went wrong, there was little chance of a warning shout. Saws, screaming diesels, and trees falling or shooting up the hill on the end of a cable made shouting pointless. Tilt, the empathy-impaired crane operator, had great skill at whipping the end of the crane around and flipping the cable and hooks down a slope.

My job was to hop through the downed timber, grab the hooks, set them in a log, and run like my ass was on fire, because the instant the hooks set, Tilt jerked the log out of the scramble, knocking timber and limbs through the known dimensions.

Being a hooker was a job for quick, reckless boys. Few lasted three seasons. Eventually they got hurt. Every year one or two in the Northwest got killed. Hookers had higher comp claims than anyone, including sawyers—that's if an outfit bothered with workers' comp in the first place, which Corkran's didn't. If bragging rights for deadly heroics were based on actuary tables, hookers would best firemen, cops, and underground miners.

Naturally I aspired to something not so deadly. Plus there was no way to make hooking easy.

It turned out I was good with a chain saw. I had a knack for dropping a tree exactly where I wanted it, running was rarely involved, and I didn't have to depend on Tilt to get me killed.

Pine forests are dry and lifeless. Acid in the needles is designed to kill off all other forms of plant life. In my list of things best avoided, conifers quickly joined cowboys and cows.

After several weeks, a few of the standing ponderosa seemed to acquire personalities. I would be on a ridge looking across the canyon at half a dozen trees and become aware of them as individuals. I wasn't surprised or shocked when they started talking to me. It seemed natural enough.

I was exhausted from working long hours in the cold, and it's possible I'd been drinking heavily and not getting much sleep. I couldn't tell whether their voices came from inside my head or not. At the time, that didn't seem important. I was having small talk with trees. For some reason my awareness of individual trees didn't interfere with my work, but then I never had to kill a tree I had a relationship with.

One day I was sitting on the stump of a tree I'd just dropped, eating my lunch and counting the growth rings. I finished lunch at the two-hundred-year mark—roughly halfway through.

There wasn't a thing I liked about conifers, but it seemed perverse to kill something that had managed to stand in the same place for four hundred years braving fire, wind, ice, and the pestilence of bark beetles and mistletoe fungus. I screwed the cap on my thermos, got in the truck, and drove down the switchbacks. The delusion of talking trees and the troubling idea of killing something that would have lived another four hundred years let me escape the woods with my skull intact.

Talking trees are not a bad thing. The world talks to us all the time. Whether we can afford to listen is another matter. The ability to disassociate the killing of trees from building houses is a trick of mental gymnastics, similar to detaching the cow from the burger.

It took us thousands of years to overcome a deep-seated reluctance to cut down a tree or alter the path of running water. Ceremonies, offerings, and prayers to a multitude of spirits and gods were required to alter the course of life. That made our lives incredibly complex. Every damn detail had to be negotiated with unseen forces. Putting all our gods in one basket simplified things and helped speed up the alterations—we had to bribe only one guy to get an entitlement.

The Bitterroot Ranch

Sam must've been in trucking for about four years. He contracted out to Haines Wholesale Grocery and drove his truck so hard he and Mother managed to save up enough for a small down payment on a five-thousand-acre ranch on the Burnt Fork Creek of the Bitterroot Valley. They bought the place from a man named Lou Miller. The ranch had simply worn Miller out, and he was happy to be rid of it. For the next twenty years, he never saw more than the interest on the mortgage. He could've repossessed it a year after they took over. Fortunately for Mother and Sam, Miller's wants were simple.

I began driving down to the ranch to help out on weekends. The place was a struggle to maintain. Most of those five thousand were up-and-down acres. There wasn't a lot of cropland, but with an extra thousand acres leased from the Forest Service, there was enough grazing for 350 head.

Mother and Sam worked the place alone much of the year. They were either too tired to fight or they turned civil when I came around. Nobody seemed to remember Colorado. They ran cows, raised a little wheat and barley, and put up hay. During thrashing and haying, they hired extra hands and were grateful for a free set.

I liked haying. The baler was ancient, but I could keep it tuned and tight, humming along, popping out perfect bales all day behind an even more ancient Ferguson tractor. After a field was cut and baled, I'd hitch Sam's team to the hay wagon and go out to pick up bales. I can't remember the horses' names, and no one's alive who would know. Both were cream-colored—a mare and a gelding. They'd been trained to skid logs and respond to voice commands. I could *gee* and *haw* them back and forth between bales all across the field. *Gee* might have been for left and *haw* for right. I could have it backward. They were so old we used them only to pull the hay wagon.

That spring, Sam had hired a hand named Dan Cassidy, who believed he'd been born a hundred years late, that he belonged back in the time before telegraph lines put an end to the Wild Bunch. It made him a little despondent, particularly when he'd had a major snootfull. Late one afternoon, after I'd greased gears, bushings, and bearings on the baler and the Ferguson, I walked across the hay meadow to the bunkhouse.

Dan had come down from the hills, where he'd been checking heifers and calves, and was sitting on a stump, swatting flits and sucking a lukewarm beer. The bunkhouse refrigerator was a GE marginal. Occasionally the compressor made a tortured gnashing sound, then shook violently, causing the refrigerator to leap forward and hop around on the cherry-print linoleum. The inside was stocked with near-cold beer, a loaf of blotchy green American cheese, and a half pint of sour goat's milk one of Dan's girlfriends had recommended for sexual enhancement. In the Bitterroot Valley, magical thinking served as a reality check. In the ice cube compartment with the missing door, Dan kept a semifrozen rattlesnake he'd saved for the bones. He intended to feed the snake to a good-size anthill and give the skeleton to the sour-goat's-milk girl. He claimed that if she kept the snake on the shelf above her bed, it would shy-off evil spirits, a kind of cowboy dream catcher, but he'd broken up with her before he found a suitable anthill, so the snake stayed at near melt waiting for the next lucky gal.

Her name was Trixie. She found Dan at the AmVets club. In Dan's words, she was a stunner who'd turned his brain inside out. When he realized she was several watts brighter than he was, he decided not to mention the evil-spirits–snake-skeleton correlation. Her intellect intimidated him, and he was already wearing his brains outside his skull. He'd found a smart, beautiful woman who understood him and still loved him. She was also fast on her feet. Soon after they met, she chased him down in the soft earth of a newly plowed field, tackled him, and consummated their love amid the furrows.

Dan was in deep and drowning. She was far more than he deserved, and he couldn't take the pressure of the relationship. When something was too good to be true, Dan's tendency was to stomp on it till it broke.

In an effort to distract him from reveling in his self-imposed devastation, I'd related the tale of the Chinese cook who was murdered in the bunkhouse in 1910, the year the great fire cut a wide swath through Montana, burning farms, forests, and entire towns, thereby rearranging the hopes and dreams of half the state. I told Dan that the Asian's ghost had been seen in the bunkhouse in the early-morning hours by numerous cowboys, most often after a hard Saturday's night in Stevensville. Some heard laughter reverberate down the stovepipe, evidence—since the cook's body was never found—that he'd been dismembered and burned. All I'd done was relate what I'd heard to take his mind off Trixie for half an hour. My strategy had unintended consequences.

The following Sunday about two in the afternoon, I came in for lunch. Dan was carefully arranging his assets in the back of his oxidized-red pick'emup, as he called it. He was pale and frayed. His hands were shaky and his eyes tight and red-lined, a condition that usually remedied itself by noon. He said he was exhausted—he'd made the acquaintance of the Chinaman, who'd kept him awake, talking till dawn. Dan didn't intend to spend another night in the bunkhouse, on the ranch, or in the Bitterroot.

When Dan left, the compressor died, and the snake rotted. I hauled the refrigerator outside and propped the door open. The maggots left a beautiful skeleton, which I considered giving to Trixie, but thought better of it.

The Slaughterhouse

I got a job at a slaughterhouse—later referred to as a meatpacking plant, and still later as a facility. We facilitated slaughter. I worked with a Spanish nobleman named Ted Pacheco who'd been deprived of all four fingers of his left hand to the second knuckle. He cooked entrails, blood, scraps, and crushed bone—shoveling the resulting mingle into an iron press that banged out highly compressed, thirty-pound cakes. After the cakes dried brick hard, I forced them into the mouth of a pulverizing hammer mill. The result was called bonemeal and included anything that couldn't be sold in Yankee Stadium.

The mill emitted a constant, nerve-racking scream, varying its pitch as it finished eating one cake and started another. It wasn't dangerous work unless you fed your hand into the mill, and only a moron would do that. I got paid by the number of sacks filled. I worked fast and kept my own schedule.

I went to work one day after I'd been up all night reading. It wasn't wise to come to work exhausted with a head full of Bedouins killing Turks and spend the day feeding cakes into the hammer mill. My mind wandered, my hand slipped, and the hammer whacked off my right thumb. I could feel it go. I yelped and jerked back. My instant response was, "Thumbs don't count, anyhow," thereby displacing the opposable thumb theory of evolution with a disposable one. I carefully pulled the thick leather mitt off. There, by a miracle of Saint Anthony, patron saint of missing limbs and digits, my thumb was still attached. I focused past the throbbing thumb to the Spanish nobleman in the cook pit. My yelp had penetrated the scream of the hammer mill. Ted was staring up at me, wondering what that stupid kid had done to himself.

I hit the kill switch on the mill and climbed down to Ted in the pit. I admitted my first response was thumbs didn't count. Ted grinned, held up his fingerless hand, and told me that story, while I held my thumb.

As a young man, he'd escaped a Colorado coal mine fire that killed thirty-nine men. He'd learned to play the violin, which helped him woo the local schoolmarm—a major accomplishment at the time. They migrated to Butte, where Ted got work as a miner. Then the Depression hit, and he got laid off. He wandered around the state looking for a job. He lucked out, finding a job as a gutter in the killing room at the slaughterhouse. The floor was a thick river of red, and the air was moist and stank with the heavy odor of warm blood. A team of horses was used to pull up the kills by their hind legs for gutting.

One day Ted was trying to fix a mess some kid had made with a cow caught in the pulley ropes. The horses were confused and jumpy, and they'd pulled the knotted mess even tighter. Ted got things partly untangled, but the cow was still dangling from a rope that had twisted and wedged under another rope. He braced himself against a timber, grabbed the rope, and gave it a yank. The rope popped onto the pulley; the cow's entire weight snapped the rope taut as a bowstring and snatched Ted's fingers free of his hand. For a moment, they lingered in the air. He stared at his suspended fingers and thought, Shit, I'll never play the violin again.

Today or even in the early sixties the doctors might have put his fingers back, but not in 1935. The loss of toes, fingers, hands, and arms was common. Because of the jobs I'd had, I knew several men with missing parts. I met a man who'd lost an arm in a train accident and claimed that doctors in Butte had connected the whole mess and got it working. He could grasp tools and raise the arm level to his shoulder. I'd never heard of such a thing, and my skepticism must have shown. The man just smiled and waved his arm. He was gentle and sweet in his pride and made me a believer.

Ted took me fishing on the Madison River. He had a small row-boat big enough only for the two of us, but it fit on top of his '54 Dodge sedan. The boat was needed to get to his favorite spot, which was out among several islands where the river widened until it seemed like a lake. We left in the dark and got into the water when it was just getting light. The water was pure and clear, the holes deep, and the currents so unpredictable it made the little islands feel as though they were floating. We fished until ten that morning, then headed home with our limit of twenty-inch rainbows.

We'd hardly said a word the whole trip, but on the way back he started talking about his life in Colorado. He told about making his own skis and winter trips into the mountains. That was before the coal mines, the fire, and the schoolmarm. I told him about the skis in the hayloft and described the little rough-cut knobs on the ends. He explained that after you'd soaked a new board in hot water you could tie a rope to the knob and bend it over a curved block shaped like the ski tip. You left the knob so you could reshape the tip if it flattened out.

I'd never told anyone about the milk barn brooms. They were ridiculous, and most people would've laughed. Ted wasn't the kind who ridiculed, so I told him about the brooms. It put a smile on his face.

Ted was quiet and intelligent. He was observant, but without that inborn curiosity that draws people beyond their zone of comfort into new lives. Had he managed to get an education, he would've been teaching anthropology in a still academic pond in the

Rocky Mountains. He didn't have the aggressiveness that lands the big jobs.

That time on the Madison with Ted was the best fishing of my life. I rarely fished after that. Sometimes, when I went back to the ranch, I'd fish along the banks of the Burnt Fork in the evening. One Saturday, I had my father's bamboo brush rod and was casting along the bank. I'd come upon a spot near the gristmill a French carpenter named La Fontaine built in 1851.

The creek widened below the mill and cut under a large cotton-wood on the far side, exposing its roots. Minuscule floating particles and darting insects filled the air where the sun slanted through the leaves. The fly I'd cast upstream was drifting down over the deep hole near the cottonwood. The fly balanced on the silky water, each hair illuminated, waiting for the strike from the black, watery universe below.

At that perfect moment, I realized fishing was merely my way of searching for that hidden thing—the secret under the surface, the mystery of the universe, the truth. It was an unconscious craving, but always there, deep in my brain, nosing around like a trout searching for a winged morsel. Fishing wasn't going to reveal anything but fish.

At the instant fishing became a metaphor, I flicked the fly off the water, reeled in the line, and went home. That was the end of fishing.

The Most Powerful Man
in Butte

I made the mistake of trying college, because a girl I liked thought I should. Of course, she soon realized she could do better and did. For me, the time I spent in college was a period of sleep deprivation and bad decisions. At least I got to read. I ended up married to Margaret, a brainy redhead with a beautiful, creamy complexion, who wanted to be a pharmacist. I worked two jobs to pay off some debts and help put her through school.

After Margaret graduated, she clerked at Smith Drug and waited for a pharmacy job to open up. In January of '62, she was promised a job in Butte. She couldn't start right away, maybe not for a few weeks, but it was suggested she move to Butte as soon as she could. So we stuffed our minimal possessions into an old Ford station wagon and drove to Butte in the middle of winter.

Margaret was sitting across from me, under the bright, fluorescent buzz—a thousand miles away on the other side of a sticky white table in a Butte café—no place to stay, twenty below outside, no job, staring at blowing snow ghosting the deserted train depot across the street. Butte was high, and the winters were cold. It seemed like it was always twenty below, except when it was thirty-five below. On the Taylor River Ranch it'd gotten down to fifty-two below, but somehow it wasn't as cold as that first night in Butte.

I can't remember details or even where it was, but we found a semiheated shotgun apartment with running water and a lightbulb. It was cold, but it was long.

The street smart said Butte was the FBI's Siberia. Supposedly, J. Edgar Hoover, a man of considerable character and a vicious, vindictive, blackmailing bulldog in satin peach pumps, sent the agency screwups to Butte. The FBI cars were government gray without hubcaps, so they were called WOHCs, or Wookies. The FBI, along with the famous Pinkertons, had protected the Anaconda Copper Mining Company—known as the ACM, or the Company—from radical influences for decades.

I had Wookies on the brain. I'd refused to be drafted into the military. Having stood on the table at my draft board meeting, declaring my noncompliance, I was suspect and in violation. I'd thought about fleeing to Canada or New Zealand, but perversely decided to stay and watch my fate unfold on home ground. For months I waited for the Wookies to come. The fear and paranoia of going to jail gave me a sixth sense for spotting enforcers. Within a couple of years, when the Vietnam War boiled over, a significant percentage of the country would develop similar instincts.

The Anaconda Company was one of the world's largest corporations. The major stockholder at the time was Juliana Wilhelmina, Queen of the Netherlands. A corporation is a legal phantom with the rights of an individual and none of the responsibilities—an ingenious bit of legalese, without which our economy would not function. If the Company killed a miner gradually and made money while he was dying, it wasn't murder, or manslaughter, or even negligence—it was the cost of doing business. If he died in an accident, his widow automatically received two hundred dollars' burial money. She didn't even have to apply, but she had to vacate the company housing within thirty days.

From the 1870s to 1918, the sun in Butte was a small red ball obscured by smoke from dozens of smelters. Airborne arsenic killed grass, trees, and shrubs. Cats licked themselves and died. Arsenic seeped under doors and into lungs.

Miners came down with silicosis. When enough rock dust got trapped in their lungs, the resulting fibrosis slowly suffocated them. If you didn't have it, it was assumed you would. The Company wasn't liable for silicosis. Patients went to die at the state hospital in Galen. Officially, Galen was called a tuberculosis sanatorium.

The smelters in Butte were closed down by 1919 when the Company built a huge smelter thirty miles west in Anaconda. The smoke stack was fifty-eight stories high. The top was sixty feet in diameter and the walls were thick enough to drive a truck around.

Ore was hauled from the mines to the smelter on Marcus Daly's shiny new railroad, the Butte, Anaconda, and Pacific—or BA&P. The rails made it the thirty miles to the smelter, but stopped seven hundred miles short of the blue Pacific.

Even after the long innocence began to unravel, the citizens of Butte were happy to have the Company as a controlling father. When Margaret and I pulled into town in the early sixties, Butte was in the doldrums of a worldwide copper glut. Most of the underground mines had suspended operations.

Several years before, the Company had started digging the Berkeley Pit, a hole half a mile wide and a thousand feet deep. After they closed the Pit, it began filling with water until it became a toxic lake that killed entire flocks of birds that had glided in for a rest on their north–south migrations.

The Pit was Butte's most conspicuous villain. We blamed it for everything that went wrong, and a lot went wrong. Trucks the size of houses hauled 170 tons of ore at a time out of the hole. Only a few men with drilling rigs were needed to set the charges to blast out an area as large as a football field. Enormous loaders filled trucks in minutes, and the trucks climbed out of the pit on a switch-back road, over the edge, and down the hill.

Before Butte became the faceless Anaconda Copper Mining Company at the beginning of the twentieth century, the hill was dominated by Marcus Daly, W. A. Clark, F. Augustus Heinze, and William Rogers, referred to on restaurant place mats as the Copper Kings. It seemed like a lot of kings for one hill.

Margaret spent her days helping out gratis at the pharmacy of the promised job. I walked back and forth through town, up and down the hill, looking for work. There was a dark, steamy laundry with old wooden vats operated by an abundant Black Irishman, his cranky wife, two plumpish daughters, and a fragile son-in-law about my age who looked as though he would've happily traded places with me. The wife asked if I was married and lost interest when I gave her a quick yes.

A butcher shop on the flats was run by a wide man with an edgy laugh. He wasn't hiring, and the place stank. The butcher shop and the laundry were operated by families—always the last to hire and first to fire.

The railroad was laying off. The men at the city shops just sneered. In a town that badly needed hope, my desperation was old news. Butte could've used a king or two.

The mines weren't even a possibility—I'd heard there were no jobs, and I had no experience. I'd spent enough time in Butte to get a head-full of underground mythology. People went in and never came out. They were crushed, suffocated, burned, or blown up. If they survived all that, silicosis took its turn. No one had delusions about a long life.

Margaret and I'd come to Butte debt free but nearly broke. The money we'd saved was almost gone. I hadn't found a job, and pharmaceutical salesmen were flirting with her. We'd never fought, but one night we got into a screamer that reminded me of Mother and Sam. I still have no memory of where we were living then, but it might have been in Walkerville, because that night I walked downhill to Spillum's Bar, which catered to miners who told gruesome tales about dismemberment and cheating wives. Lonely men go to bars, and the loneliest have women at home who've lost the habit of loving them.

The place was loud, smoky, tall, narrow, and long and kept getting darker the farther you went, until it was black and quiet, as though the chaos of the bar was pulled into the back and absorbed. I spent the last of our money for nine shots of America's most advertised, least drinkable, petroleum-based whiskey.

I left the bar and started walking. I was warm and weightless and began to drift along through the falling snow. That night I traversed the town from the Pit to the School of Mines and from Walkerville to the flats and halfway back. It was daylight when I'd sobered up and found myself at the corner of Main and Granite asking passersby the same question: "If there's a job to be had in this town, who would I see about it?" After the eighth or ninth try, a heavy Irishman with a thick beard, tiny, deeply set eyes, and a slept-in overcoat stopped and glared, then thrust his fist straight up into the blizzard of thick flakes. My eyes followed his arm up to the stub of his forefinger, which pointed to the top of the Hennessy building. With a silicosis rasp he said, "Ed Renward, ACM vice president of Western operations. Sixth floor."

I stared up through the white flakes at the sixth floor and imagined warm men in suits poring over papers, pressing numbered keys, pulling levers, doing business. I looked back to see if the bearded man was joking, but he was on the move—a black bison-shape leaning into the falling snow. I thought he was lucky to find a coat large enough to fit. He disappeared into the whiteness, and I stood on the corner wondering what to do.

Then I was in the elevator on the way to the sixth floor. The door opened, and I was standing, not in a hallway, but in an enormous room facing a secretary behind a desk. I had just walked into the ACM's center of operations. I wondered if anyone ever came up that elevator without an appointment.

There were other people in the room, but all I could see was surprise and fear in the secretary's shocked blue eyes. I was rumpled and unshaven, probably menacing to her, but I felt intimidated. She hesitated before asking what I wanted. The sudden silence made me realize that a moment before, the noise of business had filled the large room. I hadn't noticed the row of desks along the windows or the several open office doors on the opposite wall, or the men in suits who occupied them. All those eyes were on me, waiting. The words "I'm supposed to see Mr. Renward" came out of my mouth. She kept her eye on me, leaned to her right, and pressed a switch on a dark brown box with rounded corners that reminded me of the radio in Woodman. As her finger pressed the switch, it occurred to me that she was activating a trapdoor. I imagined sliding down a chute, out onto the sidewalk. She said, "Mr. Renward, there's a young man to see you. He doesn't have an appointment." Renward crackled back, asking my business. I said it was personal. There was a pause, then he said, "Send him in." Perhaps he thought I had the goods on him.

The secretary directed me to the left, past the row of offices. I found myself in a narrow corridor with smaller offices on either side. It had the feel of walking through a Pullman car. Four or five men, evidently taking a break, were leaning against the walls outside the little offices, smoking and talking. I zigzagged among them to avoid stepping on their well-polished wingtips. They watched as I negotiated past but failed to move and never stopped their chatter.

At the end of the hall was a small room and a man sitting behind a tiny desk next to a narrow door on a sliding track. The man looked alarmed. He jumped up and said I wasn't allowed, but a voice behind the sliding door bellowed, "Let him in." The man slid the door back. I nodded, thanked him, and stepped into a large office.

Renward sat behind a serious mahogany desk, silhouetted by the grime-coated window behind him. He asked what I wanted. I told him if there was a job to be had in Butte, he was supposed to be the man who could give it to me. After a long silence, he began telling me about his first job in the Mountain Consolidated Mine, known as the Con. How he worked his way up from day laborer, contract miner, foreman, engineer, mine manager, director of mines, and finally head of the Company's Western operations. I heard a blur of strange names and mine jargon, but I was startled by what he'd accomplished.

The man, who had let me into his office on a whim, was the most powerful man in Montana. He could choose the next governor, senator, or dog catcher. As he told his story, I could hear him choke up. Renward was a Norman Vincent Peale romantic, who had never convinced himself he was the man sitting behind his overblown desk. And he knew something I did not.

There was an obvious depression in Butte. It wasn't the first. Copper and the Company had always made a comeback. What Renward knew was that the Company had failed for good. The hill would close down, even the pit. He'd spent his life coming up through the ranks to be the fall guy. He was their dupe, promoted to oversee a slow, painful end to an institution that had defined his life and given him the illusion of meaning and purpose.

Renward's tale of his rise to power was a story that belonged to other men—great industrialists he'd read about as a boy in a magazine for boys. He caught himself, cleared his throat, and told me he'd make a phone call, and there'd be a job waiting for me in the rustling hall by the time I got to the elevator. I thanked him and got out.

As I walked down the narrow hall, the smoking gents stood up straight and let me pass without having to negotiate their wingtips.

Everyone nodded or said hello. These were the men who ran the Company, and therefore Montana. In 1917 the masters of the ACM had the Wobbly organizer Frank Little hanged from a railroad trestle. The sins of the sons were subtler than the sins of the fathers, but no less deadly.

I descended to the rustling hall to rustle up a job. The functionaries in the job office were curious and cautious. Word had come down from above. That made me suspect, but suspect of what? No one with clout on the sixth floor needed a job underground. Perhaps they thought I was being punished, but such cruelty was inconceivable. I remained a mystery.

Driven by desperation, I'd violated the rules of getting a job. I'd been impulsive and presumptuous, but I'd cheated the odds.

The Thirty-Two and
the Cold-Hole

The next Monday I reported to the Badger Mine, a mile northeast of Walkerville. The miners parked outside the gate and walked a hundred yards down to the gallows frame that stood over the mine shaft and supported the giant cable pulleys. Next to the shaft were the dries, a big steam-heated barn where we changed into our work clothes. The Company outfitted me with a hard hat, a headlamp connected to a battery that clipped on my belt, and safety glasses— the Company's lone concession to federal safety regulations. At the rustling office, they'd told me to bring a jacket, overalls, a lock, and rubber boots. You could get boots with steel-toe-caps or plain—the choice of having your toes sheared clean off or just crushed. I decided better crushed than sheared.

I knew lumber mills, logging, and forest fires, but the mines spooked me. The dries had a distinct odor of steam, stone, and copper. Twenty feet above, tungsten globes hung from the rafters. Clusters of clothes, boots, and gear dangled under the lights. You hooked your gear to a chain, pulled it up out of reach, and locked the chain to a post ring. The dim light barely reached the hundred or so naked men, some tough and hard, others worn thin, and a few with bellies, moving to the showers and back below the bundles and boots. The tired men were contained in silent, colorless worlds of their own. The more robust laughed and joked over the hiss of steam. This was a gulag where they allowed you to go home at night so they didn't have to feed you.

I found the foreman. He looked at his sheet, then at me. I certainly wasn't the youngest kid he'd sent into the mines, but I was easily the greenest. He said, "Go down to the thirty-two 'n' put the bulkhead on the Moose," then disappeared into the throng. I had no idea what any of that meant, or what to do, or where to go. I followed the other miners out of the dries, around a corner, and down some concrete steps into a dank room with a low ceiling. I was at the mercy of a mass of men moving in the same direction. Had they intended to leap headlong into hell, I would've leapt with them.

It became apparent someone was directing traffic. I gravitated in his direction, seeking instruction. He proved to be the cage tender, whose main job was to stuff as many bodies as possible, usually nine at a time, into small cages and send them 1,300 feet down the shaft. I asked about the thirty-two, the bulkhead, and the Moose. He said to wait, he'd deal with me after he got the others down. Forty minutes later, with the last real miner delivered to his assigned level in the underworld, the tender returned for me. I got in. He closed the door and secured the bar. There was an initial jolt, then the cage began to drop, picking up speed, screeching and slapping from side to side as we plunged 3,200 feet to the bottom of the Badger Mine.

When the cage stopped, the tender reached over the gate and swung a bar back. We stepped into an underground train station—a huge room with a vaulted, two-story-high ceiling and a metal floor. The station separated the shaft from the tunnel, or drift, and provided a landing for men and equipment. Technically a drift was a tunnel that followed an ore vein, but it had come to mean any tunnel. The European root of *drift* referred to driving cattle. Maybe the underground men were driving stone.

We left our jackets in the station and proceeded for a mile through a low drift, so low we had to stoop the entire way, walking

on railroad ties in three inches of hot water. At 3,200 feet underground the pressure of the earth raises the wall temperature to over
140 degrees Fahrenheit. There wasn't much air moving through the
drift on the thirty-two, so our shirts were sticking to our skin.

Temperatures varied all through the mine, depending on venti-
lation and depth. Sometimes you were down to your skin, and other
times you were freezing in a heavy wool jacket. A motorman who
was moving his train back and forth in a drift could go from boiling
to freezing forty times a shift.

The Moose was the airshaft for the Mountain Con. The bulkhead was made up of several thick planks that the tender and I laid
over the Moose shaft so the men working below wouldn't be killed
by loose stones that zinged down like shots from a rifle. The idea
was to slide the planks out one at a time without getting hit by a
loose rock ricocheting off the sides of the shaft. Not that there was
much you could do about it.

It went from over 140 degrees to twenty below on the next job. They
put me in a small drift called the cold-hole, which was reached from
a cage stop just below the 1,300 station. The Badger's main shaft
was also its primary air intake. When the incoming air was below
zero, the shaft and the stations were freezing. The cold-hole extended only about forty feet from the main shaft, so the freezing air
from the shaft never had a chance to warm up. Icicles hung from the
ceiling and crystal spikes grew between the rails—stalactites and
stalagmites of ice. This frozen purgatory was a little-known artifact
of cave block mining. The cave block was an underground version
of an open pit mine turned upside down.

After thousands of years of rocks crushing miners, the obvious
finally registered on someone in authority who said, "Let gravity
do it"—when rock falls, scoop it up and haul it out. This bit of genius was accomplished by digging a high, wide drift, building

forms, and pouring a concrete tunnel down the middle, leaving holes on the sides. The constant movement of the earth caused the unsupported rock above to fall, shatter, and tumble through those holes into the concrete tunnel. Gradually the area above the tunnel grew larger and larger, until it was a cavern.

Large rock often clogged the holes. If you could reach the clog with a pole, you cleared it with a charge of dynamite attached to the end. If you couldn't reach that far, someone had to crawl into the cavern, plant the powder to break up the rock, and make it back with the wire, while random rock fell from the dome of the cavern. No one would take the job except a few illegal Mexicans whom the Company bribed with an extra seventy-five cents an hour. On one shift, the Mexicans went out into the cavern, set an entire case of powder under an enormous rock, and touched it off. Unfortunately, they'd set the case on top of the concrete tunnel and blew a big chunk out of it. That shut things down for a while.

To get the ore that sieved into the tunnel to the ore cars, a scoop was rigged on a set of cables, which were pulled back and forth by an electric motor. The same setup on the surface was called a dragline, but down there it was called a slusher. The scoop pulled the ore to an opening above the tracks where the cars were moved up one at a time until ten cars were filled. Then the ore was taken to the station and dumped into a steel grate called the grizzlies.

The grizzlies kept large rock from falling two hundred feet down the chute and busting up the hydraulic doors that controlled the flow of ore to the buckets, or skips, which went to the surface. The big rocks caught in the grizzlies had to be blasted into smaller chunks.

The cave block method took out everything above the concrete tunnel, including the timbers, known as stulls, that had supported the old drifts. The stulls clogged the operation by jamming skips and conveyors, and causing general chaos down the line. It was bet-ter to pull stulls out when they reached the grizzlies and cram them through the small opening called the rabbithole, where they materi-alized in my frozen domain.

I never saw the grizzly man. He never spoke. Between blasts, he'd shove an occasional timber through the hole. I'd grab the timber and carry it back to a small flatcar. I usually loaded two cars a shift. Sometimes the cage tenders would switch the cars out during lunch, and I'd load two more. How many cars I loaded depended on where the ore came from. If a section of an old drift fell into the cave block, a lot of timbers ended up in the grizzlies.

I don't remember how long I was stuck there. The isolation and cold were more exhausting than the work. The work wasn't hard, but standing alone in a dimly lit, icy cave for eight hours is brain- and body-numbing torture. The cold-hole only lasted an eight-hour shift, but I couldn't recover between shifts. When I was awake, I dreaded going back. When I slept, I was haunted by the ice and the gray light. When timbers stopped falling out of the cave block, I was released from the cold-hole. It seemed I was there for months, but it could only have been days, not even weeks. I wouldn't have lasted weeks.

The cold-hole was the worst job I'd had, until they sent me back down to the thirty-two. They'd found a job with no takers. The overflow ore, or muck, from the skips had spilled out on the station floor of the thirty-two, then backed up in the skip shaft until it was fifty to sixty feet deep. They'd sent men down to load the spillover into small cars and take it out in the cage. Then they started blasting the muck loose in the shaft. The safe way to do this was to attach the charge to a pole, push it up against the muck, and set it off. But you can get only about twelve feet of pole through the opening at the bottom. At some point the muck is out of reach of a pole blast.

Several tons of unstable ore were packed overhead, and the only way to get to it was to climb up the framework inside the shaft, drive a bar into the overhead dome of muck, insert a charge, and climb back down, being careful not to pull the wires loose from the blasting cap. Common sense told the foreman it was time to find a desperate, expendable fool.

He sent me down with a partner. Wherever you went, you were supposed to have a partner—the cold-hole and the grizzlies being the lone exceptions. Pard was an old scrawny guy of about fifty-five with rummy eyes and bad teeth. I never heard the story about why the foreman kept him around. I'm sure there was one, and it would've involved relatives, women, or priests. The guy had the shakes, which made him useless. He just stood there, wouldn't make a move or offer a suggestion. Since I was in motion and talking, I became boss by default. My partner didn't seem to know anything, even though he'd been sent along to show me what to do. It wasn't until later that I realized he might've suffered a mild stroke. Whatever the reason, he was experiencing a malfunction. Maybe he was just smarter.

The echo of copper water dripping from the ceiling in the dim station made the place feel like a cavern. Over the years the constant dripping turned the iron floor to copper. Our headlamps made soft, elliptical patterns on the station's copper-green floor.

Thirty-two hundred feet down, the air smelled and tasted different, as though the weight of earth at each level pressed new elements from the rock, an essence more pungent and dank than that of the levels above. The dense, bitter air filled our lungs, saturated our clothes and skin, and burned our eyes.

Besides the lack of leadership and fear of falling muck, there was another problem. I had no experience with powder. No one had shown me anything, and my partner, of course, knew nothing. The powder itself wasn't the issue. I had no knowledge of capacitance, static electricity, or errant charges that might spark and set off a blast, killing me and my partner, though Pard kept his distance. I was considerably agitated by my ignorance and promised myself never to get in such a situation again, if I lived.

In theory, an explosive cap was pushed into a stick of powder. The cap's two protruding wires were then twisted onto separate long wires. These were played out across the station floor, around the corner, and a few feet down the drift, where they were touched to the terminals on your lamp battery and Big Blam. In theory.

I climbed the shaft frame to the hanging muck and rammed the bar into the dome until I'd made a hole about two feet deep. I carefully pushed a blasting cap into the stick of powder, attached the wires, pushed the stick up the hole with the bar, wrapped the wires to a shaft frame bolt, and climbed down. Pard helped play the wires across the station and down the shaft. I touched one wire to the terminal, took a breath, then touched the other—nothing happened.

Nothing. Not a goddamned thing. Except for the watery *pling*, there was no sound. No Big Blam. I'd been too nervous and in too big a hurry. One of the wires had come loose from the blasting cap. I had to climb back, pull the stick out of the muck, and reattach the loose wire. The dome of unstable muck had obviously been disturbed when I rammed the bar into it. If I couldn't get the stick out by pulling on the single attached wire, I'd have to make a second hole for another stick.

I braced myself in a corner of the shaft frame, legs splayed out, and aimed my headlamp at the hole. I pulled. The stick gave a little, then came free. I snatched it before it fell, fearing a jolt might set it off. I was right about the wires. One was loose. Reattaching it was what frightened me. I didn't know if the wire held a charge from having already touched the battery. I don't remember, but I may've touched both ends of the long wires together to discharge any residual electricity. That would've been the logical thing to do.

Then I was faced with reattaching the loose wire. I stared at the short wire and the long wire, holding them within a sixteenth of an inch of each other. I couldn't make the wires touch. Everything was focused on that space between the wires. Then I realized if it exploded I'd never know. Some people go from one stupidity to another and their luck holds. That instant, that day, mine did. I touched the wires and nothing happened. I twisted them together, got down, sprinted through the station to the drift, and touched off that damn stick. It did its Big Blam and tons of ore fell to the bottom of the shaft. Now it was the mucker's turn. We rang the tenders and waited an hour in silence for the cage.

I sat in the dark and thought about that instant, watching those wires touch. It was far more precarious to climb up that shaft and ram a hole into the muck than to twist those wires together, but I didn't know that. I'd risked my fool self for a job. I was more frightened of not working than I was of dying.

The Bar: Steve and Gracie

Steve and Gracie escaped Hollywood. In particular they escaped the humiliation of Hollywood, which seemed to be what ruined people who flirted with the movies up close for very long. It was a place where you got what you deserved plus some extra for your delusions.

Steve had been a set designer. Gracie had had speaking parts in films with stars like Stewart Granger. I hadn't heard of any of her films. That was awkward until she said, "You were just a boy." She gave me a little leer and laughed. Gracie was full of hell. They were both in their forties. Steve knew himself and Hollywood well enough to get out. Gracie didn't argue. She'd been thirty-five for ten years and hadn't had a walk-on for six.

Unfortunately, they settled on Butte to fulfill their romantic ideals. They were right in understanding that the town, in spite of its iron-plate exterior, was a hideout for passionate romantics, but they shouldn't have gone there expecting to change anything. The Butte trap was its big, generous heart. They would let you pursue your dream, and they were too polite to tell you the hole you were digging was your grave.

Steve wanted to bring live theater to Butte, and he wanted to build a bar which would support the two of them and subsidize the theater if it came to that. He bought an abandoned Episcopal church on Montana Street and a storefront on West Broadway.

I poked my head in the storefront one day and was recruited on the spot. For beers and an occasional meal, I could share Steve and Gracie's magnificent delusions. Steve had the perfect ratio of "Let's put on a show" and "I got a scheme." They needed free help, and when I wasn't working, I needed to escape the loneliness of being around a woman who'd been drawn into a life that didn't interest me. Perhaps it was a form of class warfare. We were living in the same house on different sides of the tracks. And there were the Wookies to consider.

Steve and I scavenged lumber from a condemned house and discovered a hidden staircase between double walls in the back. Eighty years before, a Chinese opium dealer had his slaves dig a tunnel from a bar across the street to the secret stairway, which led to the attic and sixteen small bunks. Four inches of charcoal beneath the floorboards absorbed the sound and fumes of the attic's illicit dreams. We used the boards for stage flats on the theory that visions emanating from the wood might inspire great performances or, short of that, delude the audience.

The mines limited my participation in the project, but I was focused on getting the bar finished. Steve got a beautiful hand-carved back bar in exchange for hauling it away. We were always thrilled and amazed by what could be had for the taking. Another time we came across a forgotten dump in the hills west of the School of Mines that had once been shared by the union hall and the Masonic temple. The dump was a treasure trove of beautiful mugs, glasses, cups, and dishes from the twenties. We'd found a time and a place where the things we coveted were free.

We started in late spring, and the bar took all summer into fall. An entire weekend could be spent nailing wainscoting to a wall. We were silent and happy in our incremental progression of vertical slats.

Cooking was not on Gracie's list of delights and eating out was expensive. She knew every way to feed us that didn't involve more effort than lighting a match under a pan of water. There were several small grocery stores that sold pockets called meat pasties— potatoes and carrots baked in a pastry shell. I don't remember the meat. The Cornish miners had imported hope, hard work, and pasties, which they referred to as "letters from home."

Montana's most celebrated eatable—a pork chop between two pieces of bread—was served hot from a greasy window on West Mercury. If you were a jerk, they'd leave the bone in. No one owned up to finding a bone in his sandwich, but the slang for getting what you had coming was "gettin' boned." Sometime later, the chop was replaced with ground pork. Not the same.

Then there were Truzzolino's turkey tamales—three times the size of a normal tamale. There was actual meat in a Truzzolino. They came frozen, wrapped in parchment, twisted, and stapled on the ends. All Gracie had to do was drop them in boiling water. The hard part was cutting the staples off a hot Truzzolino. Steve got to do that. He was handy.

Steve and I were painting the tin ceiling tiles when Gracie brought down three plates, scissors, and some hot Truzzolinos. While Steve freed the tamales, Gracie told me about the first time she and Steve had sex. She'd obviously told this story to strangers before, because Steve didn't react. I was shocked, but that was the idea. She said, "Steve just rolled off and lay there in a warm puddle," but she'd been revved up. She'd jumped out of bed, washed the dishes, did the laundry, and cleaned his apartment. "We were like bunnies—you know how bunnies do it?"

"Fast, I guess."

She gave me a wicked look. "Right. Then the boy bunny rolls off and lays there like he's dead, but the girl bunny jumps into her pedal pushers and hops into the woods, leaving the boy bunny to the predators."

I discovered I was threatened by women who were fascinated by evolutionary survival tactics. They were thinking like men. It was disconcerting to look up and see the magnified eye of a woman observing me under her Darwin scope. Steve snipped the last tamale, handed me a plate, and said, "Beware of hawks."

The Grizzlies

For the most part, the Badger and Kelly mines had gone over to the cave block system. There weren't many contract miners left on the hill. Contracts were given to miners who worked a vein in pairs. They would come in with a small front loader and muck out the ore blasted by the last shift. Each shift involved drilling the face of the drift, setting charges, and blasting. After the smoke and dust settled, the next shift came in, mucked out, drilled, and blasted—shift after shift, day after day, year after year.

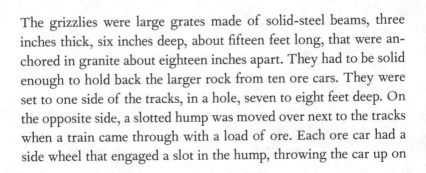

The grizzlies were large grates made of solid-steel beams, three inches thick, six inches deep, about fifteen feet long, that were anchored in granite about eighteen inches apart. They had to be solid enough to hold back the larger rock from ten ore cars. They were set to one side of the tracks, in a hole, seven to eight feet deep. On the opposite side, a slotted hump was moved over next to the tracks when a train came through with a load of ore. Each ore car had a side wheel that engaged a slot in the hump, throwing the car up on its side and dumping its ore into the grizzlies—a carnival ride for rocks.

Most of the ore made it through the grates and fell two hundred feet down a chute to the hydraulic doors that filled the skips. The big rock was caught in the grates, blasted, and busted up before it damaged the doors or the skips. Why they were called skips, I don't remember.

I got the job working the grizzlies, because the man who had the job before fell two hundred feet to his death. The foreman said the fellow wasn't wearing his safety harness and slipped between the rails. I don't remember anyone talking about the man I replaced. It was as though no one had the job before me. I thought there would've been some talk about the guy, how he died, or his family, but I learned that no one talked about death.

I liked to blast. Blowing things up was addictive. If everything went right, I'd set off up to four sticks every ten minutes—a noteworthy amount of powder. There were consequences, of course. The concussions took their toll, damaging my nerves and my eardrums.

The first thing I was told about the job was never, ever separate the foreman from his hat. In other words, let him get clear before touching off the powder. He'd fired more than one man for setting off a charge early.

An hour into my first shift on the grizzlies, the foreman stood on the tracks and watched me wire the charges. I climbed out of the hole and started down the drift toward my personally designated ignition site. I called back that I was going to blast. He turned and started down the drift. He wasn't far from the mouth of the grizzly when he said, "Go ahead." I shouted, "Are you sure?" and heard a sarcastic, "Yeah, I'm sure." I was afraid I'd kill him, but a train was due, and he was so damn sure.

The wire touched the terminal. It was a hell of a blast. My ears were ringing, and the drift was filled with smoke and dust. I started down the tracks, staring into the smoke to see if the foreman was okay. About twenty feet on the far side of the grizzlies I saw a pair of boots. The smoke thinned, and I could make out the rest of him, stretched full length between the tracks; his hard hat, still tethered to his battery, extended out another foot. His headlamp was pointing at the ceiling. For a moment I thought I'd killed the bastard. It was a tragic, forlorn scene. Even if he wasn't a very nice man, he didn't deserve to die between the tracks, facedown in the Badger. At least he'd never had time to reflect on his net worth as a human being. Then I heard him swearing. It was muffled, but I could hear words coming out of his mouth. He was damaged, but conscious.

It was always a race to break up the big rock the blast hadn't shattered before the next train dumped, but now I had to drag the foreman off the tracks before the motor car scraped him off. Then a miracle happened. His butt lifted, his knees scrunched up under his belly, and he stood up in the swirl of dust and smoke. For a moment he was still, either recovering from an out-of-body experience or deciding my fate. Then he reached down for his hard hat, turned, nodded, and walked down the drift. I scrambled into the grizzlies and hammered the big stuff through the rails before the next load hit the hump.

The same foreman had once helped himself to a bag of ammonium nitrate from the powder shed to fertilize his lawn. He evidently thought more was better. Anyone who noticed his crisp yellow lawn saw the flaw in his thinking.

I worked a shift that produced a lot of ore, most of it coming from the cave blocks. The trains came through and dumped in ten-minute intervals. It took all my youthful agility to cut and plant two to four sticks of powder between the big rocks, wire the mess to the long wires, climb out, get down the drift to touch it off and back to break up the rocks that hadn't shattered and fallen into the chute before the next train came through, and then it started all over again. The faster the trains ran, the more powder I used.

Years later, when an old miner heard I'd used as many as four sticks at a time, he gave me that dead-eyed, "you're dumb lucky" look and shook his head to indicate his superiority. My only defense was, no one told me different, and besides, I never blew out the grizzlies.

The job got easy. I liked the body-pounding roar of the trains, the cars hitting the hump and throwing their loads into the grizzlies, balancing from rock to rock, wedging charges into all the right places, the big bang, the smell and taste of the blast, then maniacally hammering stubborn rock through the rails and hearing it crash into the ore pile two hundred feet down.

Late on a shift, I'd blasted and cleared except for a big rock in the back left corner. It was about four feet long and egg-shaped. The sledgehammer was in midswing when I saw a hole in the rock. The thing was hollow. I stopped my swing, took my hard hat off, and shined the lamp inside. The rock was filled with long crystals. A thrill ran through me down to my balls. I had to stop the train. It was the biggest geode in the world. The thought came with the train—I could hear it rumbling through the main drift. Once you heard the train, it was too late to radio for it to stop. I took a long look inside the geode and jumped clear as the first car threw its load. After the last car dumped and the dust cleared, the geode was gone, crushed to pieces in the chute below. I've never been enraptured by geology, but those perfect crystals encased in gray-black stone 1,300 feet beneath the surface were the ultimate hidden treasure. I was a boy with his first fish.

My geode—and having been the only one to see it made it mine—was not the largest ever. I'm told much larger geodes have survived, but none with crystals so clear and perfect. I know, because I have a snapshot of it in my mind.

After shooting the grizzlies, I sometimes saw men moving toward me through the smoke-filled drift. If the train was behind them, it would project their shadows on the layers of smoke and colors of the blast, making their movements the gestures of giants.

Colors from blasting underground are unlike any seen on the surface. No doubt the combination of powder and ore makes its own tints—nitroglycerin fused with copper, silver, magnesium, and traces of gold—colors that exist in the visual spectrum for a fraction of a second, leaving an afterimage for our memory.

Setting off a hundred fifty rounds a shift left me a little raw. It was an extreme state, tinged with a bitter taste, the smell of the blast, and extraordinary colors. Some days I couldn't hear anything until I got home.

Underground, you went through an inadvertent selection process that allowed you to find your place, which is to say, to discover who you were in that curious world. It might not apply anywhere else, but it let you and the others know what to expect underground.

At first, being green and relatively expendable, I got one lousy job after another and wasn't told how to do them. Maybe the miners were waiting for me to ask. Except for that first night, I don't remember asking anyone anything. Why, I don't know, but I watched and listened. Being scared can make you an ardent observer.

Besides being better storytellers, miners were generally smarter than men in most other professions. Working underground had its selective aspects—the slow of mind and unlucky were maimed or killed sooner than later. Fortunately, I worked there such a short time, the hand of nature never had a chance to pluck me out.

On the surface, men tended to talk and walk and behave differently than they did underground. Some preferred the mines to life on top. Being a thousand feet down changed the way they treated one another. There was a kind of emotional compression, as though the weight of the earth and air held them in check.

Arguments never turned ballistic. The only fights I witnessed were in Spillum's Bar. Underground, the potential for a major reorganization of your body parts was a constant presence. You didn't need to add to real risks by throwing punches. We survived in the underworld, held together by some fragile element that evaded definition, even detection. Like dark matter in the universe—you know it's there, because the universe couldn't exist without it.

We had parolees, guys on the run, check forgers, armed robbers, rapists, and murderers. Underground you'd never know, and it didn't seem to matter. The mines let you escape the viciousness, uncertainties, and anxieties on the surface. We were protected from angry wives, bill collectors, mortgages, cops, the INS, and the FBI. In that respect the mines were like the Catholic Church of the Middle Ages, which sheltered criminals from civil authority. Once I got used to the underground, I never felt anxious until the shift ended, and I had to face the Wookies lurking above in the real world.

The enforcers never went down into the mines. They waited until you came up and grabbed you half-naked in the dries or at home in front of your children.

Unlike the Church of the Middle Ages, the sanctuary of the mines lasted only a shift at a time. Some men spent their hours on the surface waiting for the safety of the next shift.

I came home one evening, checked for Wookies, and opened the mailbox. There was a small card inside. The card said 4-F. It was from the Selective Service. 4-F meant they didn't want me. Ever.

The impending doom of prison lifted off my shoulders and shot straight into the sky. I was free. Saved from Wookies.

I suspected intervention by Judy Devine, the draft board secretary, in her institutional-green office on the second floor of a defunct Missoula bank, built during the last boom and guarded from the roof by imperialist lion gargoyles. She was in her midforties, wore dusty, brick red lipstick, matching nail polish, and red alligator platforms. She spoke as fast as she typed and never stopped typing. Maybe she thought I was too daft for the military, but not daft enough for prison. A switched word, a skipped space, and those quick red fingertips may have changed my life. In any case, she had sway—she had those old draft board guys wrapped around her little finger, in the palm of her hand, on a string.

I encountered only one psycho. He was a motor operator named Killer Prem. I heard he'd crushed three men to death. Maybe those deaths were accidents, no one was quite sure, but that stone-faced bastard in his hooded red parka gave me the creeps. He was still on the motor when I left. Maybe the old guys said things like that to scare the kids—"da mean motoman go'n squitch yus." I was scared of the mean motorman, all right, and kept my eyes open, but even then he damn near squitched me.

I've wondered what the mining engineers who drew up the plans thought about the parts of town that would collapse when the timbers rotted and the drifts caved in. Their corporate bosses had the stockholders to answer to, but the engineers were miners with a slight upgrade. Most had been raised in Butte. Their families and friends built the homes that would be worthless when the streets and sidewalks buckled, foundations settled, plaster cracked, windows stuck shut, and doors no longer closed. The town was a significant part of those men, yet if they wanted the cush job, the white shirt and wingtips, they had to destroy the town.

We wanted to think the community was superior to the corporation, but the corporation easily picked people out of the community and said, in effect, "Destroy your own, and we'll give you the good life." Few resisted.

We worked at the Company's whim, lived on skill and luck, and were paid enough to survive. Manki, a Czech who'd studied to be a

Catholic priest, was arrested by the communists and put in a slave labor mine in northeastern Czechoslovakia. Four years later, he helped kill the guards and escaped to Austria. He got to come to the United States because he was a Catholic, but he hated the American Church, so he worked as a miner, first in Arizona, then Butte. He told me slaves were considered property. The communists took care of their property. They fed it, clothed it, kept it healthy, and put a roof over its head. Manki was hard and bitter. The only funny thing I ever heard him say was, "Under communism I had property rights."

The town came to see the Company as a force of nature. The Company was not that much different from the fires that smolder three thousand feet beneath the surface, sucking oxygen from granite, waiting for an unsuspecting crew from a distant mine to blast through, relinquishing a long-anticipated gush of fresh air and human flesh.

Station of the Cross

One night I was put in charge of four men and given the job of shoring up an area in the main drift that was shifting. The granite was punky and breaking up. Our job was to wedge some stulls into the existing frame to support the ceiling. We'd worked for about three hours with wedges and stull timbers, but the old frame started to groan, and small rocks fell from the ceiling. When timbers groan, they're saying somethin' bad's gonna happen.

I decided to back off and find a quiet place to eat lunch where we wouldn't be disturbed by the foreman or a train. We were about fifty feet from the job when we heard the thing cave in. The dust cleared, we looked at one another, shook our heads, and went on down the drift.

The foreman found us while we were eating and asked how the job was coming. I told him we were through with that job, he'd have to send the muckers to clean up. He radioed for muckers and reassigned the five of us. I doubt the possibility of us getting killed even crossed his mind.

I got the job of rigging an air tube into a drift full of fumes where a crew had been blasting for the first half of the shift. When the air got bad, they sent me in. In the process of rigging the tube, I inhaled enough blast fumes to give me a blinding headache.

I climbed into a main drift and started down the tracks. I was just under the cave block, between an ore car and the wall, when they set off a charge. Usually they shouted something like, "Fire in the hole." But they didn't this time, and I was right under the damn thing when it went off.

I can't begin to imagine what it's like to be shelled in battle. I took a single blast and turned to jelly. It went through my body and took out several frequencies of my hearing. I felt like my head had been split open and my brains spewed across the tracks. As soon as I could stand, I continued down the drift. I could taste metal, my vision was blurred, and I had the shakes. The shaking was the worst part. I kept walking toward the station. I thought I was going to shit myself.

As I got nearer to the station, there was an old man pushing a car loaded with stull timbers. The load shifted on him, and he was trying to right things. Just as I got there, the load came down on him. I think he was screaming, but I couldn't hear anything. His mouth was open, and blood was spurting out of his hand. Then I realized his hand had been chopped off across the palm. I grabbed his wrist and squeezed until the blood stopped. We stumbled down the tracks to the station and rang down the tender.

I lost track of things for a while. I'd intended to go home, but found myself standing in the station. The place was empty. I could smell the copper and hear water dripping. The shakes and the headache had stopped. Evidently, I'd had a chance to wash up, because I wasn't bloody. Then I heard the cables slap and the cage coming down. I looked over and saw the cage stop. The tender's arm came out, threw the bar back, and opened the doors. There were two tenders. They stepped off the cage with a heavy cross made of stull timbers, carried it to the opposite side of the station, and leaned it against the wall. For a moment I thought the cross was meant for me, but they went back, rang down the next cage, and opened the door. Curled up on the floor of the cage was an emaciated, skin-and-bones Jesus Christ. The tenders grabbed him by the arms, pulled him out of the cage, and dragged him across the station.

Before they nailed Christ to the stull timbers, I realized I was in my living room, sitting on the couch in the dark. My fingers were still stuck together. I'd had an incredibly realistic hallucination. I washed the blood off and went to bed. Four hours later, I stopped shaking and fell asleep.

But the shaking never really went away. Even now, a sudden sound can bring back the feel of that blast. There are things that happen that we carry with us for the rest of our lives. Mostly we remember the bad things. The good we take for granted or we carry talismans—a photograph or a trinket—to remind us of good fortune. The bad things don't need artifacts. They live in our bones.

Billy Tolley and His Girl

Late on a Saturday afternoon I was sitting with Steve at the bar, drinking a beer, and staring at the rectangle of sun coming through the open door. My eyes had adjusted to the light, which made the interior nearly black. I felt a little buzzy but solid, like a brick on the verge of awareness, when a long shadow leaned into the rectangle. The shadow belonged to a skinny, short guy who stood in the doorway while his eyes and his brain adjusted to the dark interior. He had no idea what was going on inside. There was no sign on the building except for faded letters on the brick next to the door advertising Orange Crush and Lucky Strikes.

Steve and I drank our beers and watched. The skinny man hadn't seen us. He was drunk, lost, wanted a job, or any combination of the three. I thought the man's "Hello?" sounded wary, but that wasn't it at all. He was just shy. I came to find out he wasn't wary of much.

The skinny man was turning to go back outside when Steve called him over, offered him a beer, and motioned toward a stool at the bar. The man looked around the room, gauging our progress. That we were building a bar was obvious by now. It was also obvious that I was a kid and Steve was in charge, so he addressed Steve.

"Just off the bus." He said it flat, but in a way that was loaded. I imagined he'd been on the bus for days, or that the bus he spoke of was not real, but one of life's journeys. "I been in Deer Lodge prison five years. Got out this noon." He sat on the round Naugahyde bar stool and sipped his beer. It was a while before he looked up and asked Steve for a job. He claimed he could do damn near anything. Steve nodded and asked what he was in for.

"Stole stuff outa some rich guy's house. Got caught." He added the obvious—he wasn't a very good thief.

Steve said he was sorry to hear that, but there wasn't money to hire anyone and that the lack of work had nothing to do with his having been in jail. Steve explained that I helped out on weekends and worked for beers. He introduced me and asked the man his name.

"Billy Tolley. Mu-my family farmed out by Denton. Drought'n the bank put us outa farmin', so I tried stealin'." He chuckled.

Steve suggested he should have robbed banks, but Billy didn't know it was a joke, he just shrugged and mumbled something about his stomach. Billy Tolley was a loser, but he was gentle and his slowness was calming. He started coming around, particularly on Saturdays. Sometimes he tried to help, but he was a fumbler and, contrary to his initial claim, there was damn little he could do. I told him about jobs I'd had in high school picking up trash at drive-ins, and he managed to find three places that needed help. One was a Dairy Queen, which was a long walk, another was an A&W, and the third was the 4-B's. He offered to pay for his beer. Steve said, "Wait till you're rich."

Billy Tolley found a girl, Renee. She was bruised up, she wouldn't smile, her eyes were bloodshot from drinking, and she was a pale death white. At first she sat opposite him at a booth, but by the next week she couldn't get close enough. They held each other and whispered. When I brought them beers, she stared at her hands and said, "Thank you." She didn't smile, because her teeth were rotten. Really rotten. I'd never seen teeth like that before. By the third week, they asked me to sit down. They had a plan, and they wanted to know what I thought. Billy explained with some hesitancy that Renee worked at Fourteen South Wyoming. At the time Fourteen South was known as a house of commercial affection. They wanted to get married, but they had to get some money first. I thought he was planning another robbery, but he said he could get money from a work program to go to barber's school. Renee would quit drinking. Billy would find a job, get Renee's teeth fixed, and they'd get married. She'd have to whore until he got a job—they didn't have a choice, but she was used to whoring anyway. It was what she knew.

Nothing had prepared me for Billy and Renee. They were asking a fool kid what to do. I had a job 1,300 feet underground making $1.89 an hour. Maybe it was $1.98, but it was the highest hourly wage I would ever make. The mine was on the verge of closing, anyway. My wife, on the other hand, had a creamy complexion, a set of pearly white teeth, a good job counting pills, and customers who were always polite when she turned down their requests for sexual gratification after she'd sold them condoms. She was also developing a fascination for people with assets. I was very confused, and Billy and Renee were asking me for advice.

They studied my expression. They were hopeful, but used to rejection. These people were going to do whatever I said. I took my time and tried to look thoughtful. Given her bad teeth and red eyes, Renee wasn't going to whore much longer anyway. They would die stinking, dirty, and alone in a shed without heat.

I smiled and said barber college sounded like a great idea. I was sure it would work. Hair always needed cutting. They were giddy. They hugged and kissed. I toasted them a long, happy marriage and ten children. I felt sick. That night Margaret woke me out of a dream and asked if everything was all right. She thought I'd been crying. No, everything was fine.

Once the bar was finished, I stopped going in. It was another Butte bar. It became obvious to Steve that he loved the idea of a bar in Butte more than the reality of a Butte bar. Being a romantic, the consequences of the obvious evaded him. The closing of the underground mines had put an end to the roaring human catastrophe known as Butte. Bars and whorehouses—like their human counterparts—had been on the decline for years. There's an old line that could be Butte's epitaph: From here on down, it's all uphill, or maybe it was the other way around.

The Junior League

The Junior League, the wives-of-wealthy-men club—well-educated women married to Anaconda Copper Mining Company and Montana Power executives, and the town's wealthier physicians, bankers, and lawyers—thought it necessary and proper to bring culture to the Butte underclass. Apparently our own culture was wanting. To this end, they established a foreign film festival. Foreign films meant anything by Fellini, Antonioni, and Buñuel. There were forgotten others. Not every miner went to these movies, but those who did dressed for the occasion. The rich husbands never came.

Miners, whom I'd never have guessed owned a tie, showed up in suits and hats. The women wore their best dresses and high heels, which made them taller and perked up their butts. Culture was becoming another form of church. We'd come to be empowered, to ride the arc of New Culture. We took our wives and girlfriends, or more likely, they took us. We arrived on time, stood on one side of the lobby, and tried not to stare at the wives-of-wealthy-men clustered on the other side discussing the *Cahiers du Cinéma* article about a young French director who never put his camera on a tripod and invented cinema verité, the reality film. Little did we know what would become of that simple experiment.

We didn't like Antonioni. Fellini, at least, could tell a story—we didn't need to read subtitles, and many of us couldn't, anyway. We liked Federico because he had appetites. He stuffed us speechless and robbed us senseless. For me, it was a time of stories. Mines, films, bars, books—all were telling stories. Being fatalists, the miners told stories about fate. Fellini told stories about love.

It wasn't long before the movies stopped, not because there wasn't an audience, but because it was wrong. The Junior League ladies had good intentions. They'd been educated in Eastern schools and caught the intellectual disease of the time. They wanted to share, but discovered it was impossible to share with people whose feeble lives were controlled by their husband's heavy hands. When workers pretend they're not workers, and masters pretend they're not masters, it makes everyone uneasy. In the end, the powerful and the powerless could not share cultures, much less the same foyer.

Blown to Bits

About four or five o'clock on a Sunday morning, Margaret and I were jolted out of our sleep by an enormous blast. We lay in the dark and speculated on what had happened. When it was light, we got dressed and drove across town to see for ourselves. We were not alone in our curiosity. A good part of the town had gravitated to the slag heaps down on the flats.

The heaps had been made fifty years or more before, when hot slag from the smelters was dumped into huge forms two hundred feet long, sixty feet wide, and twenty to thirty feet high. They were laid out on the flats like dominos, with spaces between them large enough to drive a truck through.

I'd forgotten it was Sunday, so it was a surprise to see almost everyone there dressed for church. They were scattered all over the slag heaps, on top and in the roadways, in groups of two, three, or four—mothers, fathers, and children—taking a step at a time in a kind of forced slow motion. No one said a word. They just stared at the ground, searching for something. It was a Fellini movie without sound.

That morning some men were transferring a truckload of dynamite they'd stolen from the ACM powder magazine to a second truck. It was later reported the stolen dynamite was destined for the Irish Republican Army. I doubt anyone ever knew the entire story, but the police heard enough that they had the transfer staked out. A cop fired a shot into the powder. The police claimed it was an accident. Nobody but the man who fired the shot knew for sure, and nobody was sure who fired the shot. The explosion knocked out windows in houses half a mile away. There was nothing of consequence left of the thieves or the trucks.

The Junior League had prepared me for the absurd. The people of the town had outfitted themselves for their weekly meeting with God, but along the way they looked down instead of up and got distracted by body parts. Some days you go out looking for the theory of everything, and all you find is a toe.

Reincarnated from Dirt

The day they shot JFK, I was on the sidewalk in front of Gamer's Candy on Park Street in Butte. A fat man in a black Cadillac had just heard about the shooting on the car radio and stopped in the middle of the street. I stood on the curb, staring at the big man in the big black car with tailfins, and listened to Walter Cronkite report the way it was in Dallas. The Cadillac man, I, and others who'd collected on the sidewalk were as still as a photograph. We listened. The only thing that moved was Cronkite's voice, until the man in the car began to cry and tears rolled down his round, rosy cheeks.

While we listened to the broadcast, the alarm went off at the First National Bank, two blocks up on Main, followed by police sirens and finally an ambulance. Later I was told that not only had the bank been robbed, but a gentleman had raised his glass in Red's Bar to cheer the president's assumed demise and toast Fidel Castro. An offended party shot off a piece of the gentleman's ear—some claimed it was an attempted suicide. No one suggested the shooting in Red's was a conspiracy, though some claimed Butte had more JFKs on velvet than any town in the United States. Perhaps the man's sense of humor had always escaped the patrons' notice, and liberated by an excess of lubricant, his tongue had become bold. Or maybe the suicide faction had it right—the gentleman was just tired of livin'.

Once the alarms and the sirens started up, we could only catch bits and pieces of the broadcast. The rich man's tears and John Fitzgerald Kennedy's assassination are a single memory.

A week later I walked into Steve's. The place was empty. Steve had a lot on his mind. He'd discussed leaving town for the past month, and he saw JFK's shooting as an omen. Steve and Gracie were determined to start over—there was this place on the west coast of Mexico. Again, it would be a bar. For some it's always a bar, for others it's a restaurant.

I was at a dead end myself, and I was listening to Steve—whom I'd come to see not as a romantic, but as a confused, middle-aged man—fantasizing about a bar in Mexico.

I was twenty-four, risking my ass on the grizzlies for a day's pay. The mine would close in a year—if I lasted a year. I had no skills. My wife wanted a decent house and a new car and preferred to socialize with people who talked about investments. She knew her husband and his friends were living in a fast-fading world and was quick to understand that no amount of talk, appreciation, or love would change the outcome. And there was the inescapable fact that being married to a day's pay miner must have been a terrible embarrassment for her.

While I was quietly mulling my own predicament, Steve had talked himself out of relocating to Mexico—neither he nor Gracie spoke Spanish. Things were coming to a dead end for both of us. We sat silently on our black circles of Naugahyde, at the edge of depression.

The door opened, and Billy Tolley and Renee came in. The thought of Renee's rotted teeth and rummy eyes—imprints of her hopeless life—drove me into an even darker hole.

But they were alive and together. Obviously not in jail. I was a little puzzled. Both Steve and I sat up and watched. Instead of wandering in, they walked toward us. As Renee came closer, I could see her eyes were clear, and there was something different in her look, maybe better makeup, but it wasn't that. She had a glow. The whore with rotten teeth had found God or come into money. Billy declined the offer of drinks and asked Steve and me to sit down with them. We took our beers and followed them to one of the white booths. Renee and Billy sat across from us, and he told their story.

As planned, Billy had gone to barber school and completed the course. He could've said graduated, but he didn't. Then he found a job down on the flats. Renee stopped drinking, stopped whoring, got her teeth fixed, and had work at the A&W starting the next week. She flashed a smile to show her teeth. Billy's eyes were tearing. He'd been holding her hand under the table waiting for the moment. He let go, and her hand came up flashing a ring. It was new from Hennessy's, she said. "On Friday, we got courthouse married."

She reached over and squeezed my hand. "An' it's all 'cause of you." Her other hand jumped up to cover her mouth. Then she remembered and let the hand slide down. She smiled, her red lips stretched back to show off a legion of flawless, white teeth. She lifted her chin and gently bit at the air.

I wanted to say something wise and calming, at least something that made sense, but I was too wrought up, and the words got lost. Steve had to swipe his eyes with the back of his hand. It was several weeks before I realized that none of this would've happened without Steve's romantic delusions. He provided a sanctuary from cynicism, a place to bloom.

While the three males were still caught in the glow of the moment, Renee had already moved on to her dream house on the flats. She'd found a seller who would carry the mortgage. In six months, with almost no money down, she was going to get them out of that hole in Walkerville.

It was obvious she'd been the inspiration behind Billy's dream of barber school, a job, and marriage. She'd planted the seed. Now that she had teeth, she felt confident in foretelling the future, and the future held a house full of babies, love, and appliances.

She asked if I had children. She was disappointed by my answer. She wanted encouragement and pointers. All I could offer was a small memory of a baby's mysterious world. I'd had two early experiences I thought all babies must encounter.

The first was the sensation of being born again. I experienced a gradual awareness of emerging from deep blackness into consciousness. I felt slightly anxious, but I knew I'd been here before, had gone away and come back. I was waking from a nap.

Renee was intense, staring hard into my eyes. She said, "So every time a baby wakes up it feels like it's being born."

I said maybe that's why people believe in reincarnation. Steve said I was full of crap, that 99 percent of the world's population believed in reincarnation, so even if it wasn't true to begin with, so much believing would make it true. I couldn't argue with that. Renee said she was reincarnated from dirt so it didn't much matter, but she would never watch a baby wake up without thinking how it must feel to be born again.

My second memory started with being in an enclosure. Above and to one side of the enclosure was a boom of light. On the other side, something dark was moving above me. I knew the boom of light and the enclosure were not a part of me and were not like me, but I knew I was like the dark thing, and I knew the dark thing didn't know that I knew. I was delighted. It was my first secret and my first joke.

Renee ran the story through her head. I'd been too young to know words, so how could I do all that thinking without words, much less remember any of it?

I didn't have an answer. Maybe it was a dream or it had been such a strong sensation that I remembered it until words came along.

Her skepticism seemed to fade. She wanted to look into her child's eyes and try to imagine its secrets.

She put her head back and stared up at the tin ceiling. She could've been basking in the moment, but more likely she imagined the future—she was touching her new teeth with the tip of her tongue. Maybe you could imagine the future, and it would happen. Renee had imagined herself right out of Fourteen South into another world, and for the moment, she'd taken the rest of us with her.

Buddhists with Headlamps

A three-dimensional image of the underground began to take shape in my mind after working various levels and sections of the Badger, moving through drifts that intersected other drifts to other mines, blurring any sense of where one mine ended and another began. That latticework of tunnels revealed ore-rich areas where molten copper once flowed through liquid granite, churning, twisting, and folding, then cooling to solid rock. In places, pockets of punky granite needed careful attention and endless shoring, or they would give way and the drift would collapse without warning.

Surely, the maze that grew in my mind was both misshapened and limited. I was never deeper than 3,200 feet, and I doubt I traveled more than a mile in any direction through the jogs and turns that Irishmen, Finns, Norwegians, Swedes, and men of a dozen other nationalities had blasted in dogged pursuit of copper, zinc, and gold at the cost of countless limbs and lives. However distorted, I had a distinct vision of an underground defined by burrows made from desperate need and uncommon greed.

Stories and fantasies told by miners extended my tangled knowledge into the unexplored regions—caverns a thousand feet high a mile down, a geode found in the Stewart as large as a miner's shack, four-foot seams of solid copper, lunch buckets full of silver, and gold nuggets the size of apples. There were miners who swore of miracles—the Son of God floating through the main drift on the thirteen hundred, asking for a drink; another saw a man fall down a shaft, splattering against the sides until he turned to rain. The Virgin Mother, arms outstretched, rose up through the rain of the falling man. I remember the man who turned to rain, because I remember standing near the shaft and the taste of his blood. The memory is like a dream. Perhaps I only imagined the taste of him, but men did fall and when they did, they turned to rain. I didn't see the Virgin.

Life underground was a fantasy lived by blind men feeling their way through the intestines of the monster earth—dedicated to carving her a cavernous belly, stealing her copper-gold bile, and escaping alive.

Working in the mines changed the surface of the land for me. After several weeks underground I could not look at the surface without wondering what was underneath. The latticework of the underground found a conscious expression in the minds of lifelong miners, extending itself up to the surface as a way of thinking. Miners were the archaeologists of human behavior. Unlike the cowboys' simple flatness, the miners saw a deeply dimensional world. I suspect the ancient exploration of caves—finding our way into the mind of the earth—affected human thought, made us aware that something was hidden beneath the surface. Perhaps we talked to the earth by painting our stories on the walls of her caves. No doubt, we prayed for her to make us powerful so one day we would escape her complexity, depth, and grasp.

One night at the end of a shift, I set off a charge in the grizzlies on the thirteen hundred. The wires touched, I felt my body shudder from the force of the blast, but there was no sound.

Images from my entire life were rushing through my mind—images of childhood, mountains, towns, cities, jobs, people, scenes from Fellini, Buñuel, and Antonioni—all coalesced into a thought: I would tell stories, I would make films.

I'd never heard of anyone in Montana making films. It was expensive, you needed a mountain of equipment, you had to know a lot of stuff, and you had to have some exotic, God-given skills. If I made films, they'd have to be short and cheap; not movies with big, galumphing plots, but films about the way one thing affected another, about the play of things, about stuff that constantly glittered and zinged around in my head. I stood on the back of the last car of the train, heading to the station, and imagined a kind of film I'd never seen before.

When we're young, we can imagine anything and all without consequences. In the station, waiting for the cage, I started explaining my plans to Delf, a short, earthy man, and his tall partner, Enoch, whose big teeth magnified a memorable grin. We turned our lamps off, packed into the cage, and rode up in the dark. There were nine of us pressed so tight we were warm on three sides. As the cage rattled and slammed toward the surface, they listened to me chatter on about making films. I didn't shut up until we reached the top. The tender threw the bar back, swung the doors open, and released the pressure of bodies. The moment we hit daylight and twenty below, Delf looked up at Enoch and said, "I ain't made plans in thirty years."

I felt like I'd been kicked in the chest. I was ashamed for humiliating Delf. At the same time I was stunned by the notion of never making plans. It seemed like a terrible sentence, but I looked at Delf and saw a man without bitterness or irony. He'd simply made an observation.

Longtime miners usually achieved a kind of working man's grace. They had expectations—a sense of what they should do and how to behave. What was expected had been shaped by several generations of miners before them in a world perfected over time. Those who were graceful and accepting seemed like masters of the art of living.

For generations miners have searched for that place where they could give themselves to the inevitable—like a gathering of Buddhist monks with headlamps.

Working in the mills, the woods, and the mines allowed me to gain back a small piece of what I'd lost when I left the real world of mountains and rivers and animals and moved to the man-made realities of town. I would never achieve that quality of grace and acceptance I found in the miners, but they, and the work itself, had given me a richer life and new ways of seeing.

There is a thing that happens underground that can happen nowhere else—an arrangement of motion, light, and the passage of your mind and body through the earth. If you stand looking forward, on the back of the last car of a long train whose motor car is around the bend, you will be moving through a tunnel supported by stull timbers, illuminated only by the lamp on your hard hat. It feels as though reality is being projected from the middle of your head and you are always moving into a world you can never quite enter, because you are always in the dark.